Teaching and Learning in Further Education

Further education colleges now deliver education and training to more students than any other institution in the post-compulsory sector. In these colleges students from as young as fourteen to adults in late old age participate in a wide range of academic and vocational programmes. Such diversity makes FE colleges both volatile and stimulating environments in which to work. This book provides a practical guide to teaching and learning within the context of the changing FE environment and addresses the diverse nature of the curriculum and of the student body for which it is designed.

The book describes the changing context, structure and funding of the FE sector and the way in which change has impacted on staff, students and the curriculum. It examines the nature and scope of the student body, illustrated by vignettes of students of different ages, backgrounds and abilities. It also explores new models of assessment, the need for teachers to be reflective and aware of their own professional developmental needs, and gives information about support available to FE teachers.

Case studies are included to give help in considering differing student needs and how these might best be served. They also provide an opportunity for practitioners to reflect upon the changing policy context of FE and how this impacts upon students, programmes and institutions. Practical activities are also included, and these can be used as catalysts for questioning attitudes and approaches to work in FE.

Whether you are embarking on a career or already teaching, this book will help you review your approach and understanding of the process of teaching and learning in FE.

Prue Huddleston is Deputy Director of the Centre for Education and Industry at the University of Warwick. **Lorna Unwin** is a Senior Lecturer in Post-compulsory Education and Training at the University of Sheffield.

Teaching and Learning in Further Education

Diversity and change

Prue Huddleston and Lorna Unwin

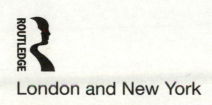

London and New York

First published 1997
by Routledge
11 New Fetter Lane, London EC4P 4EE

Simultaneously published in the USA and Canada
by Routledge
29 West 35th Street, New York, NY 10001

Typeset in Garamond by M Rules
Printed and bound in Great Britain by Clays Ltd, St Ives PLC

British Library Cataloguing in Publication Data
A catalogue record for this book is available from the British Library

Library of Congress Cataloguing in Publication Data
A catalogue record for this book has been requested

ISBN 0–415–12017–9

Contents

List of figures   vi
Preface   vii
List of abbreviations   x

Part I Further education in context

1 Where will I teach?   3

2 The student body: Who will I teach?   20

3 Diverse curricula: What will I teach?   29

Part II Teaching and learning

4 Approaches to learning   59

5 Teaching strategies   88

6 Assessment and recording achievement   111

Part III Professional development

7 Evaluation, reflection and research   137

8 Professional development   148

9 Networks and support agencies   160

Appendix: National targets for education and training   171

References   172
Further reading   178
Index   181

Figures

1.1 Council regional map   4
1.2 Full-time and part-time Council-funded provision   8
1.3 Proportion of colleges identifying risk factors to their   9
    strategic plans
1.4 Proportion of sixth form colleges identifying risk factors to   10
    their strategic plans
1.5 The elements of college recurrent funding allocations   12
3.1 Influences on curriculum design   30
3.2 The NVQ framework   34
4.1 Kolb's learning cycle   61
4.2 Teacher–learner relationship   79
4.3 Types of aims and purposes in group teaching   81
4.4 College guidance map   84
4.5 Guidance team influence on learner's pathway   86
5.1 Teaching strategies continuum   92
5.2 Reflection exercise   94
5.3 Model for effective learning   105

Preface

This book has been written, primarily, for people who are embarking on a teaching career in colleges of further education (FE) and for those already teaching who may wish to review their approaches to and understanding of the process of teaching and learning. It may also be of use to managers in FE and to people working in organisations which have a relationship with FE colleges.

The book attempts to encapsulate the dynamic and volatile world as experienced day in and day out by students and staff in the hundreds of FE colleges throughout the United Kingdom. For unless one is able to have some picture of these powerhouses of education and training, it is difficult to begin to envisage the nature of the teaching and learning which goes on within the FE sector.

To teach in an FE college as the twentieth century draws to a close is a very demanding job. At first glance, it would seem that the FE teacher shares little of the advantages enjoyed by colleagues in schools and universities. Unlike schools, colleges are open to their students from early in the morning to late at night, often at weekends, and, increasingly, throughout the traditional summer holiday period from mid-July to early September. Unlike universities, colleges are open to people of all abilities, from those adults who may be learning to read and write to those who are technically highly skilled and, again increasingly, to those who are following undergraduate and postgraduate courses. There is a heterogeneity about the student body, structures and curricular offerings in FE colleges which would send some school and university teachers running for cover. That very diversity, however, helps make FE colleges such stimulating and exciting environments in which to work as a teacher.

As we write, FE colleges are experiencing yet another period of change and there are many problems across the whole sector: there are conflicts between staff and managers about contracts of employment; battles between colleges and their funding bodies about resource levels; anger about the levels of bureaucracy associated with the validation and accreditation of courses leading to national qualifications; the emergence of a damaging competitive climate in which colleges, schools and private training providers compete for students; and concern that the increasing emphasis on externally imposed quality assurance mechanisms may dominate college life instead of teaching and learning. A recently retired FE teacher summed up the pessimistic mood which haunted many colleges in 1995:

> I have friends still working in FE who say it is like being owned, body and soul, by management. Corporatism has replaced and stifled democratic debate, and so compromised working conditions that there has been a mass exodus of previously committed and experienced teachers. Staff are no longer respected, just told to shut up and get on with it.
>
> (Macleod and Beckett, 1995, quoted in Gleeson, 1996)

Working in any sector of education, however, means that one must be prepared for change and periods of upheaval, much of which may be imposed from outside one's sector or organisation. And despite the catalogue of concerns given here, the majority of FE teachers still spend the majority of their working day helping their students to learn, to progress and to achieve.

Throughout this book, we have tried to portray the realities of college life in order to emphasise that FE teachers must be capable of adapting to many different situations and circumstances. In any one day, an FE teacher will employ a range of strategies, moving from a traditional didactic style in one lesson to being a facilitator of group work in another, from the company of mature adult students to a group of disaffected 17 year olds, and from teaching and assessing in the college classroom to the variable conditions of the industrial or commercial workplace.

Two current important reviews of FE are pending: the Tomlinson Report on special needs in FE (FEFC, 1996d) and the pending Kennedy Commission Report on widening participation. Although, in this book, we explore the challenges which face FE teachers in managing and facilitating the learning of disaffected young people, we do not cover the more specialist area of students with learning difficulties or disabilities. (See Corbett and Barton, 1992, for a discussion of these issues.)

The book is divided into three parts: Part I: Further education in context; Part II: Teaching and learning; and Part III: Professional development.

In Part I, we describe in Chapter 1 the FE world, how it is funded and the external constraints which govern the ways in which colleges can go about their business. Chapter 2 examines the nature and scope of the FE student population and introduces the reader to some real students whose needs and expectations pose challenges for teachers and support staff. It also describes the different types of staff found in colleges and the multi-skilled nature of teachers. In Chapter 3, we discuss the rich diet that comprises the curricular offerings found in FE colleges from basic skills workshops through to higher education courses.

In Part II, we explore in Chapter 4 the relationship between teaching and learning, drawing on a number of theoretical approaches which can help teachers reflect on their work and be used as a basis for examining the problems they encounter. This underpinning theory is continued in Chapter 5 where we present a number of strategies for use in the different teaching situations found in a college. In Chapter 6, we focus on assessment and recording achievement.

In Part III, we see that, as in all teaching, regardless of the sector, professional educators never stop learning about their work and spend a great deal of time reflecting on how to improve and develop their competence and levels of creativity. In Chapter 7, we discuss the concept of the reflective practitioner as it relates to both teachers and students, and the extent to which teachers can also function as researchers. The possibilities for continued professional development are examined in Chapter 8 and Chapter 9 provides information about the organisations and resources upon which FE teachers can draw for support in their work. At the end of the book, for each chapter we indicate further reading material which will help you extend your understanding of some of the complex learning and teaching concepts covered in the book.

In each of the chapters, we have included sets of questions and activities for you to consider. We have boxed these under the heading 'Reflections' and hope that you will find time to use them as catalysts for questioning your attitudes and approaches to your work in FE and for discussion with colleagues.

This book has been written in the spirit of sharing rather than preaching and, as such, reflects the philosophical basis of much of the teaching and learning that occurs in FE colleges. Our ideas come from our own experiences of teaching in colleges and, more recently, of working with FE professionals in a staff development and research capacity. We hope the book provides you with some useful and relevant information and ideas but equally we hope it provides enough challenging material to make you say: 'I think I would tackle that situation differently' or 'I can come up with a better way'.

List of abbreviations

ACAC	Curriculum and Assessment Authority for Wales
ACM	Association for College Management
ALBSU	Adult Literacy and Basic Skills Unit (now Basic Skills Agency)
AOC	Association of Colleges
APC	Association of Principals of Colleges
APL	Accreditation of Prior Learning
ATL	Association of Teachers and Lecturers
BTEC	Business and Technology Education Council (from April 1996 BTEC merged with the London Examinations Board to become EDXCEL)
CAD/CAM	Computer-Aided Design and Manufacture
CBI	Confederation of British Industry
CCEA	Council for the Curriculum, Examinations and Assessment (CCEA) in Northern Ireland
CEF	Colleges' Employers' Forum
CGLI	City and Guilds of London Institute
CPD	Continuing Professional Development
CPE	Continuing Professional Education
CPVE	Certificate for Pre-Vocational Education
CRAC	Careers Research and Advisory Centre
DfEE	Department for Education and Employment
EBP	Education–Business Partnership
EBPNN	Education–Business Partnership National Network
ERDF	European Regional Development Fund
ESF	European Social Fund
FE	Further Education
FEDA	Further Education Development Agency
FEFC	Further Education Funding Council
FESC	Further Education Staff College
FEU	Further Education Unit
GCSE	General Certificate of Secondary Education

GEST	Grant for Educational Support and Training
GNVQ	General National Vocational Qualification
HE	Higher Education
HEFC	Higher Education Funding Council
HMI	Her Majesty's Inspectorate
HNC	Higher National Certificate
HND	Higher National Diploma
HRD	Human Resource Development
ITE	Initial Teacher Education
ITO	Industrial Training Organisation
LEA	Local Education Authority
LEC	Local Enterprise Company (Scottish version of TEC)
NATFHE	National Association of Teachers in Further and Higher Education
NCET	National Council for Education Technology
NCITO	National Council for Industrial Training Organisations
NCVQ	National Council for Vocational Qualifications
NIACE	National Institute for Adult Continuing Education
NISVQ	National Information System for Vocational Qualifications
NVQ	National Vocational Qualification
PGCE	Postgraduate Certificate of Education
QCA	Qualifications and Curriculum Authority
QTS	Qualified Teacher Status
RAC	Regional Advisory Council
RSA	Royal Society for the Encouragement of Arts, Manufacturing and Commerce
SCAA	School Curriculum and Assessment Authority
SHA	Secondary Heads Association
TDLB	Training and Development Lead Body
TEC	Training and Enterprise Council
TFW	Training for Work
TTA	Teacher Training Agency
TUC	Trades Union Congress
TVEI	Technical and Vocational Education Initiative
WEA	Workers' Educational Association
YT	Youth Training

Part I

Further education in context

Chapter 1

Where will I teach?

NATURE AND SCOPE OF FURTHER EDUCATION

This chapter describes the shape and scope of further education (FE) colleges and gives particular emphasis to their diversity. In the United Kingdom, the majority of FE colleges (452) are to be found in England and there are 51 in Scotland, 29 in Wales and 24 in Northern Ireland. The FE sector is expanding, with growth rates of up to 21 per cent for full-time students and 28 per cent for part-time students projected for 1997/8 (FEFC, 1996a). The map in Figure 1.1 shows the English regional breakdown.

These colleges have their roots in the Mechanics Institutes of the mid-nineteenth century. Originally intended to provide technical education on a part-time basis for the growing numbers of technicians and craftspeople required by the industrialisation process, they grew and developed during the twentieth century to provide vocational education and training mainly on a day-release basis. For example, Huddersfield Technical College began as the Huddersfield Mechanics Institution in the 1840s, and became a technical college in 1896, whilst Lowestoft College, the most easterly college in Britain, traces its origins to evening art classes held in 1874 and courses in navigation for fishermen began in 1923.

The 1960s saw a considerable expansion in the FE sector, not just within the area of vocational education but also in the development of professional and academic courses. Some of these were on a full-time basis, often for those students who were looking for an alternative to that which was provided in the school sixth form.

The FE sector has always had a policy of 'all inclusiveness' in its provision. That is, it has provided non-selective education for everyone over 16 who wished to benefit from extended education or vocational training. In many colleges this provision now includes everything from basic education to undergraduate and professional programmes. Colleges increasingly see their role as providing for the needs of the local community as well as for a growing regional, national and, in some cases, international student clientele. They now cater for more over-16 students than the universities and school sixth

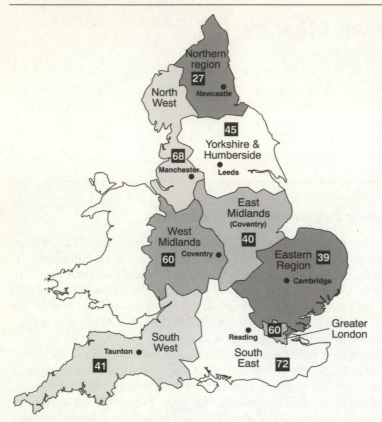

Figure 1.1 Council regional map showing the number of colleges in each region as at February 1996 and the location of regional offices

forms put together with over 3 million students in 1996 (FEFC, 1996b). In addition, it should be noted that the majority (as much as three-quarters in 1995) of students in colleges are mature adults attending part-time classes.

Until April 1993 FE colleges were under the control of their local education authority (LEA) from which they received their funding. Under the terms of the 1992 Further and Higher Education Act colleges became independent self-governing corporations with responsibility for their own budgets, staffing, marketing, course planning and provision. In England and Wales, their funding now comes mainly from two national funding bodies, the Further Education Funding Council (FEFC) in England and the Welsh Funding Council. (Scotland has an entirely different and separate education system in which colleges are funded via the Scottish Office, and in Northern Ireland, colleges relate directly to the Northern Ireland Office.) Colleges also draw funding from a number of other sources, for example their local Training and Enterprise Councils (TECs), the European Union and 'full-cost' paying customers. Where there are undergraduate and postgraduate students following programmes in FE colleges these will be funded through the Higher Education Funding Council (HEFC). For example, Birmingham College of Food, Tourism and Creative Studies, which in 1996 had the highest proportion of higher education students of any college in England and Wales, receives more than 65 per cent of its funding from sources other than the FEFC and takes students from foundation to postgraduate level. The colleges are under the direction of Boards of Governors which determine the needs of their local community in terms of vocational education and training as well as respond to the demands of the FEFC.

A typical FE college might well receive its income in the following ways:

College of Further Education: Projected income distribution		
FEFC		78.0%
TEC (including income earned for managing Youth Training and Training For Work)		3.0%
HEFC	for undergraduate programmes	5.0%
European Union	• European Social Fund (ESF) programmes for unemployed people • European Regional Development Fund (ERDF) for economic development • Leonardo and Socrates programmes for exchanges and partnerships	2.1%
Local authority	funding for own vocational and recreational classes	0.3%
Fees	tuition, registration, assessment/examination fees	3.0%
Sales	letting fees, catering sales	2.0%
Business income	short courses for local companies, other 'full-cost' courses consultancy	6.0%
Investment		0.6%
		100.0%

The inclusive nature of FE has meant that it has always provided for the needs of a very wide range of students. It traditionally provided vocational education for jobs in engineering, construction, business, hotel and catering, hairdressing and health, on both a part-time and full-time basis. Now its range of programmes and qualifications are much wider. However, most of the students in the sector are: 'striving to obtain qualifications in one or more of three broad categories: general education, vocational education and training, higher education' (FEFC, 1994a, p.7).

For some students FE represents a 'second-chance' education. This may mean that they are resitting examinations in which they were previously unsuccessful, for example General Certificate of Education (GCE) Advanced

(A) levels and General Certificate of Secondary Education (GCSE) subjects. It was estimated (DfE, 1994) that in 1992–3 about a third of FE students were studying for academic qualifications, whilst about a half were studying for vocational qualifications. Some of these students may also prefer the more adult environment of a college to a school sixth form.

For other students the 'second chance' may have come relatively late in life and may represent a return to learning after a substantial break. There are a wide range of courses available for adults wishing to return to education to update their skills, or to learn new skills. The changing nature and patterns of employment mean that there will be a continued demand for vocational training and retraining, a demand for which FE colleges are well placed to provide. The 1994 White Paper, *Competitiveness Helping Business to Win*, describes colleges as playing 'a key part in meeting the needs of employers, young people and adults for high quality, general and vocational education and training' (HMSO, 1994, p.37).

There are also those for whom secondary education has been a negative experience and who have completed compulsory education with few or no formal qualifications. Their basic literacy and numeracy skills may be poorly developed. The FE sector is able to provide for such students in a non-threatening environment and is being increasingly funded to do so. Some of this provision will be made away from main campus sites, in 'outreach' facilities. This work may be funded by the local TEC or through the ESF. Examples of such programmes are the courses for women returners.

The growth in higher education (HE) has been achieved in part by students progressing through FE by the access route or by franchising arrangements whereby colleges offer the first or second year of an undergraduate programme in collaboration with an HE institution. It is clear that the national targets for post-16 participation and achievement set by the National Advisory Council for Education and Training Targets (NACETT) will only be achieved through an expansion of the FE sector (see Appendix A). There are signs that this expansion is under way. The FEFC Chief Inspector's Report for 1993–4 (FEFC, 1994a) indicated a growth of 6 per cent overall in the sector during the first year of incorporation and the government is seeking an expansion of approximately 30 per cent in full-time equivalent students in the sector between 1992–3 and 1996–7 (DFE 1994).

Further education colleges are of five broad types (FEFC, 1994a):

- General FE and tertiary colleges   62%
- Sixth form colleges   25%
- Specialist designated colleges   3%
- Colleges of Art and Design and the Performing Arts   3%
- Agriculture and horticulture   7%

Since the FE/HE Act sixth form colleges have come under FEFC funding methodology and have been recognised as part of the FE sector rather than the schools sector. The sixth form colleges still cater essentially for the 16-19 age group rather than for the whole 16-60 age range and their programmes are still focused more on academic rather than vocational routes. However, this could well change in the future. Young people between the ages of 16 and 24 who join a government-sponsored training scheme such as Youth Training (YT) or Modern Apprenticeship are funded through a system called Youth Credits (originally known as Training Credits) operated by the TECs (or LECs in Scotland). Colleges claim part of the Youth Credit if they provide the young person with vocational education and training as part of their traineeship or apprenticeship (for more discussion of Youth Credits, see Unwin, 1993, and Hodkinson, 1996).

STUDENTS AND COURSES

The FE and tertiary colleges cater for anyone over 16 and offer a very broad range of programmes. The specialist designated colleges are those mainly catering for adult provision. In addition to the FE colleges, the FEFC also funds FE in HE institutions and some 500 external institutions, mainly adult education centres.

The following list indicates the ways in which FE students were funded in 1995–6 (FEFC, 1996c).

FE enrolments by mode of attendance and source of funding, 1995–6
Students enrolled in colleges funded wholly or partly by the FEFC:
2.7 million
of whom: 27 per cent full-time and 73 per cent part-time.

Students enrolled in colleges funded from other sources: 800,000
of whom: under 10 per cent full-time and over 90 per cent part-time.

These students were studying a broad range of programmes, the balance of which has changed considerably since the 1960s. During the 1970s there was a decline in the numbers of apprentices and day-release vocational students coming into FE colleges. The world recession of the early 1970s and the growth in unemployment, particularly youth unemployment, meant that many college engineering departments shrank whilst programmes for both adult and youth unemployed grew. During the early 1980s the introduction of government schemes for the unemployed resulted in more jobless young people coming into FE colleges.

The balance of subjects currently studied and projected for 1997–8 is given in Figure 1.2.

The ten programme areas shown in the charts of Figure 1.2 vary greatly in terms of their students, qualification aims, levels of attainment and employment opportunities. For this reason, the FE sector is 'wide and complex', and one college may also vary significantly from another. Part of this difference will

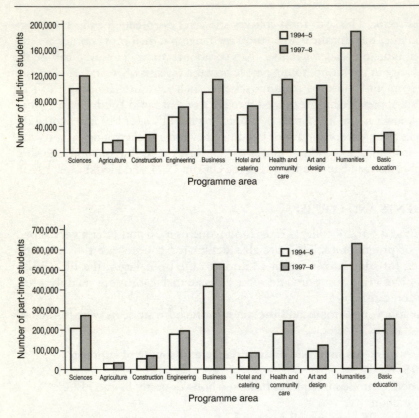

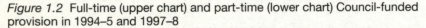

Figure 1.2 Full-time (upper chart) and part-time (lower chart) Council-funded provision in 1994–5 and 1997–8

Source: Institutions' strategic plans, July 1995; FEFC (1996a)

be accounted for by the location of the college and the immediate area which it serves. Changes in local labour markets will affect college provision; for example, those colleges which previously provided training for the mining sector have had to diversify or face closure. Engineering now accounts for only 10 per cent of enrolments (FEFC, 1994a) whereas it was previously the *raison d'être* of many FE colleges. Business studies, on the other hand, has seen an expansion and now accounts for 17 per cent of enrolments (FEFC, 1994a).

Colleges are also in competition with schools, universities and private training providers. In 1995, colleges identified the risk factors (see Figures 1.3 and 1.4) which they faced in trying to achieve their strategic goals. It is interesting to note from the figures that the greatest risk factors were shown to be competition from schools and other colleges.

Whatever the subject area, the qualifications which FE students seek fall into three broad categories:

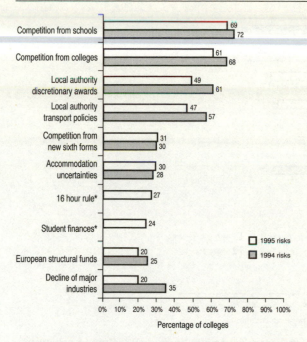

Figure 1.3 Proportion of colleges identifying risk factors to achieving their strategic plans

* Factors not identified as risks in the framework used to analyse 1994 plans

Source: 20 per cent sample of college strategic plans, July 1994; updates, July 1995 (FEFC, 1996a)

Note: One college of agriculture represents approximately 1 per cent on the chart

1 *General education:* programmes leading to GCSE, GCE A and AS level or local/regional accreditation, and some programmes which are not accredited.
2 *Vocational education:* programmes leading to General National Vocational Qualifications (GNVQs) covering broad vocational areas such as health and social care, business, manufacturing and designed to lead to employment or higher education.
3 *Occupationally specific training:* programmes leading to National Vocational Qualifications (NVQs) or other occupational qualifications.

Although the competence-based NVQ system does not require candidates to attend college courses, accreditation is based on verifying performance in the workplace, and many colleges, in association with employers, are providing training programmes to develop such competences. The government's intention for the NVQ framework to cover all occupational areas has not yet been achieved although 80 per cent of jobs are now covered by them (Beaumont, 1995). FE has traditionally been the main provider of vocational

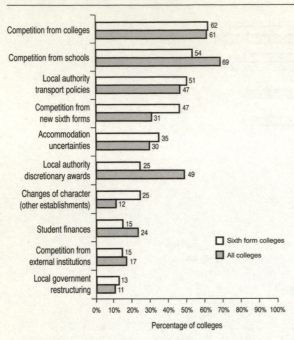

Figure 1.4 Proportion of sixth form colleges identifying risk factors to achieving their strategic plans, compared to all colleges

Source: College strategic plan updates, July 1995 (FEFC, 1996a)

Note: One sixth form college represents approximately 1 per cent on the chart

training. In addition to NVQ work, a large proportion of occupationally specific qualifications are still obtained through the FE route. Many of these qualifications might eventually be subsumed into the NVQ framework. In 1994 there were 159 awarding bodies and over 2,000 qualifications operating within the FE sector (FEFC, 1994a).

There are now an increasing number of programmes being offered in FE colleges which lead to HE qualifications. These include part-time Business and Technology Education Council (BTEC) courses, Higher National Certificates and full-time BTEC Higher National Diploma courses. Some degree work is franchised to FE colleges by HE institutions. (In 1996 BTEC joined with the London Examinations Board to form EDXCEL, but we use the more familiar BTEC title throughout this book.) Courses leading to qualifications of professional bodies, for example the Institute of Marketing, may also be offered in FE colleges. In their study of HE students in FE, Scott and Bocock found that these students tend to be 'mature, mainly local and have non-standard entry qualifications' (Bocock, 1996, p.2). They reported:

Colleges made a real effort to acknowledge the life experiences such students bring wherever possible within the curriculum. This also meant the boundaries between academic and other forms of discourse became blurred. Also the staff were accessible in ways no longer possible in much of mainstream higher education because of expansion. Cumulatively these features provided a system of learning support that helped many students to succeed and gain confidence in their return to study.

(ibid.)

Colleges still provide some courses for adults which do not lead to vocational qualifications; these are mainly leisure and recreational classes. The number of such programmes is diminishing since funding is not provided by the FEFC but usually through the local authority. The need to publish details of student retention rates and achievements and the linking of funding to these outputs may mean that colleges will be less inclined to mount programmes not directly leading to recognised qualifications.

Colleges may, however, decide to mount 'full-cost' courses where students, or their employers, are prepared to pay the real cost of a course. These include company-specific training programmes, short courses for business, seminars and workshops. Often these are provided by a separate business or enterprise unit within a college. The job titles of some members of staff suggest this trend, for example Business Development Manager, Enterprise Unit Director, Marketing Manager. The 1992 FE/HE Act gave more flexibility to colleges to expand and to enter new markets; the new funding methodology introduced in 1994 also emphasises the need for colleges to seek additional sources of funding to those provided by the FEFC. The planned growth for the sector will not be achieved through FEFC funding alone, so colleges will need to be more pro-active in identifying new markets and in attracting other funding sources.

The growth may be achieved in a number of ways. It is not simply by increasing the number of enrolments which will contribute to growth but in improving the retention rates of those who do enrol. The Audit Commission (1993) drew attention to the low retention rates on some programmes and the FEFC (1994a) has confirmed high wastage rates in particular subject areas. The new FEFC funding methodology takes account of students at particular stages of a programme and is not simply based on enrolment statistics (ibid., 1994a). This may help to achieve programme completion and contribute to growth.

Each year every college submits a strategic plan to the FEFC setting out the college's objectives and ways to achieve them. The FEFC then allocates funds to the college in the following two ways:

1 *Core funding:* the college automatically receives a percentage of the previous year's funding (in 1996, the core was 90 per cent).
2 *Above core:* the college applies for further funding based on funding units – for every unit achieved by the college above those applied for, the FEFC pays an extra demand-led allocation to encourage colleges to expand.

(See Figure 1.5.)

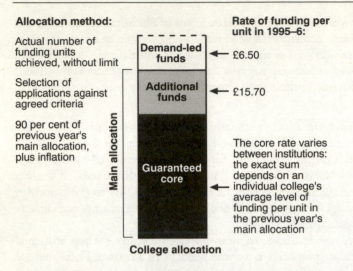

Figure 1.5 The three elements of college recurrent funding allocations

Source: FEFC (1996e, p. 17) *Introduction to the Council*

Every student enrolled at a college attracts FEFC funding units, the precise number of which depends on the course they are following, the progress they make and whether they achieve the intended outcome. Courses are costed according to an annually reviewed tariff based on the relative level of expense which a college would occur to mount and run courses. Engineering courses, therefore, carry a higher tariff than courses in business administration. A college can earn additional units for pre-course guidance, for negotiating learning plans for each student, for providing extra support for students with learning difficulties or disabilities, and for waiving fees for younger students or adults on low incomes. In 1996, the average college received some 400,000 units compared to the smallest with 20,000 units, whilst the largest received 1.6 million units (FEFC, 1996e, p.15).

Many colleges have already identified potential new markets by targeting new clients, for example mature adults, people from ethnic minorities, etc. In some cases a more flexible approach to access has been adopted by opening colleges at non-traditional times, such as at weekends and during holiday times. New courses have been developed, and some colleges have been successful in developing more flexible enrolment opportunities for students through the introduction of modular and 'roll-on, roll-off' programmes.

Colleges are required, under the terms of the 1994 White Paper (op. cit.), to plan strategically and to produce, in consultation with local TECs and the FEFC, a development plan linked to local labour market needs. Whilst this is desirable in order to plan and deliver a coherent system of vocational education and training, there is always an uncertainty about 'who will turn up on the day'. This tends to make the so-called 'FE market' volatile and it is not simply a matter of predicting demand and matching supply to it. The sector was previously criticised for being too much dominated by the supply side (Audit Commission, 1985) and much has been done to adjust the balance but the problems are not easily resolved. Since funding is dependent on enrolments and outputs there are serious resource implications if demand and supply are not reasonably well aligned.

The following extracts from an FEFC report on college responsiveness indicate the ways in which colleges are devising strategies to reach out into their communities:

> A college in one area has been successful in promoting courses for the Sikh community at a local community centre, the local hospital and an Asian women's group. As part of this programme, the college offers open learning workshops and a home-study service. The provision was effectively marketed in the local Punjabi-speaking community as a result of a bilingual advertising campaign on local radio. The proportion of students from minority ethnic backgrounds attending the college is actually higher than represented in the local population.
>
> (FEFC, 1996f, p.15)

> One agricultural college conducted market research and held interviews with 12 local poultry producers in preparation for developing poultry provision. The research identified a range of training needs, including management, marketing and personnel skills as well as stockmanship. Poultry provision began in 1991 with six part-time students. Good links with industry enabled the college to use practical facilities owned by major companies. However, the lack of such facilities on-site was a limiting factor, and the college corporation decided to build a specialist poultry unit using industrial sponsorship. Over the next three years, a total of 45 industrial sponsors provided cash or equipment, allowing the college to build a modern facility costing £45,000. The unit . . . is run as a business partnership with industry, and now provides central training for large poultry firms.
>
> (FEFC, 1996f, p.13)

Most FE colleges provide for students with learning difficulties, and much of this provision may be integrated into mainstream courses, but there may well be special courses for some of these students. For those students with multiple or complex learning needs specialist independent institutions are available.

In Chapter 2 you will be presented with a range of students which reflects the current student profile of an FE college. This profile has changed over recent years with student numbers increasing and class sizes rising. A survey conducted by the *Times Educational Supplement* (TES) in 1994, reviewing the progress of the sector during the first year of incorporation (TES, 1 April

1994) indicates a rise in average class size in 85 per cent of colleges interviewed and a corresponding rise in staff–student ratios. The largest demand for college places had come from school-leavers in 73 per cent of the sample with 24 per cent of the sample reporting an increase in adults, particularly those on state benefits. Concern was expressed over the drop-out rates on these programmes.

COLLEGE STAFF

From the above description of the nature and scope of FE, it is clear that the staff who work in colleges are faced with many competing demands on their time and energies. Those who manage the system are responsible for multi-million-pound businesses. They are accountable to different funding bodies, to local and national employers and to the FEFC inspectorate for the quality of education and training provision. These pressures may appear contradictory at times: for example, the need to provide excellence in vocational education and training at the same time as driving down costs and increasing student numbers. As one Midlands FE lecturer put it: 'it is impossible to put a financial value on people's learning needs and achievements'.

Employment patterns within the sector have changed in recent years with an increase in part-time staff, more flexible contracts, and the introduction of non-traditional teaching hours, for example during weekends. New contracts issued by colleges outline very different terms and conditions of service from what one might expect for a teacher in a primary or secondary school. Edwards has suggested that 'the trends towards multi-skilling and flexibility elsewhere in the economy are also to be found in institutions of post-compulsory education and training' (Edwards, 1993a, p.48). Staff are being required to take on new roles so that in addition to a teaching and tutorial role they may have significant administrative duties. Some FE lecturers may also have responsibility for promoting and marketing their courses. They may be expected to counsel students. Many staff have budgets to manage as well as their course teams. The introduction of distance and open learning systems has required some staff to take on the role of authors as well as develop new techniques for working with open learning students.

Edwards refers to the blurring of roles between 'lecturers and tutors, administrators and technical staff' (ibid., p.48). The TES survey (op. cit.) refers to a new, hybrid 'support tutor' who provides self-study support to students and is responsible for recording prior learning or achievement: 78 per cent of the sample colleges reported that this was already occurring in their institutions. A new or established teacher in the FE sector may be working on a number of part-time contracts in different institutions. The future workforce could comprise freelance professionals moving between colleges in response to demand for their expertise. This unpredictability in employment reflects the way in which the organisation of work in the wider society is being restructured.

The staff in FE colleges, therefore, have a wide variety of roles to fulfil and come from a diverse set of backgrounds. There will be some with academic qualifications, and others with professional qualifications who have perhaps become teachers after a substantial career in business or industry. There will be those who have qualified through a craft or technician route, who have spent a considerable time on the shopfloor or training apprentices. In addition there is a range of support staff: kitchen assistants, laboratory technicians, audio-visual technicians. There will also be clerical and administrative staff and those responsible for student services.

One project which attempted to create a map of the type of staff employed in FE colleges reported its findings under the following headings (DfEE/FEDA, 1995):

- Learning management (e.g. director of studies, head of department, curriculum manager, etc.)
- Co-ordination (e.g. GNVQ co-ordinator, college careers co-ordinator, etc.)
- Liaison (e.g. school liaison manager, employer liaison manager, etc.)
- Lecturing/teaching (e.g. senior lecturer, lecturer, tutor, community education officer, etc.)
- Learning resources (e.g. open learning staff, learning resource centre staff, etc.)
- Libraries
- Technical learning support (e.g. technicians, workshop managers, etc.)
- Assisting learning (e.g. instructors, demonstrators, language assistant, etc.)
- Governing (members of governing body)
- College management (e.g. principal/chief executive and deputies)
- Student guidance
- Human resources management (e.g. personnel director, staff development staff, etc.)
- Facilities management and support (e.g. campus manager, building and estates staff, etc.)
- Marketing and development
- Information and finance management and support

The most recently available figures record a total of 174,209 staff working in the FE sector, 63 per cent of which are in roles related to teaching and learning. In England, more females (54 per cent) than males (46 per cent) make up the teaching staff in colleges, whereas in Scotland 64 per cent are male and 36 per cent female. Over half (52 per cent) of teaching staff are employed on part-time contracts, though this figure could be a great deal higher if all the staff who work less than 25 per cent of a full-time lecturer's contract were taken into account (ibid., p.11). The fact that many FE staff start their careers in colleges after having had other jobs and professions is reflected in the figure showing that 63 per cent of staff are aged between 35 and 54.

There is no statutory requirement for teaching staff in colleges in the UK to possess a professional teaching qualification, other than in sixth form colleges which follow similar requirements for trained staff in schools. All staff responsible for the assessment and verification of GNVQs and NVQs, however, are required to achieve assessor and verifier awards under the direction of the Training and Development Lead Body. (This is discussed in more detail in Chapter 6.) Most teaching staff in FE will, however, engage at some time in teacher training or equivalent modes of staff development. Initial teacher training for FE includes the Certificate in Education, the Post-Graduate Certificate in Education and the City and Guilds 730 series of awards. (These qualifications are examined in more detail in Chapter 8 which explores professional development for FE staff.)

The job titles below are taken from a current range of college prospectuses. You may like to reflect what the job description of each of these people might be:

Director of Studies

Course Tutor

Enterprise and Development Manager

Personal Tutor

GNVQ Team Leader

Vice-Principal (Curriculum)

Publicity Officer

Manager, Open Learning Centre

Programme Manager, Health and Community Care

Head of Faculty, Hospitality and Tourism

Co-ordinator, Information Technology

Temporary Lecturer, Science (Advanced)

Chief Executive

0.5 Lecturer Business

Head of School, Learning Support.

IN THE PUBLIC EYE

The FE sector has undergone a period of rapid and continuous change over the past ten years, the pace of which has accelerated since the incorporation of colleges in 1993. In 1995 some colleges were faced with closure while others continued to grow and some may yet merge to form larger institutions. The sector is having to face pressures on its funding, accommodation and resources in a climate of increased student enrolments and output-related performance indicators. The quality mechanisms imposed through the FEFC assessment inspection process and through the FEFC Quality Assessment

Committee place further demands on the sector to prove that it is up to the job.

As well as publishing information on completion rates for all courses, since 1996 colleges have been required to publish the actual destinations (e.g. further/higher education, employment, training scheme, etc.) of all their students who achieved qualifications in the previous teaching year. The FEFC has encouraged colleges to use these destination data to spot patterns and trends and as a basis for evaluating student experience through the following types of questions:

- why is the proportion of early leavers from some courses higher than others?
- why are the percentages of students progressing from foundation to intermediate and from intermediate to advanced level courses within the college higher in some vocational areas than others?
- why do the percentages of students progressing to higher education from advanced vocational courses vary significantly from one vocational area to another?
- how strong is the correlation between the subjects studied within GCE A level programmes and the degree courses to which students subsequently progress and what are the implications of this for careers education and guidance?
- why are there significant differences between the numbers of male and female students progressing to higher education from the same or similar courses?
- are the trends in destinations of students on particular courses in step with changes made to the structures of those courses?
- are enough students gaining jobs in those industries where the labour market is expanding?
- does the number of unemployed students emerging from particular courses suggest that related labour markets are saturated?

(FEFC, 1996, pp. 17–18)

In England, the FEFC inspects colleges every four years and uses a five-point grading scale to summarise the strengths and weaknesses of the following aspects of cross-college provision:

- Responsiveness and range of provision
- Governance and management
- Students' recruitment, guidance and support
- Quality assurance
- Resources

The five-point scale is as follows:

- grade 1 – provision which has many strengths and very few weaknesses
- grade 2 – provision in which the strengths clearly outweigh the weaknesses

- grade 3 – provision with a balance of strengths and weaknesses
- grade 4 – provision in which the weaknesses outweigh the strengths
- grade 5 – provision which has many weaknesses and very few strengths

As well as giving a grade for the aspects of cross-college provision listed above, the inspectors also grade each curriculum area. Here are extracts from two inspection reports published in 1996:

College one: a technical college in the North of England
Its strengths are:

- a well-informed governing body which has a productive working relationship with college management
- a wide range of courses which reflects the needs of the community
- good and impartial guidance for students and adult returners
- suitably qualified and experienced teaching staff
- effective teaching
- good staff–student relations
- good relations with the TEC, local authority, higher education institutions and community organisations

The college needs to address:

- the poor quality of some of the course team evaluations
- inadequate procedures to enable governors and senior managers to evaluate some aspects of college activity, including quality assurance
- inconsistencies in the implementation of the tutorial system
- inadequate equipment in some programme areas
- the poor quality of some college accommodation

College two: a coastal further education college in South East England
Its strengths are:

- a broad range of vocational and recreational provision for school leavers, adults and commercial customers
- substantial commercial course provision, particularly for the offshore industry
- strong links with local secondary and special schools
- a cohesive, effective team of assistant principals
- a thorough approach to the development and implementation of some policies
- effective student guidance and support
- good standards of teaching in most subjects
- well-qualified teaching and support staff
- exceptional equipment for maritime, offshore and survival training

The college needs to address:

- the limited range of foundation programmes in some curriculum areas
- insufficient information about the college provided to the members of the corporation
- the lack of a rigorous, analytical approach to monitoring and reviewing of performance
- the need for further development of the cross-college learning support system
- the poor quality and availability of statistical data on students
- an over-elaborate, ineffective quality assurance system
- the poor student achievements in some areas
- the slow progress in staff obtaining assessor and verifier qualifications
- those parts of the accommodation which are inappropriate or in poor condition

In these extracts we have not identified the colleges. All college inspection reports are available from the FEFC (see Chapter 9 for FEFC details).

These extracts reinforce the points made throughout this chapter that FE colleges are large, complex and heterogeneous organisations. They are busy, dynamic places of learning with shifting populations of students of all ages. In the following chapters, we examine the implications of this complexity for teaching and learning.

Chapter 2

The student body

Who will I teach?

DIVERSE STUDENT BODY

One of the distinguishing features of the FE sector has always been the diversity of its student population. Since FE is essentially 'education for all', this is reflected in its student body in terms of age, gender, ability, attainment levels, economic, social and cultural background and differing learning needs. Teaching in FE presents a set of challenges which are quite different from those presented in primary or secondary education.

The following vignettes illustrate the diversity of the student body in FE:

College 1

18,096 enrolments (57 per cent female, 2 per cent ethnic minority) mainly from town but some part-time students come from wide catchment area and students in dance, music, technology and road transport technology courses are recruited nationally. Age profile: 25 per cent of students aged 16–18, 69 per cent adults and 6 per cent under 16 following school link courses.

(FEFC Inspection Report, September 1995)

College 2

17,353 enrolments (71 per cent female, 35 per cent ethnic minority) mainly from local borough and 96 per cent of students are over the age of 19. The majority attend part time and courses are offered in 20 venues, five of which are college sites.

(FEFC Inspection Report, April 1996)

Most teachers in FE will be expected to teach across a wide range of programmes which could include basic skills programmes at one end of the spectrum and undergraduate or even postgraduate work, at the other. Similarly the students may range from 16 to 65 and beyond in age. At the time of writing one London college has some 90 year olds amongst its student population as well as some pre-16 pupils from a local school. These different age ranges are not confined to particular programmes of study. An A level group, for example, will not necessarily include only those of 16–18 years as would be the case within a school sixth form.

Students in FE represent an enormous range of different circumstances and any one class or group of students will be heterogeneous in nature. In this sense, the work is real mixed-ability teaching. It is not only the ability of the students which differs, however, but also their motivation, prior experience, expectations and the way in which they are funded. They may also have very different social and cultural backgrounds and their domestic circumstances may be widely different. Some of the students may be returning to learning after a long break, others may be continuing their education but in a different environment. Others will be attempting to combine full-time employment with part-time study or juggling the competing demands of family commitments and study requirements. Some students may have physical disabilities, others may have emotional and behavioural difficulties. The teacher in FE has to be sensitive to this diversity in the planning, preparation and delivery of programmes.

If we look at the FE student profile for England, 79 per cent of the 3.5 million students enrolled at colleges in 1995–6 were adults over the age of 18 (FEFC, 1996b). Males and females are equally distributed until the age of 24 after which females predominate.

The patterns of attendance will vary between full time and part time, which can be day or evening, employment release, block release or attendance at individually designed short courses. An increasing number of students are registering as distance learners or open learners. Some students may be attending a college solely to have prior learning accredited for the purpose of acquiring an NVQ. Others may never attend the college but be taught by college staff at their place of employment.

Although FE has traditionally been the main provider of vocational education for jobs in engineering, construction, business, hotel and catering, and hairdressing, this pattern is now changing. There has been a reduction in employer-led part-time training and a growth in full-time students (FEFC, 1995a). Amongst this student population now are those who are pursuing academic qualifications, perhaps through an alternative route to the traditional school route. There are other students, of all ages, whose participation in FE is very much as 'second-chance' education, for example those who are retaking qualifications. Some students are returning after a long absence from any contact with formal education. In addition, their previous experience of education may have been essentially negative.

As we saw in Chapter 1, there are now more opportunities to enter HE via an FE route through the introduction of access programmes and 'two plus two' degrees. This has introduced a cohort of undergraduates to some FE colleges' student population. On the other hand, there are now more programmes aimed at encouraging people of all ages to improve their basic literacy and numeracy skills and some of them will be enrolled on government-funded schemes.

The need for FE colleges to market their services more actively both at home and abroad has led to an increasing number of overseas students pursuing courses in British colleges. Some of these students may be studying courses to improve their English language competence, others will be pursuing vocational qualifications.

Colleges are now having to cope with a much wider range of student abilities, including those students with learning difficulties. In 1992 the National Council for Educational Technology reported that in a survey conducted within a number of FE colleges, 75 per cent of the sample were providing for students with physical, moderate or severe learning difficulties (NCET, 1992, p.12). Much of this provision will be integrated within mainstream college provision. However, the 1996 report of the Tomlinson Committee's review of FE's provision for students with learning difficulties and disabilities highlighted the need for the sector to make further improvements and to embrace the concept of *inclusive learning* which the Committee believes will benefit all learners. Rather than categorising students with so-called 'special needs' and so pursuing a deficit model of provision, *inclusive learning* calls for colleges to develop a policy of responsiveness to every individual student's needs and to make that policy the responsibility of every member of staff (see FEFC, 1996d).

Although funding for adult education and recreational programmes has been subject to governmental cut-backs, many FE colleges still offer some provision for adults wishing to pursue leisure or recreational programmes. This adds another dimension to the work of colleges and to the student profile. Many of these students may be studying at outreach centres or in premises away from the main college site.

It is clear that the targets imposed for growth within the FE sector will mean that the student population is likely to become even more diverse. The FE teacher will be faced with more changes and challenges as colleges move towards what the FEU (1991) has called the 'inclusive college'. The inclusive college is one which is seen as catering for the widest possible student population with an enormous diversity of learning needs and where programmes may be delivered through a range of techniques. The inclusive college has to serve community needs as well as respond to a commercial market. It will also provide for those on government-sponsored training programmes.

STUDENT NEEDS AND MOTIVATION

The motivations of such a diverse range of students will obviously be widely different, and the ways in which students learn will vary in pace and style. This requires a flexible teaching approach from FE teachers in order to provide for the needs of individual learners. The teacher will also have a central role to play in other aspects of learning support, for example through guidance and counselling, both on entry to a programme and throughout its duration. Returning learners may also need support not just in the subject being studied but in how to study it.

These competing pressures on the FE teacher's time are not easy to balance when the substantial managerial and administrative loads which are inherent in most vocational programmes are added to them. How then is the new teacher in FE to prepare him- or herself to be an effective practitioner?

Reflection

We now present a series of vignettes of typical students to be found in any college. We would like you to read each one and answer the following questions:

1 As a teacher what perceptions do you have of each of these students and of their learning needs?
2 How do you think each student feels about the learning situation and about you as a teacher?

Martin

Martin is 17 years old and is studying three A level subjects full time at his local college. His school experience was rather negative although he achieved four GCSE subjects with grades A–C. His parents were not enthusiastic about his transfer to the local college at 16 and would have preferred him to have remained in the sixth form at school. His school, however, had a sixth form entry requirement of five GCSEs. Also one of the subjects which Martin wished to study at A level, psychology, was not available at school.

Since transferring to college, Martin has found the A level courses particularly demanding. He has enjoyed the social activities available at college and taken an active part in student affairs. He has enjoyed the freedom of being allowed to organise his own time although he has found it difficult to meet deadlines for handing in essays. He has recently experienced problems with writing extended pieces of work and has had some disappointing results.

Although Martin is keen to continue with his college course, his parents now feel that he may be wasting his time. They had hoped he would gain a place in higher education but they feel that this is unrealistic. Martin, however, is still optimistic about his chances although he feels that a Higher National Diploma (HND) course might be more suited to his needs. The college offers an HND programme.

Clive

Clive attends college for one day a week as part of a Youth Training Scheme. He is 17 years old and is attending a motor vehicle course which will lead to NVQ accreditation. During the rest of the week he works in a local garage and is enjoying the practical work and the opportunities of working on a range of different vehicles. He is a keen motorcyclist and likes to spend his weekends repairing friends' bikes. He resents the fact that he has no money to spend on a decent bike but hopes that at the end of the training scheme he may be kept on at the garage as a full-time employee.

He finds the college day boring but knows that he has to attend in order to qualify for the training allowance. The practical opportunities are limited because the college does not have a supply of modern vehicles on which to work. Lecturers have complained about the group and say that they would be loath to let them near a decent vehicle anyway. Nevertheless, the TEC contract for these trainees is an important source of revenue for the college.

Clive and his group do not involve themselves with college activities and spend their break times sitting around the workshops. Recently the college caretaker has complained about the group because he has found them there and when challenged they have responded with abuse. There appears to be little on offer for these students. However, Clive is aware of clubs and activities available for full-time students because his sister is taking a full-time GNVQ programme in leisure and tourism at the same college. It seems to Clive and his group that there are two systems operating, one for full-time students and one for those on training schemes. The group has asked to see the member of staff in charge of student services about this.

Margaret

Margaret is 42 and is a student in her second year of a 'two plus two' degree programme which is run jointly by her college and the local university. The first two years of the programme are delivered by the college and involve a social science foundation course followed by a first-year undergraduate programme in one area of the social sciences. Margaret has chosen to continue her studies in economics. Before starting the course Margaret had helped her husband in his building business; she had been responsible for the clerical and administrative side of the work and had dealt with the accounts and payment of salaries.

Although Margaret left school at 16 she had always pursued some form of part-time education through attendance at evening classes. She had gained qualifications in bookkeeping, typing and accounts which had enabled her to help in the family business. However, when her two daughters started their secondary education, Margaret felt she would like to have the opportunity of pursuing a full-time course. She approached her local college about possible options and was surprised to find that she could enrol on the degree programme.

She approached the first year with trepidation and found the return to full-time education extremely unsettling. Although she found she could cope with the work she was always anxious about the expectations of staff and about the adequacy of her performance. She was particularly anxious about oral presentations and disliked having to give papers to other students and to lecturers who appeared to be about half her age.

She successfully completed the first year of the programme and achieved particularly high marks in the statistics examination. She did less well in the examinations which required a more analytical approach and a reflective style. Nevertheless, she achieved a creditable result overall.

Now she is in the second year she feels more confident about the work and is doing well in her chosen specialism, economics. Nevertheless, she finds the work demanding and is anxious about the transfer to the university for the third and fourth years of the course. She fears that most of the students will be the age of her daughters. The college staff have assured her that she will be able to cope but she remains unconvinced.

Gary

Gary has been in college for six weeks on a craft diploma course in catering. He is 16 years old and left school with few formal qualifications. The catering course is essentially practical and provides the opportunity to acquire National Vocational Qualifications (NVQs) in catering and other related subjects such as food handling and hygiene. Basic numeracy and communication skills are also included in the course content.

Although keen at the beginning of term, Gary's enthusiasm began to wane after three weeks. He started to miss theory classes and by the fifth week he was turning up late for practical sessions. Staff noticed that he was not wearing correct kitchen uniform in spite of being repeatedly told about it. He appeared to resent any criticism from the staff.

The quality of his practical work is good when he is left on his own to complete a task. He is aggressive when asked to work with other students and takes extended breaks which delay the completion of any joint activities. Other students have begun to resent this and have mentioned it to the lecturer in charge. The lecturer has discussed this with Gary who has given assurances about his future conduct. Gary has been told that he will not be allowed to participate in the work experience placement unless his behaviour improves.

During a practical session Gary became involved in an argument with another student who had suggested that Gary could not weigh or add up quantities correctly. Gary became abusive and threatened the student. He also used offensive language to the kitchen assistant who has lodged a formal complaint with the vice-principal. The catering lecturer has intervened and asked Gary to discuss the matter with him fully.

Arpinder

Arpinder works for a firm of accountants and attends his local college one day a week for an accountancy course. He is 32 and decided to study for accounting qualifications because he has friends who run a successful accountancy practice. He sees the course as the first step towards achieving full professional qualifications. He realises, however, that it will take a long time. Before starting his present job he worked for a retail chain as an assistant store manager but he did not like the long and irregular hours of work.

The company for whom he works is reasonably supportive of Arpinder's attendance at college and allows him time off work to attend. However, they are not prepared to pay his fees. So far he has been able to meet the cost himself.

He is very keen to progress as quickly as possible and has found the course helpful, although he has been irritated by the repeated changes in the teaching staff. He feels that some of the other students do not take the course sufficiently seriously and that one or two of the younger group members are disruptive. During a recent busy period his firm asked him to remain at work on college days with the promise of making up the time later when he needs some exam revision time. He cannot envisage the situation improving in the foreseeable future. In addition, his father has recently been seriously ill and he has had to spend a considerable amount of time supporting his family.

He is becoming anxious about the effect this is having on his course and the possible outcome for his examination result. He feels he has invested heavily in the course in terms of financial, personal and emotional commitment. He is becoming increasingly dispirited and depressed about the possibility of not meeting the goals which he has set for himself.

Grace

For three mornings a week Grace attends basic literacy and numeracy classes run by the FE college at a local community hall. She is a single parent of 28 and has three children aged 6, 8 and 10. She had an extremely negative and disrupted school experience, having attended four different schools in a period of six years. She left school at the earliest possible opportunity without any formal qualifications. She did not expect, nor want, to have any further contact with the education system.

On leaving school she took a series of low-paid, unskilled jobs none of which lasted for very long. She has had no paid employment since the birth of her first child.

When her children started school she began to take an interest in their work and in some of the activities in which the school sought parental involvement. She was interested in helping in a practical way but when approached about the possibility of 'listening to readers' she became very anxious. She was reluctant to become involved in case her own deficiencies were exposed.

When her husband left, Grace decided to try and find some part-time employment but soon realised that it was virtually impossible to find any work unless she improved her reading and writing skills. She also wanted to improve her basic arithmetical skills. She found that there were a series of classes being held in her local community hall, just ten minutes' walk from home. The courses were funded by the Training and Enterprise Council (TEC) and the FE college had been contracted to deliver them at a series of neighbourhood sites. It was hoped that by making an initial contact with FE through an outreach activity students might be encouraged to continue their studies at the college itself.

Grace was extremely nervous about returning to study and for the first few weeks she attempted to disguise the nature of the course when talking to friends and neighbours. However, after a short time she began to gain confidence and discovered a new group of friends amongst the class members. The atmosphere was extremely supportive and the lecturers friendly. She began to look forward to the mornings spent improving her writing skills and started to enjoy reading. This new-found confidence tended to spill over into other areas of her life. She was approached about standing as a parent governor at her daughter's school.

Grace now wants to continue her studies with the intention of gaining some qualifications. She has discovered that the next stage of the programme will be held in the college and not in the local hall. She is reluctant to travel the 5 miles (8 kilometres) to the college but she is even more reluctant to become a student there. The prospect of entering a formal educational institution is threatening; she is concerned about her ability to cope with the work.

George
At 35, George has been unemployed for the past 18 months. Prior to that he was employed as a storeman at a manufacturing company. The company was forced to close resulting in some 350 job losses. Some of the skilled workers eventually managed to find alternative employment but the large number of unskilled workers, like George, found it virtually impossible to find work.

George and several of his old workmates now attend college as part of the government's Training for Work Scheme. This scheme is open to those who have been unemployed for more than six months. Funding for the programme is provided by the government through the TECs. The TECs are responsible for managing the programmes locally and may contract FE colleges to provide the off-the-job training element. All programmes must lead to the acquisition of NVQs. Trainees are paid a weekly rate, the receipt of which is dependent upon attendance at the programme. Colleges receive payment for the trainees, part of which is related to successful outcomes.

George is attending a painting and decorating training programme. He is hoping that even if he does not secure employment in a company, he may be able to become self-employed. In addition to the practical elements of the programme, sessions on how to complete job applications, interview techniques and presentation skills are provided by college staff. Having already suffered 18 months of unemployment, George is unsure about the value of some of the programme in helping him to secure a job.

Sommiya

Sommiya is a pupil in the sixth form of a comprehensive school. She is studying three A level subjects and is hoping to continue her studies in higher education. Her school is only offering two of the subjects which she is studying and she has to attend the local FE college for the third subject. There are franchise arrangements between the school and the college. For five hours a week Sommiya travels to the college and joins the A level business studies group. There are three other pupils from the school who join the 15 college students for the classes.

The class is mixed in age and ability; some of the students are part time, others are full time. There has been a succession of staff teaching the course, many of whom are part time. Sometimes classes have had to be cancelled. There are, however, one or two lecturers to whom the pupils relate well and who appear to take an interest in the pupils' work and progress.

Sommiya is, nevertheless, anxious about the arrangements for a number of reasons. School pupils have to wear school uniform and are obviously distinguishable from the college students. There appears to be little liaison between the head of the sixth form and the college. College staff do not attend the parents' evenings, or any other meetings, at the school. She does not like the atmosphere in the classes and is reluctant to ask questions in case she exposes any inadequacies which she feels she has. The other school pupils feel much the same but are reluctant to say anything about it. They are worried about jeopardising their chances of gaining a place in higher education.

Sue

Saturday courses are a relatively recent development at Sue's local FE college and have received a fair amount of publicity in the local media. A wide range of courses are offered from recreational and leisure classes to courses leading to business and professional qualifications. Sue has enrolled on a ten-week short course within the Saturday college programme entitled: 'How to market your business'.

Sue has recently set up a small business providing household cleaning and ironing services, and employs five people on a part-time basis. The company has bought two vehicles and hired some office accommodation. This has involved some financial outlay and Sue is afraid that she may not be able to sustain the initial level of business growth. She realises that she needs to improve her marketing and promotional activity and, for this reason, has enrolled on the college course. The fees are quite expensive for her because the course is a 'full-cost' course. Nevertheless, she hopes that the outlay will be worthwhile and that business will improve.

She is not too happy about giving up her Saturdays for the course but realises that this is the only way she can attend. Sue is anxious to secure value for money for the investment which she has made in course fees, and hopes that the experienced college staff will be a useful resource on which she can draw.

Hussein

Hussein is part of a group of overseas students studying at an FE college for an HND in electrical engineering. The college has established a relationship with Hussein's home country and each year students from there apply for entry to the college. The college has a tutor designated to support the overseas students. This tutor also makes recruitment visits overseas and interviews prospective students.

The overseas students are taught alongside home students for some parts of the course but have additional classes in English and some other subjects. Hussein and his group are enjoying the course and like the relaxed atmosphere of the college. They are finding some difficulties with their accommodation and in organising their workload. They are not always sure what is expected of them because the teaching methods and organisation of work are very different from those which they have previously experienced. They are not sure if they should raise this with the student liaison officer.

Phyllis

Phyllis is 50 and has recently joined an adult 'return to learn' programme at her local FE college. The timetable is arranged to suit individual needs and interests and it is possible to build a programme from a wide range of college courses. Phyllis has decided to concentrate on word-processing and basic office skills. She is greatly enjoying the college environment and the opportunity which it has provided for making new friends. There are times when she would prefer the course to be better organised, and has already spoken to the head of adult studies about it.

One aspect of the course particularly concerns her: the work experience placement. She will be expected to complete a period of work experience during the course and she feels that this is quite unnecessary for someone of her maturity. She is also concerned that she may be placed in a company with which she has contact on a personal basis. Her husband is a prominent solicitor in the town. She is hoping she may be able to gain exemption from this part of the programme although the lecturer in charge has said that it is an integral part of the course. Phyllis hopes she may be able to have a word with the vice-principal about it.

Each of these students will have developed their own perspective on learning and will communicate that perspective through their behaviour in the classroom, workshop, tutorial, seminar group and so on. Their prior experience of education will have shaped their attitudes to learning, to teachers and to their fellow students. These issues are explored in detail in Chapter 5 and in Chapter 6, where we will return to these vignettes and consider which teaching and assessment strategies might be most appropriate for helping students such as these to learn most effectively.

Chapter 3

Diverse curricula

What will I teach?

Just as the range of students in FE colleges is too wide to enable it to be described in tidy categorisations, to talk about an FE curriculum as if it were a homogeneous entity would be totally misleading. However, as the FEFC's chief inspector has pointed out:

> There is no single further education curriculum but further education does have curricular traditions.
>
> (FEFC, 1994a, p.54)

These curriculum traditions are: general education, general vocational education, job-specific training, higher education and adult education. Such divisions are not as simple as they might at first appear because even within these broad bands there is often a wide range of courses or programmes of study on offer. Colleges may also differ from each other in the curricula which they offer because of differences in their size, culture and location.

It is not the purpose of this chapter to discuss the appropriateness, or inappropriateness, of particular curricular models or to embark upon curriculum design. Nor do we intend to describe what an optimum post-16 entitlement might be. These issues have been debated elsewhere and considerable attention is at present being focused upon the need for reform in post-16 education (see Finegold *et al.*, 1990; Richardson *et al.*, 1993; Dearing, 1996; among others). It should be noted that this phase of education has been particularly resistant to change and the divide between vocational and academic routes has yet to be bridged. Nevertheless, there are some compelling reasons for reform, not least among them the need to improve the quantity and quality of our vocational education and training and to enhance our competitiveness, particularly with Germany, France, Japan and the USA (Green and Steadman, 1995).

The purpose of this chapter is to familiarise the new or intending teacher within FE with the curricular traditions which exist and with the range and diversity of curricular offerings within any one college. It is also important to note that the post-compulsory curriculum is subject to constant change. This is inevitable since there are a large number of stakeholders in the curriculum. Squires (1987) has suggested that:

It is at this point that the 'radical monopoly', to use Illich's phrase, of the education system breaks down, and a plethora of institutions and interests become involved.

(Squires, 1987, p.96)

Figure 3.1 is intended to indicate the large number of influences which may be impacting upon curriculum design. In addition, the balance of these influences will shift in response to changes in government policy, the numbers and types of students enrolling, the variations in funding mechanisms and so on. This raises questions about the control of the curriculum. Are education professionals within the FE sector increasingly managers of the curriculum rather than curriculum designers since much of the curriculum is externally imposed?

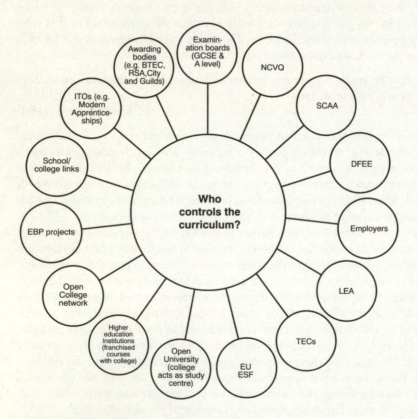

Figure 3.1 Influences on curriculum design

There are several reasons why FE curricula are so complex and diverse. A major reason is the shifting nature of the student population. As we saw in Chapter 2, there are now more full-time students participating in education beyond 16 than has previously been the case, whilst the number of independent part-time student enrolments increased by 3 per cent over the same period and part-time employer-led students declined by 7 per cent. These students are not only more numerous but also more diverse, including students with specific learning needs. This means that the curriculum offerings will need to be more diverse to cater for such a range of students. Differing modes of attendance and patterns of learning may also determine what the curriculum looks like.

Students who enter FE colleges do so at different ages and stages of their educational development. Achievement is not age related as it tends to be in the compulsory school sector, particularly since National Curriculum testing relates assessment to performance at key stages, at the ages of 7, 11, 14 and 16. In an FE college a GCSE in history, for example, can be taken at 17 or 70, whilst students may be achieving basic numeracy at 35 or even older.

If the concept of lifelong learning is to take hold this means that individuals could be moving in and out of colleges throughout their lifetime. In the future they may not even have to attend the college but will be able to access learning programmes by a range of routes, for example through computer-based learning.

The 1996 Higginson Report made recommendations for an £84 million investment in hi-tech initiatives for the FE sector in order to increase the use of new technology in FE (FEFC, 1996g). This technology, it is suggested, would increase the potential level of learning support for students and provide opportunities for open learning. But students will need support in accessing such information and in mastering the skills required to use the new learning technologies effectively. Thus, many colleges now have Learning Resources Centres. These are usually 'drop-in' centres where students can use the technology available in order to complete assignments or where they can access additional units to support other learning.

This trend will increasingly lead to more individualised learning programmes with students being able to 'pick and mix' different units and elements of courses in order to meet their own needs. Whilst this may open up the whole college curriculum provision to a much wider clientele than has previously been the case, there are implications for student guidance and counselling. Students need help in accessing parts of the curriculum which meet their needs. They also need guidance in constructing a coherent and integrated programme of learning from the wide range of offerings available. In this situation the FE teacher becomes a facilitator of learning rather than a provider. The issues raised here will be further developed in Chapter 5 but the following extract from an FEFC inspection report illustrates the strategies which colleges can employ to meet the needs of individual students:

The college is committed to meeting the needs of individual students. In some areas of work, an individual programme of study will be negotiated if

existing courses are unsuitable. This enables students to join full-time classes on a part-time basis. In other areas, the structures of courses have been modified to enable more people to attend. For example, part-time health and social care students can join a modular programme which provides flexibility and choice both in mode of study and the duration of the course. The college also provides workshops in information technology, numeracy, and communications, which students can attend as they choose.
(FEFC Inspection Report, April 1996)

The range of courses on offer will also be dependent upon the size of the institution and upon its location. Traditionally colleges have served their local communities and have been dependent upon local companies sending their employees on day-release programmes, usually at a craft apprentice or technician level. Notable examples were the colleges in parts of South Yorkshire and Nottinghamshire which were almost entirely dependent on the local mining industry for their students. Pit closures have subsequently meant that these colleges have had to diversify to seek and exploit new markets. Similarly, many large engineering departments have contracted or closed down. Against this background, new courses catering for the burgeoning demands of the information technology industries and for the service industries have been developed. All of this will affect the curriculum offerings of a college. The following extract from an FEFC inspection report illustrates how a college in the South East of England is meeting the challenge of closer links with Europe:

The college is a lively participant in European links. The European Business and Language Centre offers courses to companies. Clients have included the major ferry operators and Eurotunnel; a number of concerns with substantial export interests; and retailers such as Tesco and Marks & Spencer, whose staff need to be able to sell in at least two languages . . . . The European Business and Language Centre now has funding from the Esme Fairbairn Foundation to develop open-learning materials; to link the college campuses electronically; and, with substantial further funding from the European Union, to introduce an audio-conferencing network with seven colleges in other European countries. There are a dozen exchange agreements with colleges in France, Germany, Denmark, Belgium and Sweden. These produce over 100 student exchanges each year, with financial support from the European Union. In addition, about 25 students cross the Channel in each direction for work experience. There are courses in the college which have preparation for employment in Europe at their heart. These include a degree in European business and finance, a course for bilingual secretaries, and a Business and Technology Education Council (BTEC) national diploma in leisure studies which is jointly run with a private college in Arras.

(FEFC Inspection Report, January 1996)

In drawing up strategic plans for their institutions, college managers are supposed to pay attention to the needs of the local labour market and to reflect these in their provision. Funding is often tied to the ways in which courses meet the needs of the local community. However, this is sometimes a difficult task since local labour markets can be volatile and predicting future training requirements is not an exact science. There is also a further consideration in that the demand from students may not match the supply of jobs within the local, regional or even national labour market. Pressures for increased student numbers and, hence, increased funding may persuade colleges to offer those courses which are popular irrespective of job opportunities.

Reflection

The diversity of curriculum provision is revealed in these titles from the classified pages of the educational press. What type of curriculum do you think is offered in these faculties/departments or divisions?

Faculty of the Built Environment

Department of Hospitality and Tourism

Department of Health and Social Care

School of Science

Division of Sport, Leisure and Tourism

Faculty of Business, Management and Humanities

Faculty of Visual Communication

Faculty of General Education and Student Services

You might also want to consider how these different aspects of a college's provision relate to each other.

Since the establishment of the National Council for Vocational Qualifications (NCVQ) in 1986, whose work will be discussed later in this chapter, there has been an attempt to try and encapsulate all qualifications, offered at both compulsory and post-compulsory stages of education and training, into one overarching framework (Figure 3.2).

The 1996 Dearing Review examined the complex system of regulation governing award-bearing courses in England, Wales and Northern Ireland, which has the following structure:

Awarding bodies: six for the GCSE and A level, three for GNVQs, and over 100 for NVQs.

Regulators: for GCSE and A level – School Curriculum and Assessment Authority (SCAA) in England, the Curriculum and Assessment Authority

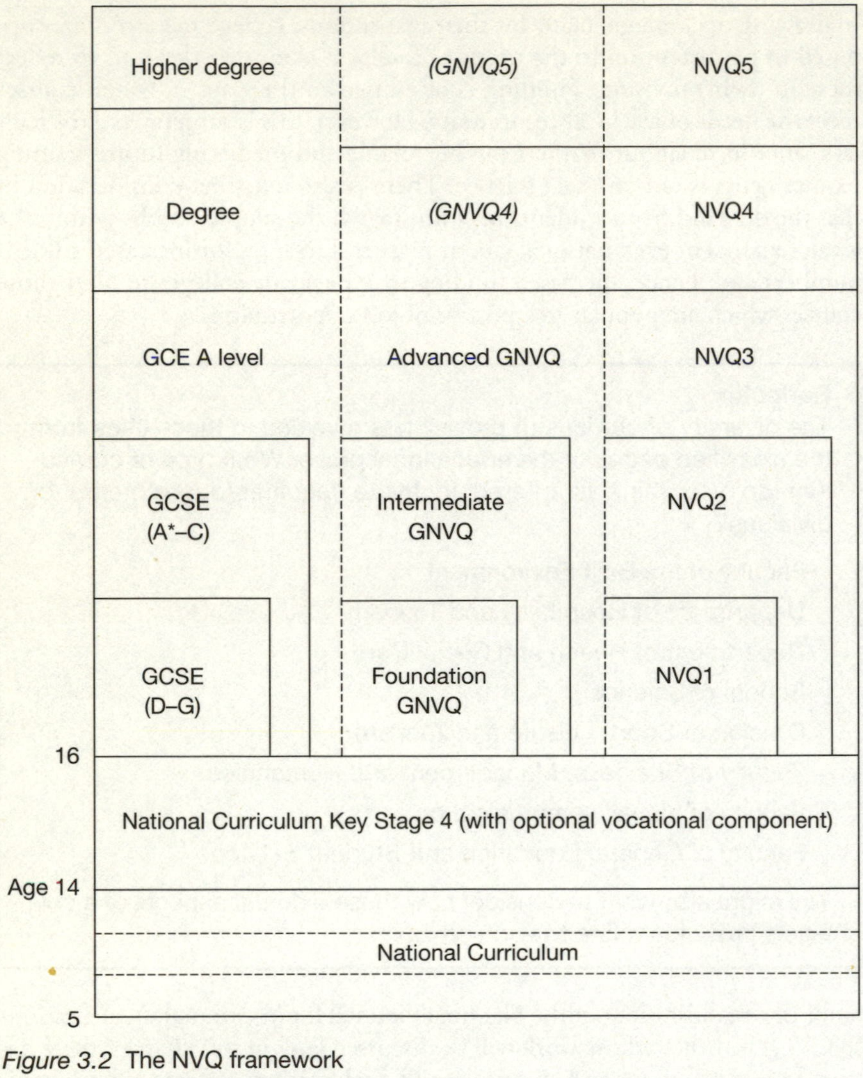

Higher degree	(GNVQ5)	NVQ5
Degree	(GNVQ4)	NVQ4
GCE A level	Advanced GNVQ	NVQ3
GCSE (A*–C)	Intermediate GNVQ	NVQ2
GCSE (D–G)	Foundation GNVQ	NVQ1

16

National Curriculum Key Stage 4 (with optional vocational component)

Age 14

National Curriculum

5

Figure 3.2 The NVQ framework

for Wales (ACAC) and the Council for the Curriculum, Examinations and Assessment (CCEA) in Northern Ireland. For NVQs and GNVQs, the National Council for Vocational Qualifications (NCVQ).

This structure is further complicated by the following features which Dearing identified:

1 In Northern Ireland, the CCEA is responsible for awarding and regulating GCSEs and A levels whereas in England and Wales these functions are separate.

2 Under the current arrangements academic awards are separate from applied and vocational awards.

3 The awarding bodies offering A levels and GNVQs compete with each other.

4 The three GNVQ awarding bodies (BTEC, RSA and City and Guilds) currently have exclusive rights to award GNVQs.

As a result of the Dearing Review, NCVQ and SCAA are discussing ways in which they might merge their responsibilities and the situation in Wales and Northern Ireland is also being reviewed. In October 1997 a new agency, the Qualification Curriculum Authority (QCA) will come into being. Since January 1995, BTEC, RSA and City and Guilds have been collaborating in a Joint Council of National Vocational Awarding Bodies. Dearing's concern, probably shared by thousands of teachers and managers in the post-compulsory sector throughout the country, is for greater coherence in the system:

> The (Dearing) Report argues that the structure of bodies for regulating and making awards should reflect the recent merger of the Government's responsibilities for education and training into the Department for Education and Employment. This will help to bring greater coherence into the framework of qualifications and challenge pervasive attitudes inherited from the past towards the relative worth of achievement in the academic and vocational pathways.
>
> (Dearing, 1996, p.3)

Perhaps it is appropriate now to look at the differing types of curriculum provision found within our FE colleges. The main curricular strands outlined by the FEFC Inspectorate will be used for purposes of classification although it should be remembered that students may combine elements from different curricular strands to form a programme of study. For example, students may combine a General GNVQ programme with an A level. They may also combine some NVQ units with a professional qualification.

GENERAL EDUCATION

A level curriculum

Most of the provision within the general education curricular tradition is either GCE A level or GCSE. Official records show that 'A level accounts for over 90% of the work of sixth form colleges and 41% of all GCE A level examination entries are from students enrolled in further education sector colleges' (FEFC, 1994a, p.13). For students pursuing A levels in a sixth form or FE college there is usually a wider choice of subjects and of examining boards than is the case in a school sixth form. The table below indicates the results achieved by students on A level courses by type of institution in 1994:

Source of entrants	No. of entrants	% pass A–E	% pass A–C
Schools			
18 year olds	364,000	83	52
19 year olds and over	52,000	72	38
Sixth form colleges			
18 year olds	79,000	83	50
19 year olds and over	23,000	73	35
Other FE colleges			
18 year olds	30,000	70	36
19 year olds and over	95,000	62	31

Source: FEFC (1994a, p.54)

As you can see from the table, considerable numbers of young people and adults pursue A level courses in colleges. The overall standard of passes is lower in colleges than schools but one should remember that FE colleges (not necessarily sixth form colleges) accept students with lower grades at GCSE than is the case in most school sixth forms.

The curriculum is determined by the examination boards which prescribe the content of syllabuses and set and mark the examinations. Students are free, subject to the capacity of the college, to choose which subjects they will study at A level. Whilst full-time students may take a programme of three A level subjects, there are other students who may study one A level on a part-time basis by evening attendance. Some may combine an A level with a GNVQ programme.

It could be argued that there is no real A level curriculum since the programme a student follows will be based on individual subjects. In this kind of model a teacher's attention is naturally focused upon achieving the desired number of student passes and at acceptable grades. There may be a danger of 'teaching to the test' rather than considering the development of the whole individual.

This situation may be exacerbated by the fact that a proportion of students taking A levels in colleges may be resitting examinations in which they have previously been unsuccessful. Since entry to HE is normally dependent upon achieving specified grades at A level there is pressure on students and teaching staff to concentrate on 'getting through'. As a teacher your lesson planning will be informed not only by the syllabus but also by the content of past examination papers.

There were attempts to modularise the A level curriculum in the late 1980s and to increase the amount of coursework assessment, though this latter move was seriously curtailed by the 1991 White Paper, *Education and Training for the 21st Century.* Coursework assessment is now limited to 20 per cent except in some practical subjects. Modularity has, according to the Dearing Review, been 'warmly welcomed' and adopted by schools, colleges and universities. Its critics, however, continue to stress that the traditional linear A level is a more effective measure of a candidate's ability as it tests, within one final examination, all the skills, knowledge and understanding which the candidate has gained over the whole programme.

The arguments for reforming A levels have formed a part of a long-running debate about the nature and provision of post-16 education and training. It is not the purpose of this book to revisit that debate, but for those of you who are interested in pursuing this further there is extensive literature on the subject. (See, for example, DES/WO, 1988; Finegold *et al.*, 1990; Nash, 1992; Dearing, 1996; Hodgson and Spours, 1997.)

GCSE curriculum

The second major area of general education provision within the FE sector is that of courses leading to GCSE. There has been a long tradition in FE for students to enrol in order to resit GCSE examinations in which they were unsuccessful at school, but these numbers are dropping as young people choose to make a fresh start by enrolling for a GNVQ or other vocational education course rather than retaking GCSEs. Some students, of course, may be tackling GCSE subjects for the first time, perhaps combining one or two of these with other qualifications. As with the A level programmes, curriculum content will be determined by the examination syllabuses issued by the examining bodies. Examinations are externally set and marked. There is also the opportunity for a limited amount of coursework assessment.

For those teaching on general education programmes which are accredited by examination boards, the content of the curriculum is, therefore, prescribed. The flexibility comes in the way in which teachers interpret the content and in the manner in which they seek to deliver it. The question of teaching style will be considered more fully in Chapter 6. You will, no doubt, wish to reflect upon the type of approach, or variety of approaches, that you might wish to adopt when teaching on general education programmes.

The starting point will be the syllabus issued by the examination board and it is from this that the teacher will need to plan a coherent scheme of work. This will then be broken down further into individual lesson plans. You may already have noticed that in this curricular tradition there is an emphasis on input, or knowledge to be imparted, to achieve a particular outcome – that is, success in the examination.

GENERAL VOCATIONAL EDUCATION

Let us now turn to the curriculum tradition of general vocational education. The FE sector has always been the main provider of general vocational education in this country. During the 1980s there were some developments within schools in both pre-vocational and vocational education through initiatives such as the Certificate of Pre-Vocational Education (CPVE) and the Technical and Vocational Education Initiative (TVEI). However, since the introduction of GNVQs in 1993, which we discuss in more detail below, the involvement of schools in this area of work has increased considerably. In many parts of the country schools and colleges are in direct competition for GNVQ students. GNVQs are, however, not the only vocational education programmes offered by colleges.

Vocational qualifications (not GNVQs or NVQs)

There are still programmes leading to Business and Technology Education Council (BTEC) awards – BTEC, National and Higher National awards – which are well respected by employers and which pioneered an integrated curricular approach:

> BTEC courses, in common with some other vocational programmes, require an integrated and multi-disciplinary approach in their core modules. The emphasis is on the application of knowledge to realistic business or working environments rather than purely on the understanding of theoretical concepts. The development of work related skills is an important feature of the programmes. Assessment, which is based on coursework assignments, may be developed in conjunction with employers.
>
> (Abbott and Huddleston, 1995, p.6)

Other awarding bodies, for example City and Guilds (C & G) and the RSA Examinations Board (RSAEB), also offer qualifications which have not yet been converted to NVQs or GNVQs. Similarly, there are qualifications awarded by professional bodies which have not yet been subsumed within the NVQ framework. The banking sector, for example, has continued to use its own professional qualifications rather than embrace the NVQ model.

At the time of writing, the DfEE was reviewing the development of GNVQs and NVQs in the light of several critical reports and studies which have been published since the early 1990s. For the foreseeable future, it would seem that most colleges will continue to offer courses leading to qualifications which lie outside the GNVQ/NVQ structure.

GNVQs

The 1991 White Paper, *Education and Training for the 21st Century*, announced a proposal for the phased introduction of GNVQs into colleges and school sixth forms. These new qualifications were intended to offer an alternative route for those remaining in full-time education beyond 16. They were to offer a broad preparation for employment or HE and were intended to develop the skills, knowledge and understanding required for the related occupations.

In addition, the government announced that these qualifications were to have a parity of esteem with academic A levels. Indeed, the then Secretary of State for Education, John Patten, said they should be thought of as vocational A levels, a theme taken up by Sir Ron Dearing in his review of qualifications for 16–19 year olds. Sir Ron prefers the term 'Applied A level', which was suggested to him by the National Council for Industry Training Organisations (NCITO):

> The name, Applied A level, has the advantage of bringing home to every-one that the qualification matches A level as a distinctive approach to learning, based on the application of knowledge. To many the thought of studying something that is related to practical applications but is part of the A level family will be attractive. It would help to give parents a better understanding of the value society places on the GNVQ.
>
> (Dearing, 1996, p.71)

In 1992, pilot GNVQs were introduced into 107 schools and colleges, involv-ing 8,500 students in one or more of five broad vocational areas: health and social care, leisure and tourism, business, art and design, manufacturing. Further vocational areas have since been developed, including: information technology, construction and the built environment, hospitality and catering, science, retail and distributive services, media: communication and produc-tion, and management studies.

GNVQs now form a major part of the 16–19 provision in schools and col-leges and by the beginning of 1996, three years after they were piloted, some 66,000 students had gained the award. Spours (1995) has suggested that the GNVQ curriculum model has its roots in the different vocational initiatives that developed in the 1980s, namely:

1 The NVQ methodology for defining standards and assessment.
2 The BTEC First and National Diplomas, which are integrated group awards.
3 CPVE's promotion of active learning strategies and portfolio approaches to recording achievement.

The first of those initiatives, namely the development of NVQs within a competence- and outcome-based model of education and training, was the strongest influence on the nature and design of the GNVQ. Although we dis-cuss NVQs in more detail later in this chapter, it is useful here to explain how the outcome-based model which underpins both GNVQs and NVQs came to be introduced to the UK in the 1980s.

The development of this model in the UK has its roots in the MSC's 1981 Report, *A New Training Initiative* (HMSO, 1981), though it had been influ-ential in the USA since the 1960s in the context of teacher training (Hyland, 1994). In its report, the MSC flagged the need for vocational training to be based on occupational standards, an idea which was stressed again in the 1988 White Paper, *Employment for the 1990s*.

there must be recognised standards of competence, relevant to employment, drawn up by industry-led organisations covering every sector and
every occupational group, and validated nationally.

(ED, 1988, p.30)

These standards of competence were to be drawn up by Lead Bodies, com-
prising employers, professional bodies, training organisations and others,
representing occupational sectors (e.g. construction, engineering, hotel and
catering, business administration, etc.). The Lead Bodies worked with the
Standards Methodology Unit of the Employment Department (since 1995,
part of the merged Department for Education and Employment) and the
NCVQ which was established in 1986. The definition of competence with
which the Lead Bodies were asked to work was: 'the ability to perform the
activities within an occupation or function to the standards expected in
employment' (Training Agency, 1989, p.6).

In identifying standards of competence, the Lead Bodies use a methodology
called functional analysis which involves 'breaking the work role for a particular area into purposes and functions' (Mitchell, 1989, p.58). These 'purposes
and functions' are expressed as competences which are grouped together to
form units (individual competences are called elements). In carrying out their
analysis, Lead Bodies work at five levels of competence as follows:

Level 1: competence in the performance of a range of varied work activities,
most of which may be routine and predictable.

Level 2: competence in a significant range of varied work activities, performed in a variety of contexts. Some of the activities are complex or
non-routine, and there is some individual responsibility or autonomy.
Collaboration with others, perhaps through membership of a work
group or team, may often be a requirement.

Level 3: competence in a broad range of varied work activities performed in
a wide variety of contexts and most of which are complex and non-routine. There is considerable responsibility and autonomy, and control or
guidance of others is often required.

Level 4: competence in a broad range of complex, technical or professional
work activities performed in a wide variety of contexts and with a substantial degree of personal responsibility and autonomy. Responsibility
for the work of others and the allocation of resources is often present.

Level 5: competence which involves the application of a significant range of
fundamental principles and complex techniques across a wide and often
unpredictable variety of contexts. Very substantial personal autonomy
and often significant responsibility for the work of others and for the
allocation of substantial resources feature strongly, as do the personal
accountabilities for analysis and diagnosis, design, planning, execution
and evaluation.

(NCVQ, 1995, p.20)

Unlike NVQs, GNVQs are not competence based but outcome based as the NCVQ explains:

> Although the structure of GNVQs is similar to NVQs, their purpose and content differ significantly. NVQs set the national standards of competence for occupations and professions. NVQ requirements are directly related to those of the workplace and most of the learning and assessment for NVQs is carried out in the workplace itself. The award of an NVQ confirms that the holder has demonstrated that she or he is competent to perform in the relevant job or occupation. The award of a GNVQ does not imply that a student can perform competently in any occupation immediately on qualifying, but rather that she or he has a broad foundation of learning upon which to build.
>
> (NCVQ, June 1995, p.12)

Whereas NVQs span five levels, GNVQs, at the time of writing, are limited to the first three levels of the NVQ/qualifications framework:

Foundation GNVQ　　　　NVQ Level 1

Intermediate GNVQ　　　NVQ Level 2

Advanced GNVQ　　　　NVQ Level 3

For a picture of how GNVQs fit within the overall qualification framework see Figure 3.2, p.34.

This new system of qualifications, and indeed the whole notion of a competence-based model itself, has many critics (see, for example, Smithers, 1993; Hyland, 1994; Hodkinson and Issitt, 1995; Bates *et al.*, 1995). It is not, however, the purpose of this book to debate the appropriateness or inappropriateness of a competence-based model of vocational education and training. What is important for the purpose of the intending or practising teacher in the sector is an understanding of how these different systems operate and of the ways in which curriculum design is affected.

The defining features of GNVQs are as follows:

- They are vocationally specific qualifications relating to broad vocational areas.
- Performance is measured in terms of outcomes (statements of achievement).
- Assessment is carried out through a series of coursework assignments rather than through one externally set and marked examination.
- Evidence of achievement is collected throughout the programme to form an individual student portfolio.
- The qualifications also include key skills. Prior to the 1996 Dearing Review, the term *core* skills was in common use but has now been superseded by the term *key* skills.

The Foundation and Intermediate GNVQ programmes are intended to take normally one year's full-time study and the Advanced normally two years' full-time study. From September 1995, 14–16 year olds have been able to follow specified units in order to complete just over half a GNVQ programme, known as the Part One GNVQ.

There are two types of GNVQ unit available: vocational and key skills. Key skills units comprise communication, application of number and information technology and are mandatory for all candidates. They must be passed at the appropriate level for the award: for example, Advanced key skills for an Advanced award. All GNVQ courses are also expected to develop a range of personal and study skills.

Units are further divided into those which are mandatory for all awards, irrespective of the awarding body, and those which are optional and specific to a particular awarding body. A candidate may also take additional units to enhance the award at all levels but does not need to complete such units in order to achieve the award satisfactorily.

The introduction of such radical changes to the nature and structure of general vocational awards has been a cause of major upheaval in colleges, and more so in schools. It is not surprising, then, that a new teacher may feel bewildered by the seeming complexity of the structure, pedagogy and assessment procedures involved in such a system. In terms of structure the position may be summarised as follows:

Advanced   15 units in total

    8   mandatory units
    4   optional units
    3   mandatory key skills

Intermediate   9 units in total

    4   mandatory units
    2   optional units
    3   mandatory key skills

Foundation   9 units in total

    3   mandatory units
    3   optional units
    3   mandatory key skills

Any additional units which students take will be recognised in the student's record of achievement (see Chapter 6). The award will be granted when all the mandatory, optional and key skills units for that level of award have been satisfactorily completed. The outcomes for the award are expressed as statements of achievement.

Before moving on to the content of teaching on such programmes, it is necessary to understand a little more about the structure. It has been noted that GNVQs are unit-based qualifications; the unit is the smallest part of a GNVQ qualification that can be accredited by an awarding body. Each unit is made up of anything from two to five elements. Performance criteria are set for each element describing what a candidate must do in order to meet the requirements of the element. In each element a range is identified, which indicates the depth and extent of coverage required by the candidate. Evidence indicators indicate the minimum evidence a student needs to provide to demonstrate achievement. Below is an extract from the Advanced GNVQ specification for Manufacturing:

STRUCTURE OF ADVANCED GNVQ IN MANUFACTURING

SUMMARY OF MANDATORY UNITS

Unit 1   Design Specification (Advanced)
1.1   Prepare product specifications
1.2   Develop potential design proposals
1.3   Select and recommend design solutions

Unit 2   Communicate Product Design (Advanced)
2.1   Record and communicate designs and specifications
2.2   Prepare and present design proposals

Unit 3   Manufacturing Systems (Advanced)
3.1   Investigate manufacturing systems
3.2   Investigate production processes
3.3   Evaluate equipment and machinery for production

Unit 4   Production Costs and Schedules (Advanced)
4.1   Calculate and compare production costs of products
4.2   Produce production schedules

Unit 5   Process Operations (Advanced)
5.1   Process materials
5.2   Carry out and monitor assembly and finishing procedures
5.3   Package products and prepare for dispatch

Unit 6   Quality and Control (Advanced)
6.1   Evaluate quality assurance and quality control systems
6.2   Test and inspect products at key stages of production

Unit 7   Work Practices (Advanced)
7.1   Investigate responsibilities to customers and product consumers
7.2   Contribute to production teams and working groups
7.3   Identify health and safety standards for individuals and the workplace

Unit 8   Environmental Impact (Advanced)

8.1   Evaluate the environmental impact of manufacturing processes
8.2   Evaluate the management of hazardous materials
8.3   Investigate the use of energy in manufacturing

(*Source:* RSA Examination Board)

You will probably be perplexed as to how this might be transformed into a scheme of work, or, indeed, into individual classes, especially if your own experience has been on academic programmes. The curriculum model of GNVQ is based upon some key elements:

● the emphasis on an outcome-based approach which is independent of the mode or duration of study;
● a close relationship between individual learning and assessment which allows students to build up their own portfolios of evidence for assessment;
● flexibility in the ways in which outcomes may be achieved allowing for a variety of learning experiences.

The inclusion of key skills, through an integrated approach, is part of the curricular design, although in practice this integration has been difficult to achieve. Even where integration has been achieved it has still met with criticism (see, for example, FEU, IOE and Nuffield Foundation, 1994; Capey, 1995). The curriculum design is also based on the notion of providing broad vocational knowledge and generic skills suitable for progression to occupationally specific training or vocationally related HE courses.

The Dearing Review (1996) has emphasised that GNVQ is still at a developmental stage and that there are likely to be further modifications. Nevertheless, Spours (1995, p.38) has indicated that there are some curricular strengths in the GNVQ design, namely:

● their organisation around assessed units could be the basis for encouraging a step-by-step approach to achievement and a flexible approach to credit transfer between qualifications;
● strong formative assessment, an active approach to learning and the compilation of coursework portfolios encourage students to manage their own study and acquire the habit of lifelong learning;
● GNVQs include a wide range of vocational areas and key skills which have not previously been associated with nationally recognised qualifications.

You will already have recognised that teaching and learning on GNVQ programmes are different from those encountered on traditional academic programmes. In GNVQ programmes the emphasis is on developing the skills of the learner, to enable him or her to become more self-reliant. The responsibility has to shift from the teacher to the learner but these are skills which have to be cultivated. It may be difficult for teachers who have been accustomed to 'leading from the front' to change to a more student-centred approach. Equally, it may be difficult for students to come to terms with a more flexible approach.

The last three years have witnessed an enormous degree of change in the pattern of provision of general vocational qualifications in our FE colleges. The range of GNVQ courses and the numbers of students have increased dramatically. Such rapid change has obviously brought in its wake a number of issues still requiring resolution. A 1995 FEFC report drew attention to the need for improved staff development for teachers involved in the delivery of the new qualifications (FEFC, 1995a). It is recognised that there is a need for clearer guidance on curriculum and assessment.

NVQs and job-specific training

FE has a long tradition of providing job-specific training for both young people and adults covering a wide range of occupational sectors. The provision of vocational training was the *raison d'être* of many early technical colleges and much of this provision was on a day-release basis. Employers generally funded this training and were sometimes represented on college advisory boards. In the main, however, employers would have to place employees on courses which were available at colleges and had very little influence over what would be provided or when or how this would be achieved. In this sense, provision was supplier led; that is, colleges offered a range of courses structured around a traditional 36-week college year and it was anticipated that demand would follow supply.

In addition to day-release provision, colleges have always provided evening classes for those wishing to pursue job-related qualifications in their own time. Many of those achieving vocational qualifications in the past have done so by attending evening classes for anything up to five years or more.

The awarding body with the largest number of such qualifications is the City and Guilds of London Institute (CGLI). On the other hand some awarding bodies are very small, perhaps only offering a couple of qualifications. Although many of these qualifications are now subsumed within the NVQ framework and others are in the process of being converted to NVQs, there is still a large amount of vocational work within the FE sector which is outside the NVQ framework. Figures held on the National Information System for Vocational Qualifications (NISVQ) reveal the 'numbers of traditional vocational qualifications continue to exceed awards of NVQs, despite a recent growth in the latter' (DfEE, 1995) Although the NISVQ covers only 75 per cent of all traditional awards, it is estimated that, on this basis, the number of traditional vocational qualifications awarded each year is just under three-quarters of a million.

In December 1995, the millionth NVQ was awarded; however, this relates to the millionth NVQ certificate and does not represent a full award. The tables below indicate the numbers of traditional vocational awards and the numbers of NVQs awarded during the past four years.

Traditional vocational awards
1991/2   737,000
1992/3   781,000
1993/4   773,000

Growth in cumulative total of NVQ certificates awarded:

1990   20,217
1992   221,644
1994   628,143
1996   1,203,159

Source: NCVQ 1996

Of course not all these qualifications are awarded through FE colleges. In 1993/4 NISVQ records that approximately 43 per cent of traditional vocational awards (i.e. not NVQs or GNVQs) were made to candidates who were examined or assessed at an FE centre. Note that this does not imply that the training took place at the college but that assessment was carried out there. It is clear, however, that FE still remains the major provider of vocationally specific training both of NVQs and of traditional vocational awards.

The next section will focus specifically on the impact of NVQs on college provision since this has introduced a significant change in the way in which teaching and learning take place. It is important to recognise that an NVQ is not a course of study and it is not necessary to undertake a specific training course before competences are demonstrated. NVQs confirm that the holder possesses the competences required to carry out a specific job.

The majority of these awards are available within the FE sector although some are delivered within companies to their own employees. The reluctance of some employers to become involved with the delivery of NVQs has meant that FE colleges have been at the forefront of development and implementation. The barriers to implementation perceived by companies have been highlighted in a number of recent reports (IES, 1994; KPMG Peat Marwick, 1994; CBI, 1994; IES, 1995; Beaumont, 1996).

Each NVQ comprises a number of units of competence as follows:

Each NVQ comprises two or more units, for example, *Level I Catering and Hospitality (serving Food and Drink – Bar)* has the following units:

● Maintain a safe and secure working environment
● Maintain customer care

The defining characteristic of the qualification is that it is based on the notion of competence, evidence of which is derived from the candidate's performance in the workplace, or under simulated working conditions. The structure of the qualifications also differs from that of more traditional vocational awards.

Each NVQ comprises a number of units usually between six and twelve, but this will vary according to the occupation and level. A unit is the smallest part of an NVQ for which a candidate may be awarded a certificate. NVQs are available at five levels (see Figure 3.2 page 34).

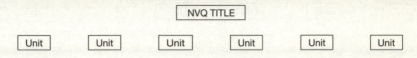

To gain the full NVQ a candidate must complete all the mandatory units for that NVQ.

Each unit is broken down into a number of elements. An element summarises the activities on which the candidate will be assessed. For example, a candidate completing a unit within a Retailing NVQ on Dealing with Refunded Goods and Complaints will have to demonstrate that s/he can complete a refund/exchange of stock.

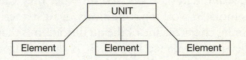

For each element a series of performance criteria are given, these are the outcomes which are expected from the activities outlined in the element. For example, if the candidate were dealing with a refund or exchange of stock, s/he would need to demonstrate that the correct amount of cash had been refunded or that appropriate stock had been selected and exchanged.

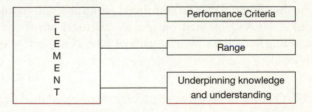

You will see that there are two further boxes attached to the element. Range indicates the situations in which the work is to be carried out and helps to contextualise the activity. For example, our candidate completing the element on stock refund/exchange would need to show that s/he was competent to deal with the activity when goods appeared to be suitable for exchange and also when they appeared damaged. The final box deals with underpinning knowledge and understanding. In addition to the demonstration of competence candidates are expected to have the necessary underpinning knowledge and understanding to perform effectively. Our candidate would need to know, for example, about the implications of the Sale of Goods Act on the return of goods.

The whole model may be illustrated diagrammatically as follows:

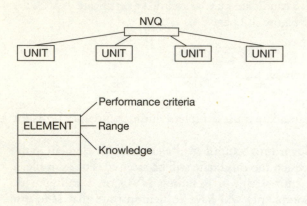

For each element candidates are assessed on what they can do in the work-place, or under simulated working conditions, against a series of performance criteria. The defining characteristic of the qualification is that it is based on the notion of competence, evidence for which is derived from the candidate's performance in the workplace. In addition to the demonstration of competence candidates are expected to have the necessary underpinning knowledge and skills to perform effectively. Critics of the qualification (Smithers, 1993; Hyland, 1994; Richardson *et al.*, 1995) have argued that it is the lack of underpinning knowledge and skills which makes the qualification deficient. FEFC (1994b) has suggested that:

> The contribution of NVQs to vocational education and training would be enhanced if NCVQ insisted on greater clarification of the knowledge, understanding and core skills elements of each NVQ before qualifications are accredited.

> (FEFC, 1994b, p.6)

Although NVQs were designed as essentially work-based qualifications, many of which would be taken by adults already in employment, the largest proportion of uptake has been by young people in initial training. It is estimated that 75 per cent of all NVQ units studied by young people are currently funded through Youth Training (YT) (Payne, 1995) which is perhaps unsurprising given that the funding methodology for YT requires that trainees be working towards a minimum of NVQ Level 2.

Assessment methods for NVQs include workplace observation of performance, skills tests, practical projects, assignments, written and oral questioning. Because of the need for candidates to demonstrate competence in the workplace, colleges have had to find suitable work placements for full-time students and unemployed students on NVQ programmes. This has not always been easy for colleges particularly since there are so many competing demands on employers to provide work placements. Some colleges have been able to provide realistic learning environments, for example in college restaurants. For other colleges it has been much more difficult to provide a simulated work environment. The FEFC has indicated that in engineering this may be more difficult since workshops 'are not always adequately equipped to meet the needs of NVQ assessments' (FEFC, 1994b, p.14). Some employers are also doubtful about the validity of assessment undertaken in a simulated environment.

NVQs are not dependent upon any particular mode, duration or location of study. This is one of several significant changes which colleges have had to face in reorganising their provision for those wishing to acquire NVQs. Candidates may claim credit for competence previously acquired providing that they can furnish sufficient evidence to demonstrate such competence. This process is known as the accreditation of prior learning (APL). Colleges show enormous diversity in their capacities to handle APL effectively.

The development of competence-based curricula in FE colleges has highlighted the need for some significant changes of approach in course delivery. These may be summarised as follows:

- the need for more flexible and responsive provision which can accommodate individual student needs;
- the development of learning support materials and learning resource centres which students can access individually according to their own needs, with or without the help of a lecturer;
- the modularisation of curricula, although this is by no means universal, to enable students to 'pick and mix' units which they require in order to complete an NVQ, rather than having to follow a complete programme;
- the development of partnerships with employers in order to ensure an adequate supply of work placements for students;
- the design of simulated work environments within colleges, for example, college restaurants, hairdressing salons, vehicle maintenance workshops, to allow students to demonstrate competence under the same conditions and pressures as they would in employment;
- the need to develop adequate systems of guidance, advice and counselling to enable students to access the appropriate parts of the curriculum;
- the incorporation of support structures to enable students to build portfolios of evidence and to identify learning opportunities within the workplace and within the college.

These may be seen as pre-conditions for the flexible college. However, whilst the curricular offerings are so diverse, lecturers may find themselves moving between programmes during the course of a working week.

Reflection

How does the teacher juggle these possibly competing demands?
How can the potential learners seek impartial and informed advice?
How does modularisation of the curriculum affect the teaching
    timetable?
What are the implications for teachers of a modularised curricu-
    lum?
If students are allowed to 'pick and mix' units, how can they build a
    coherent programme of study?

The fact that such questions, and many more, are raised by the introduction
of competence-based models suggests that there are, and have been, some significant challenges to colleges in introducing the new qualifications. Perhaps
the most significant impact lies in the fact that because NVQs are specified in
terms of outcomes rather than inputs and can be assessed in any context
where competence can be appropriately demonstrated, colleges do not have
the monopoly in job-specific training.

Colleges are in competition with private training providers and with companies 'in-house' training programmes. Cost may be an important factor
when employers or TECs decide where to place their training contracts. In the
new climate of competition colleges are competing not only with companies
and private training providers but also with each other.

A more detailed examination of such issues lies outside the scope of this
book. However, as a teacher in the sector you will naturally be concerned
about the curriculum offerings available to students and how best to accommodate their learning needs.

HIGHER EDUCATION (HE) AND ADVANCED STUDIES

HE generally refers to those advanced courses usually, though not exclusively,
provided by a university or by its constituent or associated institutions.
Advanced in these contexts refers to courses which are deemed to be beyond
A level, or equivalent, standard.

Although some FE colleges have always provided a certain amount of
advanced work, for example through Higher National Diploma (HND) and
Higher National Certificate (HNC) programmes, the provision of degree-level
courses is relatively recent. Nevertheless, some colleges have expanded their
provision rapidly in this area through franchising arrangements with universities. As we saw in Chapter 1, one Birmingham college receives a greater
proportion of its funding from the HEFC than from the FEFC.

It is not the purpose of this book to debate the nature and form of the
HE curriculum; this has been considered elsewhere and there is an established literature on the subject. The intention is to highlight the developments

which have occurred within the FE sector in its relationship with HE institutions.

Squires (1987) suggests that 'the pattern of undergraduate studies in the U.K. depends on two things: where one studies and what one studies' (Squires, 1987, p.130). He then goes on to explore some of the features of academic and professional courses and draws attention to developments in the modularisation of some undergraduate programmes. In those universities where modularisation has been whole-heartedly embraced, the course unit or module becomes the essential element of the programme. In its most extreme form students may 'pick and mix' across a very wide range of units to build a whole programme. Each unit may be assessed and accredited on completion until a full degree has been built up. There are obviously various stages along the continuum from what Squires (ibid.) has described as a 'holistic' to an 'aggregative' curriculum.

One of the reasons for drawing attention to these developments is to suggest that once the curriculum has been unitised in this way then the place in which it is studied becomes less important provided there is adequate quality control. The Open University allows students to study through a variety of means and in widely dispersed locations. The unifying factor is, of course, the content of programmes which is centrally regulated. By devolving delivery in this way, universities can reduce their costs, or rather not incur further costs, whilst increasing student numbers.

The delivery of some parts of undergraduate programmes in colleges has enabled students to access the HE curriculum locally. Relationships between colleges and HE institutions may vary. In some cases colleges are delivering the first two years of a degree programme, with the third and fourth years being delivered in the university. In other cases, colleges may deliver the whole of an undergraduate programme. There may be franchising arrangements in place or colleges may have their own programmes accredited by an HE institution. Sometimes the HE institution may not be local to the college. There are further examples where colleges may be running whole, or part of, degree programmes from several different HE institutions.

Where FE colleges are delivering programmes through franchising arrangements then curriculum content will be a given. There will also be control over the staffing of programmes and other resource issues. Standards of assessment will be monitored and verified, examinations will be set by the university.

Those involved in teaching such programmes in colleges may be located within a separate department or unit specialising in HE courses. This will not always be the case, though. HE courses may fall within the remit of a Department of General Education or within a curriculum area, for example, Business and Management.

Students on HE programmes may have come through special access courses which the college offers, and many of them will be mature entrants. As teachers you will need to consider these factors in developing your teaching strategy.

If you return to Margaret, the HE student described in Chapter 2, you will see that she has particular learning needs as an HE student, some of which derive from a lack of confidence.

There is a continuing debate concerning the role of FE in HE provision. Some FE practitioners argue that colleges should concentrate on the delivery of high-quality vocational education and training and that they should 'not turn themselves into universities' (TES, 9 February 1996). Nevertheless, it seems likely that much of this growth will have to come via the FE rather than the HE route given Lifetime Learning Target 2:

> By the year 2000: 30% of the workforce to have a vocational, professional, management or academic qualification at NVQ Level 4 or above.

ADULT EDUCATION

The term 'adult' as applied to education is not easy to define. For some it has connotations of anything beyond the phase of compulsory schooling, whilst for others it may be regarded as post initial education, that is the period beyond initial HE. Some institutions may use age 25 to distinguish between ordinary and mature students whereas for funding purposes 19 is frequently regarded as the difference between youth and adult status.

The scope of adult education has always been, and is, extremely wide. There are some institutions which exist primarily to teach adults, for example the Workers' Educational Association (WEA), the Open University and adult education services, where they still exist, provided by local authorities. (For a more detailed discussion of adult education provision see Fieldhouse and Associates, 1996) Adult education may also be engaged in through a whole range of informal mechanisms, including, for example, church groups and voluntary organisations. In its widest sense adult education may be described as any form of education or training in which adults engage. The current interest in the fostering and development of lifelong learning will focus attention on the ways in which, and the means by which, adults engage in continuing education and personal and professional development.

For the purposes of this book we are focusing on the provision for adults in the FE sector where, as we have seen in Chapter 1, the majority of students are over the age of 19. Although most courses will not be specifically targeted at a particular age group, some will naturally be more appealing to younger rather than older students and vice versa. There are, however, some programmes which are definitely targeted at adults, for example, those involving government schemes for the long-term adult unemployed, such as Training for Work. There are also programmes, often funded by the European Social Fund (ESF), which are designed to meet the needs of those adults wishing to return to work, particularly women.

A proportion of adult provision will cover basic education. These programmes tend to focus on the achievement of basic literacy and numeracy skills and will often include the development of a range of interpersonal and social skills. Topics such as applying for jobs and interview techniques may be covered. Some adult programmes will also include an introduction to specific vocational areas.

An example of this type of programme is provided by a West Midlands college which currently offers NVQs in hairdressing for adult returners. The lecturer in charge of hairdressing reported that the skills development and confidence building inherent in the course design had enabled some of his students to gain employment before the end of the programme and in areas other than hairdressing, for example reception work.

Whilst this is a very significant outcome for the adult student, it does not help the hairdressing lecturer in achieving the targets for his or her department. The department's funding will depend not only upon students enrolled but also upon course completion and outcomes, that is NVQs achieved. This calls into question a funding methodology which is based upon a 'payment by results' principle. In terms of the adults involved, eventual employment is a significant outcome.

Squires has suggested that 'the older meaning of adult education confined it to two or three headings: liberal, recreational and basic' (1987, p.177). More recent definitions, and indeed those adopted by DfEE and NACETT, tend to regard adult education as continuous and ongoing, in fact any form of education, training or development in which adults engage. Informal settings may be just as significant as formal areas in this context. There is a sense in which nothing may be discounted.

Recreational classes for adults have always been provided by FE colleges. The funding for such programmes comes from the local community, not from the FEFC. These programmes have been seriously curtailed during recent years. In some areas they have been retained because adults have been able to pay a full rather than a subsidised cost. In other areas the programmes have been redesigned to lead to NVQs, or units towards them, and they have, therefore, been able to attract funding, for example from local TECs.

There is also an increasing interest in continuous professional development amongst employed adults. In certain professions it is a requirement in order to continue practising, or to be allowed continued membership of professional organisations. The introduction of appraisal processes in the workplace may also highlight areas for professional and personal development. Colleges are now looking at ways of meeting some of these individual and company developmental needs.

It will be clear from this diverse picture that the adult education curriculum is 'more diverse in terms of aims, content and form than anything that precedes it' (Squires, 1987, p.207). It is quite impossible to talk about an adult education curriculum. It is perhaps more useful to think about the ways in which adults learn and the strategies which we as teachers might develop in order to help them learn more effectively. These themes are returned to in Chapters 5 and 6.

This chapter has attempted to outline the range and diversity of the curriculum post-16. As a teacher you will be constantly re-examining your position in relation to these differing curricular models. It is not only you as a teacher – your students too may be exposed to a range of curricular models.

Reflection

If you return to the students in Chapter 2, you will see that several of them are following a mixed curricular model. This means that their experiences, as learners, may be quite different in different parts of the programme. This is not just because they may be taught by different staff but because the content and, more importantly, the pedagogy of the separate elements may be different. For example, Margaret is an HE student, but she is also a mature student. Gary is following a general vocational education programme with some job-specific elements. You might like to consider the programmes being followed by the other students. To what extent are they having a mixed curricular experience?

The following example of an innovative scheme for engineering trainees (recruited through Modern Apprenticeship) in a major motor manufacturing company outlines the ways in which the post-16 curriculum might become more flexible. Here a curriculum has been designed to suit the specific training needs of both the trainees and the company. The design has been realised by selecting those elements of different curricular models which meet the requirements for a flexible, skilled labour force.

Learning on the Modern Apprenticeship

Apprentices are combining the GNVQ at either Intermediate or Advanced levels with NVQ Level 2 and 3 as appropriate. The core skills units provide breadth and flexibility to the training which it is felt would not be the case if it were purely an NVQ programme. Some of the core skills units are achieved through a week's 'outward-bound' style of residential programme which involves all the apprentices and some of the college staff and company personnel. This takes place at the beginning of the programme. At this time students are also introduced to the concept of portfolio building and shown how to collect evidence to meet both GNVQ and NVQ requirements.

On completion of the GNVQ and NVQ the apprentices will then move on to either an HNC or a degree programme. The strength of the scheme is that it allows flexibility between and across different routes and the apprentice is not artificially restricted from moving from what was formerly a 'craft' route into a 'technician' route. The introduction of the scheme has caused colleges and company training personnel to work closely together and fundamentally to change the curriculum model.

The model recognises that learning takes place both in the college and in the workplace. The assignments which apprentices complete as part of the GNVQ are work-based assignments. That is, they have been identified from the work placements which students undertake in the company. This requires both workplace supervisors and college staff to identify jointly the learning opportunities within the workplace. Once these have been identified, and there is no reason to believe that there would be any shortage of such opportunities, assignments are designed which will enable the apprentices to reflect upon the learning experience and to demonstrate what they have learned.

In this model the assignment is at the heart of the learning process rather than being something which is added on at the end of a period of instruction. The specifications for the NVQ and GNVQ indicate what has to be achieved; the assignment is a means of achieving them. Perhaps more importantly it links the learning with workplace experience and ensures that what is being learned is both realistic and relevant. In the past employers have sometimes complained that college practice did not mirror current workplace practice. As one head of department put it: 'When I came here a few years ago, students were still hammering lumps of metal.' No account had been taken of the changes in manufacturing processes and the developments in computer-aided design and manufacture (CAD/CAM). He went on to say: 'That has all changed here now; this programme has been developed with our partners in the company and reflects current practice. Teaching can be carried out by both company and college staff on either college or company premises; the whole thing is much more flexible.' The college staff even wear company overalls.

In this model the apprentices have to take responsibility for their own learning. The objectives of the programme are stated at the outset, and the unit specifications clearly demonstrate what has to be achieved. The apprentices have to decide how, when and where they will achieve them. There is, of course, support from both college and company staff and each apprentice is provided with a company mentor to support him or her through the programme. There are deadlines to be met and the apprentice has to decide how best to meet them. In this curricular model a great deal of the 'ownership' of the programme has been devolved to the apprentice.

(*Source*: Huddleston, P., 1996)

Part II

Teaching and learning

Chapter 4

Approaches to learning

> When adults teach and learn in one another's company, they find themselves engaging in a challenging, passionate, and creative activity. The acts of teaching and learning – the creation and alteration of our beliefs, values, actions, relationships, and social forms that result from this – are ways in which we realise our humanity.
>
> (Brookfield, 1986, p.1)

In order to meet the challenge of teaching in the FE sector, it is essential to have some knowledge of the different theories which explain how people learn. As we discussed in Chapter 2, you could be teaching students whose ages range from as young as 16 (possibly even 14) to those in advanced old age, all of whom will have spent some years being taught in other educational institutions, in informal settings, and possibly in their places of work. You will, therefore, be confronted with people who have a great deal of experience as learners. And that experience will be of a particularly personal nature. For some of your students, their learning experiences may have been entirely pleasurable, whilst for others learning may be equated with anxiety and even pain. You will meet students who lack confidence as learners and many who find it difficult to know how to learn for themselves without being totally dependent on a teacher. The nature of a person's prior learning experience has a profound effect on their approach and attitude to further learning activity. As such, teachers do not start with a clean sheet. It may seem unnecessary to point out that people, whether they be teenagers or adults, learn in different ways but it is a truism whose implications can be lost in the hectic whirl of the average teaching day.

Just as your students will approach their learning in different ways, you too will have developed your own strategies for acquiring knowledge and understanding and for learning new tasks. And that very personal approach to learning will influence your approach to and style of teaching.

Reflection

Give some thought to the following questions and try to answer them as honestly as possible. You could also try them out on a friend, partner or member of your family.

1 What was the last thing you learned?
2 Do you attend a regular class of any kind, for example keep-fit, camera club, local history? If you do, why do you attend and how did you get started?
3 Do you enjoy learning? Do you, for example, enjoy learning from books, listening to lectures, watching experts, finding out answers for yourself?
4 Do you consider yourself to be a *good* learner? How would you define a *good* learner?
5 Given your answer to question 4, were you a good learner at school? Have you improved as a learner since leaving school?
6 Is there anything which prevents you from learning?

In answering the questions above, you may have revealed aspects of your persona as an adult learner which even you find surprising. The last question, for example, may have brought forward a certain personal barrier to learning which you have not articulated before.

Your answers may also reveal something about your own personal definition of what learning means. You might, for example, agree with the 'behaviourists' who say that, in order to claim learning has taken place, a person's behaviour has to change (see Skinner, 1968). The 'behaviourist' school of thought was pre-eminent in the 1950s and 1960s, particularly in the USA through the work of B.F. Skinner, and had a great influence on workplace training and the programmed learning approach adopted in correspondence courses. Indeed, the competence-based approach (discussed in Chapters 3 and 6) has been criticised as being a return to the techniques of behaviourism. What the 'behaviourists' overlooked, and as a result are now seen to be the 'bad guys' of learning theory, is the contribution and consciousness of the learner.

Kolb, whose work has been influential in adult education and workplace training, defines learning as 'the process whereby knowledge is created through the transformation of experience' (Kolb, 1984, p.41). His 'learning cycle' claims that learners progress through four stages (Figure 4.1), each of which can be entered first, on their learning journey.

Whilst being praised for its contribution to the development of learning theory, Kolb's model has also been criticised for being too simplistic. For example, Jarvis (1987) has pointed out:

consider the situation where a person is reading a complex mathematical tome and is involved in abstract conceptualisation from the outset: the next

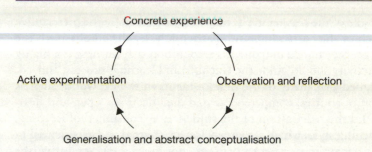

Figure 4.1 Kolb's (1984) learning cycle

stage of the learning process might be reflection rather than active experi-
mentation and so the arrows would need to point in both directions. In
addition, Schon (1983, pp.49–69) discusses the idea of reflection-in-action
in which they occur almost simultaneously. Hence there may be stages of
Kolb's cycle that are not sequential.

(Jarvis, 1987, p.18)

Despite the flaws in his model, however, Kolb's key contribution is his emphasis on the central importance to learning of *experience.* There is a general
consensus among adult learning theorists that the experiences which adults
have gained during their lives play an important part in any learning activity
on which they embark. Those experiences can have both a positive and negative effect. They can help adults contextualise and conceptualise new
information but experience can also hinder learning by reminding adults of
past failures. The recognition that adults learn in different ways and that each
adult comes to learning with a unique set of experiences has contributed to the
development of the theory of 'experiential learning', echoes of which are to be
found in the work of Piaget and the American educationalist, John Dewey.
(See Piaget, 1970 and Dewey, 1938.) In its simplest form, experiential learning recognises that adults approach any learning activity with some
preconceived idea about what it is they are about to try and learn. This is
because of the wide range of experience they already have and so they do not
approach learning with a totally blank mind. A great deal of teaching, in all
sectors of education, undervalues this prior experience in learners and tends to
follow what the Brazilian adult educator, Paulo Freire, called the 'banking'
concept of education:

Education thus becomes an act of depositing, in which the students are the
depositories and the teacher is the depositer. Instead of communicating, the
teacher issues the communiques and makes deposits which the students
patiently receive, memorise, and repeat.

(Freire, 1974, p.58)

Although the role of the teacher in FE may be constrained by the prescriptive nature of much of the curriculum and, particularly, by the emphasis on the assessment of predetermined outcomes, a recognition that learning is a highly personalised activity should guide the teaching and learning process. Indeed, it could be argued that many of the developments in the FE world, such as modularisation of courses, competence-based qualifications, open and flexible learning, and the redefinition of the student as a 'consumer' of learning, necessitate teaching styles which are largely learner centred and experiential in emphasis. The danger in treating students as consumers, however, is that the 'product' (e.g. a module or a qualification) they are 'buying' becomes more important than the learning process. Whether they are learning on their own or in groups, students should not be seen as, or even allowed to be, simply passive participants.

For some FE teachers, the promotion and advocacy of learner-centred and flexible approaches to teaching and learning by management are to be viewed with suspicion and even cynicism as Wilmot and McLean found when they evaluated one college's attempts to introduce flexible learning:

> The thread that runs through teachers' discussion about flexible learning is that it is being promoted for non-educational reasons. Several teachers feel that flexible learning is an educational justification for an economic measure. An important observation among teachers is that encouraging students to become self-motivated is not a cheap option. The economic pressure for larger class sizes and shorter class contact time militates against workshop style delivery – and not for it. Likewise economic pressures leading to less contact time with students may reduce opportunity for supervised discovery methods of learning, which take more time – as one teacher observed: 'Nothing can be done more quickly than telling students all the answers' . . . They (teachers) are not opposed to flexible methods which enhance the process of guiding the students to more independence, but there are two sources of tension between teachers and managers. First, teachers are anxious that management's priority of cost-effectiveness will mean that flexible learning is interpreted in ways that are not educationally desirable. Secondly, teachers point out that management do not directly observe student responses to flexible learning styles and, at times, evince unwillingness to accept that some independent learning strategies do not result in positive outcomes for students.
>
> (Wilmot and McLean, 1994, p.103)

A QUESTION OF AGE: THE CONCEPT OF ADULTHOOD

You may be surprised by the references to adult learners and adult learning when we began this chapter by acknowledging the fact that you could be teaching people as young as 16. If you were teaching in a school, you might regard all students up to the age of 18 as children and would probably, therefore, turn to theories of how children learn for some insight before preparing to teach. People mature differently and there are some 12 year olds who demonstrate greater sophistication as learners than many twice or even three times as old. Colleges of FE have always seen themselves as being different to schools in a number of ways but a key difference is in their attitude to students. Students in colleges have left the compulsory stage of education and entered the non-compulsory world in which they will be required to take responsibility for their own learning. Although, in reality, significant numbers of students in the 16–19 age bracket may have been persuaded to attend college by their parents, from the college's point of view they have chosen to attend as opposed to being obliged to attend by the State. The following quotations from college prospectuses illustrate this:

> We treat our students as adults who want to take responsibility for their own lives and who will thrive in the supportive and lively atmosphere of the College.
>
> (Sixth Form College)

> The college prides itself on creating an adult atmosphere in which all students are treated with respect and seen as individuals with individual needs and aspirations. In return, we ask our students to behave responsibly and make the most of their opportunities at college.
>
> (College of Art and Technology)

That colleges actively promote themselves as being 'adult oriented' reflects their appreciation of the fact that young people in the 16–19 age bracket, who could continue their post-16 education in schools, are attracted to FE colleges precisely because they want to get away from the 'child-oriented' ethos of their secondary education. As they enter the second half of their teenage years, these young people will be developing a sense of *self* which, according to Rory Kidd (an influential writer on adult learning), 'is essential to all learning' (Kidd, 1973, p.127). Attending college offers young people the chance to develop this sense of self within a context which allows social interaction with people of all ages. It is not surprising, then, that colleges devote considerable resources to ensuring that the social and student support facilities they provide are of a high enough standard to encourage social interaction in addition to that which takes place in the formal learning situation. For the more mature students in a college, development of a sense of self may also be a central feature of their college experience, particularly if they are returning to learning and studying for the first time in a number of years. In their research with American women mature students in HE, Belenky *et al.* (1986) asked these women to try and describe how they saw themselves. One woman said, 'I don't know . . . . No one has told me yet what they thought of me' (p.31).

Reflection

It might be useful at this point to revisit the vignettes in Chapter 2 and consider the ways in which the development of a sense of self applies to those students. Consider these questions:

1 How might Martin's parents affect his personal development?
2 Can Clive develop a sense of self within his current peer group?
3 How might Margaret overcome her self-consciousness about her age?
4 How could Grace be helped to transfer with confidence to the college?

In Chinese culture, there is a tradition which says that people cannot be classed as adults until they are married. In the UK, the legal system has a curiously confused approach to adulthood. For example, a 16 year old can marry but cannot vote, drive a car or be served with alcohol in a public place. Employers, too, often display somewhat illogical attitudes to age in their recruitment strategies. For example, some employers advertise for experienced and skilled people yet only consider applicants under the age of 35, whilst others categorise all 16 to 19 year olds as lacking enough maturity. Given the spread of student age in an FE college, you could find you are teaching people a great deal older than yourself one day, followed by a day when your students are very close to your own age.

HOW DO PEOPLE LEARN?

Stephen Brookfield, whose quotation opened this chapter, has said:

> To specify generic principles of learning is an activity full of intellectual pitfalls. Even if we leave aside the variables of physiology, personality, and cultural background, we still have to consider the implications of those developmental theories that hold that adults function in very different ways when responding to the societal and personal imperatives required of them in young adulthood, midlife, and old age. This suggests that the generic concept of adulthood is so broad and oversimplified as to be of limited use as a research construct.
>
> (Brookfield, 1986, p.26)

Brookfield goes on to recognise, however, that a number of people have contributed since the late 1950s to the creation of a theory of adult learning which has proved to be important to both learners and teachers:

Gibb (1960) – adult learning must be problem and experience-centred, provide feedback, and have learner-set goals.

Miller (1964) advocated cognitive models of learning above behaviourist models.

Kidd (1973) placed importance on lifespan, role changes, egalitarian relationship between teacher and student, self-directedness of adults, meaning of time and the prospect of death.

Knox (1977) – adults learn continually and informally, achievements modified by individual characteristics, learning is affected by physical, social and personal characteristics, and by content and pace. Adults underestimate their ability and allow school experience to dominate, prior experience can both hinder and advance capacity to learn.

Brundage and Mackeracher (1980) identified 36 learning principles including: adults learn throughout their lifetimes, they construct meaning through experience, they learn best in situations which value the status of the learner and when they are in good health and stress-free, they need clear goals to learn new skills, they enjoy a combination of individual and group activity.

Smith (1982) – adults have four key characteristics: multiple roles and responsibilities, many accumulated life experiences, experience of a number of development phases (physical, psychological and social), and anxiety and ambivalence about their learning activity.

The theorists cited by Brookfield all recognise the significance of internal and external pressures which impact on any adult's capacity for learning. One study of adult learning, carried out in Canada by Allen Tough and reported in 1971, was particularly influential in seeking to identify the ways in which adults differed in their learning from children. Tough observed the ways in which adults plan and organise their own learning and how they set about acquiring knowledge and understanding. His key finding was that adults are 'self-directed' in their learning for which 'more than half of the person's total motivation is to gain and retain certain fairly clear knowledge and skill or to produce some lasting change in himself' (Tough, 1971, p.6). Tough's findings built on earlier work in the USA by Johnstone and Rivera who found that a huge number of adults were engaged in learning outside the formal adult education system, which they termed 'independent self-study' (Johnstone and Rivera, 1965). This and later studies of adult participation in learning showed how the amount of adult learning could be wildly underestimated if the only measure was the numbers attending formal classes in institutions. By recognising the determination of adults to further their learning and that this motivation made them much more self-directed than children, the need for the development of distinctive models of adult learning theory was advanced.

One of the most distinctive theories has been put forward by Malcolm Knowles who developed the concept of 'andragogy' (from the Greek *aner*, (stem *andra*), which means 'man') which stresses that children and adults approach learning in different ways and that this should be taken into consideration by those who help adults learn. Knowles noted the following differences between adults and children:

1 Children see themselves as dependent – adults see themselves as independent.
2 Adults bring experience to learning and value that experience.
3 Adults are ready to learn for specific reasons as their development is linked to the evolution of their social role – children's development is physiological and mental.
4 Children see much of their learning as being for the future – adults learn as a response to the here and now.

Whilst much of this work has a common-sense ring to it, there is a danger that the individual learner becomes lost in a sea of generalisations. The vignettes in Chapter 2 show how dangerous it is to generalise. Take, for example, the case of Clive whose behaviour as a learner seems to have more in common with the characteristics of children as identified by Knowles above, rather than with those of self-directed adult learners. There is a sense, too, with Grace that she may still be at a dependent stage as a learner owing to a lack of confidence, despite her age and experience.

Reflection

Given below is a list of instructions based on the Japanese art of Origami for making a salt cellar. (When made up, some of you may recognise the object as one which was, and may still be, popular at school for playing a game of choices.) In order to learn how to make this object, you could do one of the following:

1 Go through the instructions step by step as you would an instructional manual.
2 Ask a partner to assist you – one reading, one folding the paper.
3 Ask a partner to make the object first and then demonstrate to you as in a typical class in which, for example, the teacher demonstrates how to ice a cake or set up a chemistry experiment.

Using one of the above methods, have a go at making the object and record your experiences. When reflecting on your performance, try to consider the following questions:

1 Do you learn best by yourself or do you like/need the support of someone else?
2 Do you follow instructions to the letter or do you improvise?
3 Would you have worked better from a picture?
4 Do you prefer to be shown how to do something?

If you have the time and/or the opportunity, ask a fellow adult and a child (under the age of 13) to attempt the same exercise and compare their learning experience with your own.

Paper folding instructions

1 TAKE AN A4 SHEET OF PAPER
2 PLACE PAPER PORTRAIT WAY UP
3 FOLD BOTTOM RIGHT HAND CORNER AT 45° UNTIL IT MEETS LEFT HAND EDGE
4 TAKE SCISSORS AND CUT OFF RECTANGULAR UNFOLDED SECTION OF PAPER, AND DISCARD
5 UNFOLD SQUARE PAPER
6 MAKE ANOTHER DIAGONAL FOLD, SO THAT THERE ARE NOW TWO DIAGONAL FOLDS WHICH CROSS IN THE CENTRE OF THE PAPER
7 UNFOLD
8 TAKE THE LEFT EDGE OF PAPER AND FOLD OVER TO MEET RIGHT EDGE
9 UNFOLD
10 TAKE BOTTOM EDGE OF PAPER AND FOLD OVER TO MEET TOP EDGE
11 UNFOLD
12 YOU SHOULD NOW HAVE A SQUARE PIECE OF PAPER WITH TWO DIAGONAL FOLDS AND TWO SQUARE FOLDS WHICH CROSS IN THE CENTRE OF THE PAPER
13 FOLD ALL FOUR CORNERS, ONE AT A TIME TO MEET THE CENTRE POINT
14 TURN WORK OVER
15 FOLD ALL FOUR CORNERS, ONE AT A TIME, TO MEET THE CENTRE POINT
16 TURN WORK OVER
17 PUSH DIAGONAL FOLDS TOGETHER AND OPEN OUT THE POCKETS IN EACH OF THE CORNERS TO PRODUCE A 'SALT CELLAR'

When you analysed your approach to and experience of the paper folding exercise, you may have found yourself engaged in Kolb's learning cycle. You might also recognise some of your experience in the following eight-stage model of learning which has been advocated by Gagne, an educational psychologist who developed and extended some of the early work on behaviourism. We have summarised and adapted Gagne's model and suggest that the term 'learning' be seen as encompassing knowledge, skills and understanding:

Stage one   *Motivation*
(Student's motives and expectations identified and
brought in line with teaching objectives)

Stage two   *Apprehending*
(Teacher gains student's attention by various means)

Stage three   *Acquisition*
(Knowledge, skills and understanding acquired by
the student in a form in which they are ready to
be lodged in the memory)

Stage four	*Retention*
(Student is helped to memorise and assimilate new learning)	
Stage five	*Recall*
(Student encouraged to retrieve learning ready for application)	
Stage six	*Generalisation*
(Student transfers learning to range of situations)	
Stage seven	*Performance*
(Student tries out newly acquired learning)	
Stage eight	*Feedback*
(Student is helped to judge performance and reflect)	

As with all models, this one has a simplicity which can be misleading – teaching and learning can often be a messy business and individuals do not, necessarily, want to have their learning confined within a chronological framework. Clearly, the stages shown above can be fused and their order might be rearranged or disrupted in order to reflect particular circumstances. It is, however, a useful model for teachers to keep at the back of their mind when they are planning teaching sessions and it can be used during sessions as an evaluation tool if a teacher feels the right amount of progress is not being made. We will return to this model in the next chapter when we examine teaching strategies.

Another theorist whose work offers useful insights for understanding how people learn is Bloom who distinguished between learning which takes place in the cognitive domain and that in the affective domain (see Bloom, 1965). For Bloom, cognitive learning runs in parallel with affective learning so that at the same time as a learner develops knowledge, his or her behaviour as a learner is also developing. The affective side to learning can be seen as a way to introduce some kind of value system to the learning process so that as one acquires knowledge, one also learns to appreciate the role that knowledge plays which, in turn, encourages the learner to be committed to the process.

BARRIERS TO LEARNING

There are an infinite number of barriers to prevent people from learning, some of which are external in nature, perhaps caused by domestic or financial difficulties, and some of which are internal, arising from psychological or physiological problems. In addition, teachers can, of course, create barriers for their students. These barriers might be created as a result of the following:

- a teacher's personal behaviour towards a student;
- the choice of teaching technique;
- lack of attention to the teaching environment, for example too much noise, room too hot or too cold, not enough light, etc.

> **Reflection**
> Consider the ways in which you have been prevented from learning during your life and, in contrast, try to identify anything which has been a positive support to your learning. Make your notes in two lists:
>
> List one: Barriers to Learning
>
> List two: Support for Learning

In the lists you made, you may have identified your family or domestic relationships as a feature in one or perhaps both lists. Clearly, domestic life has a major impact on the way in which children and teenagers learn, but it can be forgotten that young and mature adults can be equally affected by their domestic environment. In his study of married, male, full-time university students in Canada, Lauzon makes the following comment:

> The decision to become a student and the subsequent changes in the student's personal identity will necessitate changes in family members and patterns of family interaction. One way of conceptualising these changes is to examine the student from a familial systematic perspective. This perspective views the family as the *main* unit of study; all family members are subsystems of the main family system. Any change experienced at the subsystem level will necessitate change at the system level. In the case of a family where one member experiences changes in social roles, responsibilities, beliefs and/or values, other members will be required to make changes in order to accommodate the change at the level of the system (Satir, 1983). Hence not only must the individual adapt but the family must *also* adapt. The decision of the adult to become a full-time student forces all family members to make some behavioural and emotional adjustment. The bulk of the adjustment, however, would appear to occur in the husband/wife relationship rather than the father/child relationship . . . . Despite the obstacles and demands placed in front of, and on, the adult student, they continue to pursue their dreams. As one respondent put it: 'It's the dream that keeps me going. Knowing that something better is just over the horizon.' But sometimes the dream turns to a nightmare and the world of the adult student falls apart. A few months after this study was completed the researcher had the opportunity to talk to one of the respondents. He reported that he was currently engaged in a vicious divorce and custody battle and attributed the breakdown of his marriage to his being a student. Sometimes the dream just isn't enough; education for the adult can be costly.
>
> (Lauzon, 1989, pp.43–4)

Only a minority of adult learners end up in the regrettable position of the one quoted above but Lauzon is right to draw attention to the stress and tensions which having a student in the family can create. Although his research was based on male, full-time university students, Lauzon's conclusions about the impact on family life and the adult learner would seem applicable to female as well as male students and to a wide range of learning situations. Before writing this book, one of the authors was responsible for running a series of residential training courses for in-company trainers and supervisors. Many of the participants on these courses had not attended a course of study for several years and often not since they had left school. One of the most interesting aspects was to observe the changed behaviour of some of the women who attended the courses. These particular women had not stayed away from their partners and children before and came away worrying about how their families would cope without them. One woman related in detail how she had filled the freezer with meals and separately labelled packs of sandwiches for lunches and had arranged for a neighbour to be on stand-by to wash and iron items of clothing at a moment's notice. By the end of the third day of a one-week course, the women began to question their attitudes and by the end of the course they were threatening domestic revolution. The last thing the group facilitator wanted was to cause mayhem in families but the power of the learning situation, and particularly the chance to draw support and ideas from peers, was considerable for those women.

In her study of why mature students leave FE and HE courses before completion, McGiveney (1996) reminds us that whilst women students tend to cite family commitments as their main reason for withdrawing from courses, men tend to cite problems with the course, finance and employment-related issues. But McGiveney also points out that it would be unwise to stereotype adult learners as potential course 'drop-outs':

> several studies have found that mature students are currently slightly more likely than younger ones to complete courses. It has been suggested that this may be because students who remain in full-time education mainly because of the erosion of job prospects for school leavers are unlikely to be totally committed to study (Payne and Storran, 1995), whereas adults with work experience and those who have made considerable sacrifices in order to participate in further or higher education will be far more highly motivated.
>
> (McGiveney, 1996, p.111)

Teenagers and young adults can find that being a student does not sit well with their life outside college. There are a number of difficult issues with which young people may have to grapple:

- personal identity and life goals
- sexuality
- the generation gap with their parents
- their status in society

- personal finances
- balancing part-time work with their studies
- relationship with siblings
- relationship with peer group
- coping with living apart from their family

In addition to any personal problems they may have, young people in the late 1990s are aware of the fragile nature of the labour market and recognise that they may have to be prepared to change career several times during their working lives. Indeed, the problems faced by young people are of concern throughout the European Union as a recent CEDEFOP report highlighted:

> The youth phase has become more extended in duration; established and normative sequences of transitions are breaking up into much more variable and individually less predictable patterns; many young people's material circumstances have deteriorated in absolute or relative terms; lifestyles and values are also shifting and becoming more pluralised. At the same time, of course, macrosocial and economic change in Europe is producing new structures of opportunity and demand in the labour market; and systematic social inequalities have by no means declined, but have rather intensified and become more complex.
>
> (CEDEFOP, 1994, p.6)

It would be ridiculous to give the impression that all young people are suffering from stress or experiencing significant hardship, but many of them do encounter problems which will have an impact on their ability and motivation to learn.

Research carried out in Cheshire, by one of the authors of this book, sought the views of 16–19 year old FE students as to where and when they encountered barriers to learning (see Unwin, 1995). They identified seven areas of concern:

1 Teaching and learning styles
2 Curriculum issues
3 Progression between courses and institutions
4 Peer group relationships
5 Financial worries
6 Level of family support
7 Labour market pull

The young people who were interviewed were studying full time for either A levels or GNVQs (Intermediate and Advanced). They came from different social backgrounds, some lived in rural areas, others in urban settings, and they were all part way through a two-year course. As they talked about their experiences at college, they reflected on their school-days and compared being a student then to now. The following quotations have been selected to show

how the learning of young people is affected by the actions of others and also by their own perceptions of their personal ability and situation:

Learning styles (notably study skills and transition from one style of teaching/learning to another):

At school you were made to work and you had the teacher telling you what to do . . . college is different: I like it but I have to do it on my own now . . . it's hard.

I wasn't used to all this taking notes, they seem to want to cram as much in as possible. I don't think I'm enjoying it as much as I thought but perhaps it's because I'm worried about how I'm going to get through all this stuff.

We seem to get a load of assignments to do all at once, six or seven just before Christmas but none for ages. Why can't they be more consistent?

It would help if we had the books we need, the library is useless.

My friend helps, she's good at using her notes and she can write the assignments – I wish they would show you early on how to do what they want. I feel as though I'm a little kid again, as if I haven't been to school before; it feels stupid but I want to get through.

It depends on the lessons, some are really good. Organisation, they need to be more organised so that we can plan our time better.

My mate left because he couldn't get his stuff in on time. There's another lad who will leave too, he's had enough. They should spend some time at the start making sure you know what you're doing.

Curriculum and timetable (nature of chosen course may not meet expectations, prove to be too difficult, be too far removed from their previous experience, too much freedom):

I've made the wrong choice – my fault. I didn't really know what I wanted to do and now I'm stuck with it.

I chose the course [A level] because it followed on from my best subjects at GCSE but it's nothing like the same. I'm amazed at this; they should have told us it was nothing like the GCSE.

I wanted a job really but my parents said stay at school. The courses go together, I suppose, but I'm not interested as I don't want to go to university.

Being at college is much better than school but we do waste time – like when we have, say, three hours in the middle of the day free we go into town and so there's not much point going back for an hour at 4 p.m. School made you turn up; here it's a lot easier to miss lessons.

Progression (level of difficulty may be far higher than the recognised feeder course prepared them for)

The BTEC First was dead easy and we did lots of projects together. Now [the National] it's all taking notes and learning tons of subjects. You're not as involved as a student as last year.

The GCSE science course I did was totally simple. A levels are something else. I've had to spend ages trying to cram because of the difference. We just weren't prepared.

It must get the teachers down that we find the course too hard but we were told we could come on it because we'd passed last year. I might leave. I'm a bit fed up with not doing well, gets you down.

Peer group (relating to a new group of people can cause problems, yet the need for group support is vital):

In my group we're all glad we're not in the other group – they mess about and seem weird.

We all help each other. The residential at the start of the year was brilliant. I didn't know anyone when I came here as my friends had gone to another college, but I've got a great set of friends now. I wouldn't like to be left out.

Our group gets on my nerves . . . the teachers don't like the group but nothing gets done.

Some people in the group can't do the work so the teacher has to spend ages with them . . . why do they let these people on the courses?

Financial (issues here range from actual poverty to peer pressure related to dress and possessions):

The costs of this course [BTEC art and design] are incredible, I've just spent another £12 on paint and next week we've got to have some thick card that costs a fortune. I reckon I spend about £5 a week on materials and sometimes it's a lot more.

You can't survive without a job.

My course expects you to go abroad on a trip and we had a residential weekend to pay for.

Family support (domestic difficulties cause pressure at home; some students leave home to live independently):

There's nowhere to work at home.

My dad is out of work . . . he's really down so I just moan at college . . . I've got to moan somewhere.

I've got a room now but I won't be able to afford it so I'll have to leave and get a job. The college helped, gave me some money, but it's no use.

Labour market pull (temporary jobs, albeit low paid, are available in all areas):

There's a German supermarket opening in Crewe soon . . . jobs at £6.00 an hour. Lots of my friends are going to go down there and see what it's like.

This agency lets you ring up when you've got some free time and gives you part-time jobs, so when I've got a day off college or I've not got any assignments due in I ring up. It's better than having a regular job like my mates . . . I can fit my college work in better.

We all know we should finish our course but if there was a job some of us would go for it . . . I know this lad who's earning £150 a week.

The financial difficulties experienced by young people deserve comment. The majority of those interviewed explained that they required money for equipment related to their courses, for food and clothes. There was some evidence of peer pressure as regards fashion and appearance but, in general, young people were struggling to find enough money to meet their everyday expenses.

Mature adults can face many of the problems identified by the younger students above, particularly if those problems are introduced by their teachers and the college in which they are studying, or if they are created by external pressures. In addition, mature students are more likely to face health problems and have the general burden of the responsibility for managing households.

For many mature women, their barriers to learning are wrapped up in the very fact of being female. Their lives tend to be more disrupted than men's as they take time out of education and careers to raise children or to support partners. The following comment from a 30-year-old mother of three captures the battle which some women have to gain lost ground:

I'm just getting to the point where everybody else starts. Do you understand what that means? Most people, when they leave home or graduate from high school, already have an idea of what they are worth. An idea that they go out and conquer the world. I'm just getting to where everybody else is at.
(Belenky *et al.*, 1986, p.53)

In order to support women who are returning to learn and who may feel threatened or ill at ease in the company of male students and tutors, some colleges run women-only courses. Maggie Coats, who advocates such courses, found from her own research (Coats, 1994, p.118) that there are both advantages and disadvantages for the women who attend:

Advantages

- allows women to gain confidence from shared experiences and group support in a non-threatening environment;
- encourages women to locate their own personal experiences in a wider social context and thus understand those experiences;
- provides a secure base from which to go out into wider society and to which women can return for further support and encouragement.

Disadvantages

- the experience of women-only provision can only be transitional and women will lose the support of the group when they progress to further education, training or employment;
- the relevant practical support needed may not be available in other provision.

Whilst many would argue against separating men and women for educational or training purposes, the issues which concern the advocates of women-only courses apply to the central issue of the impact of gender on learning.

Reflection
Consider to what extent your own gender might influence the way in which you will teach and relate to your students. For example, if you are a young man, how will you relate to mature women or to young teenage girls? If you are a young woman, how will you cope with teaching a class full of 18-year-old male apprentices or a room full of aspiring managers from the private sector? How will your students see you? (see Further Reading)

THE TEACHER–STUDENT RELATIONSHIP

At the beginning of this chapter, we explored some of the theories which seek to explain how individuals approach learning and stressed that a person's learning style will influence their approach to teaching. There is a long-running column in the TES in which well-known people from all walks of life recall the special characteristics of a teacher who, at some point in their lives, had a particular impact on them. Other newspapers and magazines often carry similar features, the common link between them being that individual teachers have the power to affect people's lives, sometimes in quite dramatic ways. The comedian and author, Ben Elton, who left school at 16 to do a drama and liberal arts course at an FE college in Warwickshire, has written about one of the college's drama teachers:

> He believed that drama was an essential part of life, that you shouldn't have to want to be an actor to enjoy it but that you should see drama as a way

of learning, a way of understanding life and other people . . . . He believes, passionately, that young people should be encouraged (with great vigour) not to shrug their shoulders and say 'Oh . . . it's all crap', not to be cynics but to get involved. He led by enthusiasm and I believe that the greatest gift a teacher can have is that ability to enthuse, to inspire with interest, to get people involved . . . He was a good teacher. He did the formal bit thoroughly and made it interesting . . . In setting up that course Gordon was a major, major influence on my life. He was a ball of energy. He enabled me to stay in education at the same time as sort of leaving it, and he did fundamentally affect my growing up.

(TES2, 8 September 1995, p.20)

To be praised by an ex-student in this way would make any teacher feel proud and, of course, most teachers, at some point in their careers, receive thanks and best wishes from their students. Most of the time, however, as in the rest of life, any gratitude which students feel tends to go unspoken and teachers have to plough on in the hope that their work is appreciated. Just as teachers can have a very positive effect on their students, they can sometimes be a negative force and there are many people who would claim that their insecurities and blocks about learning stem from a certain teacher who made them feel inadequate. The teacher–student relationship is, therefore, a complex and dynamic one and, as such, needs to be treated with care.

The following table lists a number of labels which can be applied to someone in a 'teaching' role and to someone in a 'learning' role.

Teaching role	*Learning role*
Teacher	Student
Instructor	Trainee
Trainer	Learner
Tutor	Apprentice
Facilitator	Participant
Supervisor	Candidate
Mentor	Pupil
Demonstrator	
Coach	
Lecturer	

Each of these labels carries with it a great deal of terminological 'baggage' and much has been written about the power of labels in determining behaviour. For example, the term 'facilitator' is used widely in management training where it is regarded as being much more learner centred than terms such as lecturer or teacher. On the other hand, teachers in FE colleges are usually referred to as 'lecturers' despite the fact that many of them spend very little time giving 'lectures'. From the point of view of learners, how they are described could denote how they might expect to be treated, the culture and ethos of the institution, and the context in which they are learning. Terms such as 'trainee' and 'apprentice', for example, are generally used in work-based settings, though the term 'trainee' might also be used in colleges for young people on youth training schemes. Labels can also change so that a 'student' might become a 'candidate' at the point when he or she is going to be assessed; a 'lecturer' becomes a 'tutor' when seeing a student for an individual tutorial meeting.

Teaching in a college will require you to switch between the different roles suggested by each of the labels listed above. Whatever your subject area, you might, in any one session, carry out the following functions:

- spend ten minutes giving a lecture;
- facilitate a group discussion;
- demonstrate how to use a piece of equipment or perform a certain task;
- spend a few minutes with individual students to give them specific tutoring;
- supervise small groups of students carrying out project work.

To be able to switch from one role to another certainly requires flexibility, but it also demands that the teacher is able to recognise which role is the most appropriate in a given circumstance. (Chapter 6 provides more detail on choosing and applying teaching strategies.) Rory Kidd (1973), building on earlier work by John Dewey, has described learning as a 'transaction' to which both the learner and the teacher have to bring something of value for both parties to feel the 'transaction' has been effective and produced the desired outcomes. In order for this to happen, teachers and learners have to get to know each other and be prepared to change and adapt. This may take time but the process can be accelerated through the willingness of the teacher to create an atmosphere which encourages the following:

- enables students to articulate their learning needs;
- enables students to identify and discuss any barriers which might prevent them from learning;
- enables students to develop the confidence to share their own ideas and actively contribute to the learning situation;
- provides students with constructive criticism and praise so that they feel supported and, in turn, learn how to support each other;
- encourages all students to achieve at their own pace, regardless of ability;
- encourages both teacher and students to work together with a sense of community and shared purpose;
- promotes respect for individuals within the learning community.

As Ben Elton found with his drama teacher, the individual approach and personality of each teacher mark them out as being distinctive, and so teachers differ as much as their students. Indeed, it would be a very dull day for a student if all teachers were the same. In terms of maintaining order within the teaching situation, whether it be with one or a group of students, teachers will certainly behave in different ways and choose different methods for ensuring that both teacher and students concentrate on their joint purpose in coming together. As teachers gain in experience, keeping control of the proceedings becomes a subconscious activity, so that neither the teacher nor the students are aware that control is being exerted. Students, too, can be encouraged to develop self-discipline, to control their behaviour in respect of the community in which they are learning, and learn how to maintain order as a group. A useful model for sharing ideas about control and order is transactional analysis (TA) which was developed by the American psychologist, Eric Berne.

Berne calls TA a 'theory of social intercourse' and used it to help people understand and improve their behaviour towards others. He wrote:

> Observation of spontaneous social activity, most productively carried out in certain kinds of psychotherapy groups, reveals that from time to time people show noticeable changes in posture, viewpoint, voice, vocabulary, and other aspects of behaviour. These behavioural changes are often accompanied by shifts in feeling. In a given individual, a certain set of behaviour patterns corresponds to one state of mind, while another set is related to a different psychic attitude, often inconsistent with the first. These changes and differences give rise to the idea of *ego states*.
>
> (Berne, 1970, p.23)

Berne identified three ego states which, he believed, people move regularly in and out of during their daily lives:

Parental

Adult

Child

Of the three ego states, the Adult (demonstrated when a person is in control and displaying maturity) is thought to be present in everyone but often needs to be uncovered or activated. The Child state can be exhibited in two forms: the adapted Child, who modifies behaviour under the influence of a parent; and the natural Child, who is freed from parental influence to be creative or to rebel. In this latter state, the Child can be petulant and difficult to handle. The Parental state also has two sides: firstly, it can be authoritarian ('Do as I say'); secondly it can be nurturing ('Let me help you').

Berne's hypothesis is that problems occur when these ego states are at cross-purposes. For example, if someone who is in the natural Child state meets someone in an authoritarian Parental state, then they will have trouble communicating. Similarly, if someone in the Adult state meets someone in the nurturing Parental state, they will feel frustrated or even patronised. The trick, as far as being a teacher is concerned, is to recognise both your own ego state and that of your students. You can also use TA as a model for handling colleagues and running meetings.

The teacher–student relationship will, of course, like any other interpersonal relationship, be constantly tested and there may be some occasions when it breaks down completely. In the main, however, the relationship will work because most of the people involved will realise that, if it is effective, then life for everyone will be happier.

Some of the pressure on the relationship will come from external forces which the teacher or students can do little about and which can have a positive or negative effect. The following model (Figure 4.2) illustrates how those external forces, as well as the internal feelings of teachers and students, can impact on the teacher–learner relationship. The model (adapted from Unwin and Edwards, 1990) is overlaid with three bands – class, gender and race – which exert influence throughout society and from which no relationship can be exempted.

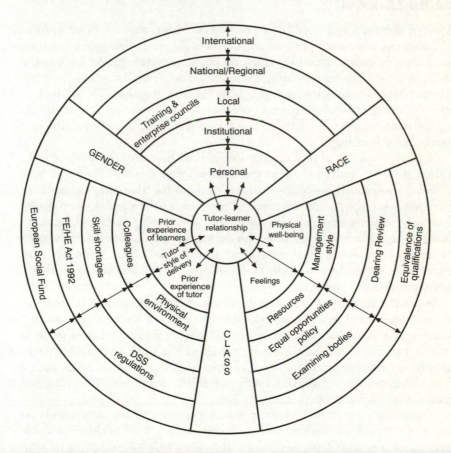

Figure 4.2 Teacher–learner relationship

> **Reflection**
> You might wish to make your version of the model to reflect the par-
> ticular circumstances in which you are working. You may, for
> example, expand some of the bands so that you can include more
> variables. One way of creating your own version is to use coloured
> card. The model could also be used with students as a way of
> encouraging them to identify the variables which affect their rela-
> tionship with you as a teacher and/or as a group of learners. This
> works well as a group activity so long as individuals are not forced
> into isolated positions.

GROUP LEARNING

Most of the teaching you will do in FE will be with groups of students. As in
all sectors of education, pressure on resources demands that group teaching
(and often of groups of considerable size) is the dominant mode. Despite the
managerial reasons for favouring group-based learning, however, there are
distinct benefits which students gain from learning together. We will look at
specific strategies for achieving effective learning in groups in Chapter 6 but,
for the moment, we will briefly explore the general benefits to be gained from
group-based learning.

We have paid a great deal of attention in this chapter to the needs of individual students and you saw in the student vignettes in Chapter 2 how
different those needs can be. By bringing students together, they can begin to
learn how their own needs compare and contrast to others and develop shared
strategies for advancing their learning and for overcoming problems. Learning
in groups can often be much more fun than singly and can facilitate the con-
tinuation of learning once the formal session has ended. Students may
continue to discuss ideas outside the classroom or workshop and apply themselves creatively to group tasks.

Given the emphasis in FE on individualised learning, and particularly on
the outcome-based model as advocated by the NCVQ, there is a danger that
learning in colleges may become too individualised. Whilst groups of students
may be together in the same space, they might all be working completely separately on different tasks or units of competence. For Wildemeersch, such a
scenario represents a 'farewell to dialogue and a welcome to individualised
technicism' (Wildemeersch, 1989, p.68).

The collegiality created by group-based learning can act as an important
locus of support for students who lack confidence, have problems outside
college, or who gain extra motivation from the discipline of having to keep
up with their peers. The teacher can capitalise on that collegiality to encourage the more able students to help others. Jaques (1992) has stated that

	Task	Socio-emotional
I N T R I N S I C	Expressing selves in subject	Greater sensitivity to others
	Judging ideas in relation to others	Judging self in relation to others
	Examining assumptions	Encouraging self-confidence
	Listening attentively	Personal development
	Tolerating ambiguity	Tolerating ambiguity
	Learning about groups	Awareness of others' strengths and weaknesses
E X T R I N S I C	Follow-up to lecture	Giving support
	Understanding text	Stimulating to further work
	Improving staff/ student relations	Evaluating student feelings about course
	Gauging student progress	Giving students identifiable groups to belong to
	Giving guidance	

Figure 4.3 Types of aims and purposes in group teaching

Source: Jaques (1992)

groups operate at both a task and a socio-emotional level and within both intrinsic and extrinsic dimensions. (See Jaques' diagram in Figure 4.3.) He notes that there is a tendency to concentrate on the extrinsic dimension and explains:

> Teaching is often solution-orientated rather than problem-orientated and seems to take external requirements as its starting point rather than the needs and interests of the students. Moreover, a lack of attention to the socio-emotional dimension means that many of the task aims cannot be achieved. Without a climate of trust and co-operation, students will not

feel like taking the risk of making mistakes and learning from them. To achieve this, the tutor would have to balance a concern for academic standards with a capacity to understand and deal with the workings of group processes as well as an attitude of generosity and praise for new solutions to old problems.

(Jaques, 1992, p.72)

There are groups and groups, of course, and not all will provide the collegiality referred to above. Rory Kidd states that there are three characteristics which have to be present in a group if effective learning is to take place:

1 A realisation by the members of the group that genuine growth stems from the creative power within the individual, and that learning, finally, is an individual matter.
2 The acceptance as a group standard that each member has the right to be different and to disagree.
3 Establishment of a group atmosphere that is free from narrow judgements on the part of the teacher or group members.

(Kidd, 1973, p.80)

SUPPORT SERVICES FOR STUDENTS

One of the most important ways in which learners can be supported is to give them access to a range of support services. Such support can include advising them as to the most appropriate modules in a course, how to stagger their studies to fit in with professional demands, how to seek financial support for fees, and putting them in touch with professional counsellors if personal problems become too difficult to handle alone. A great deal of support can be provided by organisations and teachers by actually listening to students and interpreting their needs correctly.

A major issue here is the extent to which individual teachers accept that they have a role to play in supporting learners above and beyond putting across the actual subject matter of a particular course of study. In particular, the teacher can have a significant impact on a student's sense of well-being as McGiveney emphasises with this quote from an FE teacher talking about part-time students:

The reality of formal part-time study is that individual tutors can make or break a learner's experience. The tutor is central to the creation of the essential, supportive social environment of the classroom which reduces drop-out. We can talk till the cows come home about the vital importance of guidance but we are seriously in error if we do not acknowledge the pivotal guidance role of the tutor for the part-timer. For many the teacher is the guidance system.

(McGiveney, 1996, p.135)

Egan's (1975) three-stage model of the *skilled helper* originated in his work as a counsellor, but it can be usefully adopted by teachers as a basis for supporting individual students:

Stages	*Steps*
Stage 1	Exploration
	Focus on specific concerns
Stage 2	Developing new perspectives
	Setting specific goals
Stage 3	Exploring possible ways to act
	Choosing and working out a plan of action
	Implementing the plan
	Evaluation

Colleges arrange their student support services in recognition of the fact that students' support needs stretch from, for example, help with basic skills such as literacy and numeracy, to careers information, but also include the need for access to a confidential service to deal with very private matters. The following details from a college prospectus show how one college defines student support in the broadest terms. Its services combine, under the heading of support, to provide a lively environment in which students can feel they are cared for by the institution (see also Figure 4.4).

Student Support at Hertford Regional College
- Learning support for students with learning difficulties and/or disabilities who feel that they need more support than is normally provided by the college. Support is also generally available to students with sensory or physical disabilities, specific learning difficulties and other severe learning needs.
- English and maths workshops for students who have difficulties with spelling and writing English and/or require help with number work.
- Language support is available for all students whose mother tongue is not English.
- Student services are available to provide students with extra help and guidance of a practical or personal nature during their courses.
- Personal tutors to give support both in relation to study and other matters where needed.
- A Students' Union which represents the interest of all students in the college by encouraging sporting and recreational activities and providing financial support for leisure and social events organised by the students.
- Purpose built centres which provide an opportunity for students to meet together in an informal atmosphere. There are also facilities for table tennis, pool, darts, video games and music.

	Entry	On-programme	Exit
Educational guidance	• **Programme choice:** guidance officers • **Specialist programme advice:** programme area advisors • **Placement and referral:** admissions tutors • **Self-assessment and specific learning needs:** assessment and support officers • **External training and educational opportunities:** guidance officers and routeways counsellors • **APL advice:** guidance officer	• **Management of learning:** tutors • **Support for tutorial planning and development:** guidance officers • **Transfer and learning support advice:** guidance officers • **Retention counselling [individual and group]:** guidance officers • **Individual retention counselling:** careers service	• **Progression planning and preparation:** tutors • **HE choice and applicant support:** tutors and careers service
Personal and welfare guidance	• **Learner support provision:** guidance officers • **Financial planning to support study:** guidance officers • **Transition counselling:** guidance officers	• **Personal support:** tutors • **Financial welfare, legal and learner support:** guidance officers • **Personal counselling:** guidance officers • **External referral to specialist agencies:** guidance officers • **Crisis and emergency support:** guidance officers • **Student representation and complaints:** guidance officers	• **Examination stress:** guidance officers • **Practical, financial and personal support for transition:** guidance officers
Vocational guidance **Specialist guidance**	• **Career and progression planning:** vocational guidance officer and careers services [16–19] • **Post-results guidance [GCSE and A level]:** careers service and guidance officers • **First-language counselling and assessment:** routeways counsellors	• **Individual vocational guidance:** careers service and vocational guidance officer • **Careers education:** tutors, vocational guidance officer and careers service • **Educational counselling for refugees and asylum seekers:** refugee council officer and world university service officer • **Progression counselling for students with learning difficulties and disabilities:** specialist careers officer • **Assessment and support for students with specific learning difficulties:** assessment and support officers	• **Transition and application skills [individual and group]:** tutors, vocational guidance officer, careers service and routeway • **Progression counselling for students with learning difficulties and disabilities:** specialist careers officers

Figure 4.4 College guidance map. Tutors provide a first-line service and ensure that students have access to advice and guidance on all matters affecting their learning. Guidance officers provide a flexible, comprehensive service which offers an immediate and accessible response to the range of guidance needs.

- Sports facilities include a wide variety of sports clubs and access to playing fields, gymnasiums and a sports hall.
- The Careers Information and Guidance Service will help students make choices about their future education, training, employment or career. The services include a career library, computer aided guidance, one-to-one interviews and open workshops. Areas covered include career research, Higher Education, job search strategies, C.V. preparation and interview skills.

One of the most formalised mechanisms for helping students adapt to college life and feel welcomed is induction, which can last anything from half a day to two weeks.

Reflection
Imagine you are about to start a course in a college. What items would you want to see covered in an induction programme? As you make your list, consider the circumstances of the students we introduced you to in Chapter 2.

The following extracts from FEFC inspection reports show the types of induction programmes currently in use in colleges. You might wish to compare your ideas for induction with the items listed below:

Induction One
Part-time and full-time students benefit from a well-documented induction process which is customised to suit individual courses and access centres. The quality of induction seen was generally good, although the teaching in some of the sessions was mechanistic and there were few opportunities for students to participate. Students are provided with a handbook which gives useful information on their course and college life in general. The handbook also contains a learning agreement which sets out students' entitlements and obligations whilst on their courses. Signature to this document confirms acceptance of the contents and this document has been used in student disciplinary hearings.

(FEFC Inspection Report, January 1996)

Induction Two
All new students receive a general induction which is well-organised by student services. A friendly and welcoming atmosphere is created in the main hall where stalls display the different services available to students. Tutors take or send their students to make contact with student services. Meetings are arranged by means of a special booking sheet which also provides a check on which groups have used the student services. If necessary, tutors can book follow-up visits to the study centres and counselling services for

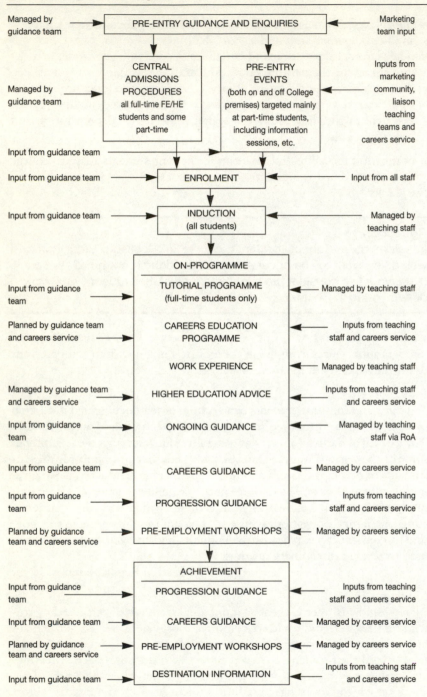

Managed by guidance team → PRE-ENTRY GUIDANCE AND ENQUIRIES ← Marketing team input

↓   ↓

Managed by guidance team → CENTRAL ADMISSIONS PROCEDURES all full-time FE/HE students and some part-time

PRE-ENTRY EVENTS (both on and off College premises) targeted mainly at part-time students, including information sessions, etc. ← Inputs from marketing community, liaison teaching teams and careers service

Input from guidance team

Input from guidance team → ENROLMENT ← Input from all staff

Input from guidance team → INDUCTION (all students) ← Managed by teaching staff

ON-PROGRAMME

Input from guidance team → TUTORIAL PROGRAMME (full-time students only) ← Managed by teaching staff

Planned by guidance team and careers service → CAREERS EDUCATION PROGRAMME ← Inputs from teaching staff and careers service

WORK EXPERIENCE ← Managed by teaching staff

Managed by guidance team and careers service → HIGHER EDUCATION ADVICE ← Inputs from teaching staff and careers service

Input from guidance team → ONGOING GUIDANCE ← Managed by teaching staff via RoA

Input from guidance team → CAREERS GUIDANCE ← Managed by careers service

Input from guidance team → PROGRESSION GUIDANCE ← Inputs from teaching staff and careers service

Planned by guidance team and careers service → PRE-EMPLOYMENT WORKSHOPS ← Managed by careers service

ACHIEVEMENT

Input from guidance team → PROGRESSION GUIDANCE ← Inputs from teaching staff and careers service

Input from guidance team → CAREERS GUIDANCE ← Managed by careers service

Planned by guidance team and careers service → PRE-EMPLOYMENT WORKSHOPS ← Managed by careers service

Input from guidance team → DESTINATION INFORMATION ← Inputs from teaching staff and careers service

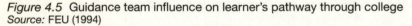

Figure 4.5 Guidance team influence on learner's pathway through college
Source: FEU (1994)

their students. All tutors receive training in induction. They are also given a handbook containing details of all the support and facilities. Similarly, students receive a handbook which sets out the college's charter and lists the facilities and staff responsible for each service.

(FEFC Inspection Report, April 1996)

A key deficiency with many induction programmes is that they tend to be one-off events, whereas the process of induction should carry on throughout a student's lifetime in the college. That is, at various points in his or her career in the college, a student will need to be inducted into a new stage, to meet new tutors and fellow students and so on, or to be reinducted with parts of the college or course long forgotten. Figure 4.4 shows how a college's guidance and support system should span all aspects of college life from student entry through to student exit.

Chapter 5

Teaching strategies

FLEXIBILITY AND ADAPTABILITY

In the opening chapters of this book, we described the complex world of FE and emphasised the need for teachers to be flexible and adaptable in order to meet the demands that their managers, students and external agencies will put on them. It is worth remembering, too, that the pressures on FE colleges to recruit as many students as possible mean that teaching staff will be faced with some people who have a wide range of learning difficulties.

FE teachers are now seen as 'managers of learning', involved in a range of activities which stretch beyond the day-to-day business of teaching in a classroom or workshop. Young *et al.* (1995) have proposed that the work of FE teachers has shifted during recent years as follows:

from subject knowledge to curriculum knowledge

from teacher-centred pedagogic knowledge to learner-centred pedagogic knowledge

from intra-professional knowledge to inter-professional knowledge

from classroom knowledge to organisational knowledge

from insular to connective knowledge

Instead of being a teacher who is solely concerned with his or her own subject specialism, FE teachers now have to understand how their specialism 'connects' with the rest of the college's curricular provision and how generic (or core) learning can be facilitated through that specialism. In moving to a more learner-centred approach, FE teachers will have to 'manage' the process of learning as a whole and not simply be concerned with transmitting knowledge and skills. As 'managers of learning', teachers will need to seek the help and support of other professionals in their college, including non-teaching staff, and they will be members of course teams. The shift from 'insular' to 'connective' knowledge recognises the way in which FE teachers have to be aware of and build on their students' prior educational experience and their future needs. An FE college represents a transitional stage for many students as they progress from school education through FE and on to work-based training and/or HE.

In Chapter 1, we provided extracts from the FEFC inspection reports of two colleges and noted how, in carrying out their task, the FEFC inspectors observe teaching sessions throughout a college and grade them using the five-point scale. Their reports concentrate, in particular, on the organisation and management of the learning situation and note the strengths and weaknesses of the following:

- level of coherence of schemes of work
- level of teachers' subject expertise
- level of rapport between staff and students
- clarity of aims and objectives
- appropriateness of the pace of learning
- range of teaching techniques in use
- opportunities for students to participate actively
- quality of resources, for example handouts, workbooks, visual aids, etc.
- clarity of assessment criteria
- classroom/workshop management, for example punctuality of staff and students, behaviour of students
- quality of feedback on students' work
- quality and usefulness of set tasks and appropriateness of coursework
- quality of record keeping to inform students of their progress

The following extracts from 1996 inspection reports indicate the range of teaching skills which the inspectors are looking for:

> In poorer teaching sessions, the pace of learning was slow and teachers used only a small range of teaching strategies. The differing abilities of students were not always sufficiently addressed. The coursework was insufficiently challenging. The poor punctuality of students, which was a common feature in many courses, affected course management and impeded learning. The poor attendance of students was also a concern on some courses. Some feedback to students on their assignment work was insufficiently informative, failing to indicate errors clearly or explain the allocation of marks.
>
> (FEFC, 1996, Inspection Reports)

> In construction, a significant proportion of the teaching took place in the workshops and was of high quality. Underpinning knowledge was taught using well-designed learning materials and textbooks, but maximum benefit was not obtained from this development because students had not been taught the study skills required for independent learning. Working relationships between students and teachers were excellent partly due to the respect that students had for the expertise displayed by their teachers.
>
> (FEFC, 1996, Inspection Reports)

Many humanities sessions were enriched by the infectious enthusiasm of teachers who used current references and illustrations to bring subjects alive. In history sessions, students used computer disk read-only memory (CD-ROM) databases and computer software to interrogate information and build up databases of historical facts. Students of English and communications experienced a good range of learning activities which included a lot of practical work in small groups. In one excellent GCE A level class, the teacher had prepared a range of resources for group work, including computers loaded with interactive packages on synthesised speech. Within a short time, and working through a graded series of exercises, students became aware of the importance of phonemes in the study of language.

(FEFC, 1996, Inspection Reports)

Engineering staff were enthusiastic and enjoyed good relationships with their students. Lessons were of an acceptable standard but the work lacked variety and often failed to stimulate students. Students were expected to listen to lectures or to copy notes from the board for excessive periods of time. In better lessons, good use was made of handouts and of question and answer techniques, and teachers linked theory to industrial practice.

(FEFC, 1996, Inspection Reports)

In hairdressing and beauty therapy, there were comprehensive, well-organised schemes of work supported by appropriate assignments that took into account students' differing abilities. Teaching was generally well planned. Good handouts were provided for hairdressing students, although there was limited use of workbooks to support independent learning. In some practical sessions in hairdressing the work was insufficiently demanding. The low number of clients in the public hairdressing salons meant that the opportunities for assessing students' practical skills were limited. In most sessions, there was insufficient integration of science, design, information technology and business studies.

(FEFC, 1996, Inspection Reports)

CHOOSING A STRATEGY

What I hear, I cannot remember
What I see, I do remember
What I do, I understand
          (Chinese proverb)

Students attend colleges to acquire skills, knowledge and understanding related to their area of study, whether it be English literature, welding, social care or applied statistics. Separating out the skills, knowledge and understanding components within any one learning encounter is not, of course, a straight-forward process as in most encounters the three are bound together.

Given the underpinning complexity of the learning encounter in terms of content, there is also the diversity of your potential students to consider. You are clearly going to need to develop a range of strategies for helping your students to learn effectively. Once you gain some experience as a teacher, you will find that you can create your own strategies which reflect your personality and are designed to respond to your students' particular needs. Always remember that different strategies work differently for different teachers. You may be the sort of person who will never be comfortable giving a lecture or facilitating a role-play exercise but able to get excellent results from designing group-based problem-solving exercises. Then again, you may shine as a lecturer, providing your students with stimulating talks which capture their imaginations. Gaining confidence as a teacher is important and all teachers tend to stick with the strategies with which they feel most comfortable. Your students, too, as we saw in Chapter 5, have their own preferences when it comes to teaching strategies. There is a danger, therefore, that both teachers and students can settle into a cosy learning relationship in which neither is challenged or pushed into expanding their learning horizons. On the other hand, if the teacher disregards the preferences of the students and sticks to the teaching strategy they feel least happy about, then the learning environment is put under stress and the outcomes may be unsatisfactory for both parties.

In choosing an appropriate teaching strategy, you have to consider four equally important issues:

1 Given a specific curriculum objective to be achieved, which teaching strategy will be most effective for transmitting the necessary *skills, knowledge and understanding* to your students?
2 How can you ensure that your students will fully participate in the learning process so that they *learn for themselves* rather than just listening to or watching you demonstrate *your* learning?
3 Given your knowledge of the group of students, how can you incorporate their *prior learning* and overcome any *barriers to learning* they may have?
4 How much *time* can you allow for this particular curriculum objective?

There are a number of strategies at your disposal and they can be arranged on a continuum (Figure 5.1) which stretches from teacher-centred methods at one end to those methods which encourage students to take more responsibility for their own learning at the other end.

The chart in Figure 5.1 is not judgemental. It is not saying that giving a lecture is wrong or that the best way to teach is to engage students in role plays and problem-solving exercises. It is, however, a means of illustrating how different teaching strategies will affect different learning outcomes.

Teacher centred  **Learner centred**

Lecture   **Question/answer session**   **Research-based project**

Examination

Demonstration   **Worksheets**   **Group work**

Video conference

Video/audio cassette

     Structured reading   **Self-directed study**

Instructions   **Discussion**

     Practicals   **Trial and error activity**

     Tutorials   **Role play**

Figure 5.1 Teaching strategies continuum

AIMS, OBJECTIVES, GOALS AND LEARNING OUTCOMES: 'WHAT ARE WE SUPPOSED TO BE LEARNING HERE?'

Every student comes to their course with preconceived assumptions about its content and will react differently to its separate components. In addition, each student will have certain expectations about how much he or she will gain from the course. The course team has to be aware of such complexities in the student profile when constructing the learning materials and will attempt to cover as many of what it judges to be potential areas of interest. In terms of choosing the inputs or content of a learning programme, it is the teacher or course team, in most cases, who has the main responsibility. Once a learner begins to study, the teacher's control begins to diminish. What goes into a learning programme and what comes out at the other end may not, necessarily, be all that closely related, as Rogers explains:

> The planning agent (teacher-provider) initially determines the goals of the learning process. The agent has in mind certain expected outcomes, the results that will flow from the learning undertaken in changed attitudes and behaviour. However, most of the student participants come with their own intentions, which may or may not be the same as those set out by the agent; they will use the learning opportunity for their own purposes, to achieve their own outcomes. Each of these sets of purposes influences the other. The teacher's intended outcomes to help shape the learners' expectations, and the learners' intentions and hopes should affect the formulation of the teacher's intentions. Both sets of proposed outcomes may well be different yet again from the effective outcomes of the educational process. Since those being taught consist of a mixed group of learners, each of whom

responds to the learning in a different way, there will always be a series of unexpected outcomes. The teacher-agent needs to keep these differences in mind when planning the learning encounter.

(Rogers, 1986, p.12)

In the case of competence-based programmes, the NCVQ would argue that teaching inputs must be determined by the prescribed competences in the various elements and units of the NVQ or GNVQ, but we would argue that the teaching and learning relationship is more sophisticated than even the purest competence-based approach would assume it to be. And, in most other sorts of programmes, teachers and learners still have some freedom to strive for undetermined outcomes. It is important, therefore, for teachers to be able to identify the aims and objectives of a particular teaching session, albeit with the flexibility to amend their original ideas. Furthermore, there are valuable opportunities here for teachers and students to work together to determine what each wants in the way of learning outcomes and so negotiate a micro curriculum.

The language of learning can be so complex as to suppress understanding. Indeed, many professional educators and trainers, and particularly academics, are guilty of constructing a highly technical and often impenetrable set of terminology which shuts out teachers and students alike. It is common practice for teachers to set aims and objectives when designing learning programmes, so what is the difference between aims and objectives and learning outcomes? Furthermore, what might be the value of specifying or identifying the outcomes of learning? The following passage from a report of research into learning outcomes in HE is useful here as its central message is equally applicable to FE:

> Aims and objectives are primarily the language of course designers. They describe what the course sets out to do and can tend to preserve traditional course structures by discouraging comment and input from other voices: professions, employers, government and students. Learning outcomes, on the other hand, describe what graduates are expected to be able to do and do not relate directly either to courses or to any particular methods of teaching and learning. They can include both knowledge of the subject and the intellectual and personal qualities which are developed as a result of in depth study of a subject. The explicit and detailed nature of the learning outcomes makes it easier for those outside HE, government, employers etc to understand the nature of the HE curriculum and to make realistic inputs to its development. Learning outcomes also make it easier for students to understand what is expected of them and to take greater responsibility for their own learning. This can be a means of developing alternative approaches to teaching and learning resulting in greater flexibility and wider participation in HE.

(UDACE, 1991)

Reflection

In this reflection, we hope you will engage in some lateral thinking about learning outcomes from the point of view both of the teacher and the learner. Similar exercises to this are often used in relation to developing communication skills.

Study Figure 5.2 and follow the instructions – you will need a partner to help you. The basic outcome should be for your partner to achieve as close a representation of the original drawing as possible. When you have finished the exercise, you might find it useful to discuss with your partner the following questions:

1 To what extent was the basic outcome achieved?
2 Can you identify any other outcomes of this exercise in terms of (a) your learning and (b) your partner's learning?
3 In terms of the overall outcomes of this exercise, how important was the achievement of the basic outcome?

You could extend this exercise by reversing your roles, though you would, of course, need to use another diagram!

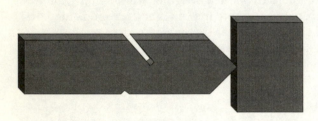

Instructions

1 Study the picture and consider how you would describe it to someone.
2 Sit back-to-back with a friend/colleague who has not seen the picture and give him or her a sheet of paper and a pen.
3 Give verbal instructions to enable your partner to draw the picture.
4 When the new picture is complete, examine it to see how closely it matches the original.

Figure 5.2 Reflection exercise

The teaching and learning involved in the exercise you have just carried out will have reflected the personalities, capabilities and learning styles of the two people involved. As the teacher, you will have had to:

- think carefully about the nature of the instructions you supplied;
- communicate those instructions effectively;
- listen carefully to your partner's questions and reactions.

In judging the success of the exercise, that is in terms of how closely your partner managed to reproduce the diagram, you will have considered to what extent each of you contributed to the exercise. Over and above the physical reproduction of the diagram, you may have discussed other outcomes: for example, your partner may have learned that he or she needs to practise following verbal instructions. By simply concentrating on the physical outcome, we can miss a great deal of associated learning which could include generic or transferable skills.

If you look in the index of the overwhelming majority of books about education, at any level, you will be lucky to find more than a handful of entries which have any specific reference to learning outcomes. You may find the word 'objectives' listed in a few and you will certainly find the word 'curriculum' in most. Indeed, you will find whole books devoted to the discussion of what makes up a curriculum, how it is planned and managed, modularised and marketed. This is not to suggest that educationalists have not been concerned with learning outcomes but that the process of learning has been largely seen in terms of what goes in rather than what comes out. Trainee teachers spend a great deal of time constructing lesson plans detailing how they will cover a particular subject in a given period of time. Most curriculum planning takes the form of a stockpot into which ingredients are thrown until the chef decides there are enough to make a decent soup. Some thought will be given to the balance of subjects, the depth to which each should be discussed, and, importantly, the presumed expectations of the potential learners. At some point, the curriculum planners will have identified certain broad aims by which their deliberations and choices are guided. These aims tend to relate to the whole curriculum or large parts of it:

> Not infrequently, such statements reflect philosophical or educational beliefs and values. Statements of aims are generally vague and tend to have little operational value (descriptively or prescriptively) in relation to the planning, development and implementation of curricula. They can, however, act as a 'reference' against which the tenability of more specific statements of intent (e.g. curricula goals and objectives) can be appraised.
>
> (Heathcote *et al.*, 1982)

Heathcote *et al.* found that three recurrent themes emerged when they analysed a range of curriculum aims taken from FE courses:

1 Promotion of the individual's personal and intellectual growth.
2 Meeting the needs of the individual in relation to the individual's societal and physical environment.
3 Meeting the needs of society itself.

They further found that when curriculum aims were translated into more specific goals, it was to serve two closely connected but alternate functions: the first function involves the teacher acting as an agent for the curriculum planner by teaching directly to tightly defined goals; the second function sees the teacher as a much freer agent who interprets the curriculum planner's goals in the context of each specific group of learners.

The pre-eminence of either function depends, according to Heathcote *et al.*, on the following variables:

1 The amount of direction which the curriculum planner wishes to impose on the implementing teacher.
2 The extent to which the curriculum emphasises student autonomy in relation to learning outcomes.
3 The ability and previous experience of the students for whom the curriculum is intended.
4 The curriculum planner's perception of the constraints imposed and opportunities offered by the subject matter.

We would add a further and, in the light of the competence-based approach, increasingly dominant variable which concerns the teaching or learning system within which the teacher has to function.

Heathcote *et al.* distinguish between the use of curriculum aims as a base from which the curriculum planner exerts control over the teacher who delivers the curriculum, as opposed to a 'staging post' where control passes to the teacher who then translates the aims into more specific objectives. They see the first approach as being objectives based and the second as being process based. The distinction here is that the process-based model focuses on the role of the teacher who adopts appropriate pedagogical methods in order to achieve the broad aims of the curriculum. Under the objectives-based model, the activities of the teacher are seen as merely the means to an end, that is the attainment by the students of the specified learning objectives. In the case of distance learning materials, the materials themselves become the main 'agent' of the course team but involve a tutor or 'secondary agent' who interprets the materials for students.

The objectives model of curriculum development in the training field first appeared in the USA with Franklin Bobbitt's *How to Make a Curriculum* in 1924, and was greatly refined in the 1940s by Ralph Tyler, and later in the 1950s and 1960s by R.F. Mager. The attraction of this model is that it systematically defines the skills and knowledge required to accomplish tasks and, in doing so, presents to teachers and trainers clear guidelines for selecting appropriate teaching methods and, most importantly, for designing an assessment programme. As Mager points out:

If you don't know where you are going, it is difficult to select a suitable means for getting there. After all, machinists and surgeons don't select tools until they know what operation they are going to perform . . .

Instructors simply function in a fog of their own making unless they know what they want their students to accomplish as a result of their instruction.

(Mager, 1962)

What is looked for is a change in behaviour on the part of the learner, change which Bloom's *Taxonomy* (1965), widely adopted by both teachers and trainers, classifies into three domains:

Affective – attitudes and emotions
Cognitive – knowledge and information
Psychomotor – practical or physical skills

Each domain is sub-divided into a hierarchy of categories which demonstrate the different levels at which a learner may operate or be asked to operate. Bloom has been criticised, particularly for separating the cognitive from the affective, and other people have developed alternative taxonomies (see, for example, Gagne, 1988). Despite the criticisms, however, Bloom's domains and categories, when taken together, do provide a useful and fairly straightforward structure of learning. As such, they can be used as a basic template for the teacher when planning learning sessions and can also be used for the purposes of evaluating the effectiveness of a particular session.

The *affective* domain has five categories:

Receiving (taking in messages and responding to a stimulus)

Responding (taking responsibility by responding and seeking to find out)

Valuing (recognising that something is worth doing)

Organising and conceptualising (the individual develops his or her own way of arranging responses to stimuli and develops particular attitudes based on a set of values)

Characterising by value or value concept (bringing together ideas, beliefs and attitudes in a coherent whole)

The *cognitive* domain has six characteristics:

Knowledge (facts, categorisation of facts and knowledge in general, theories and abstractions)

Comprehension (making sense of what things mean and how they relate to each other)

Application (applying knowledge to different situations)

Analysis (breaking down knowledge into its constituent parts to gain a clearer understanding of the whole)

Synthesis (bringing together the separate constituents to create a new whole, which involves making choices)

Evaluation (reflecting on knowledge and making judgements)

The *psychomotor* domain, as developed by Harrow (1972) from Bloom's work, has six characteristics:

Reflex movements (in response to stimuli)

Basic fundamental movements (build upon reflex movements)

Perceptual abilities (used to interpret stimuli and behave accordingly)

Physical abilities

Skilled movements (involve practice)

Non-discursive communication (involves creative and artistic behaviour)

Behavioural objectives have been heavily criticised by many people (see Eisner, 1985) for a number of reasons and, as we discussed earlier, too much emphasis on a predetermined outcome can result in a dangerously narrow approach to learning. All teachers, however, do need to have a sense of what it is they want their students to achieve by the end of a particular session and over a certain period of time. Those 'objectives' might be largely predetermined and written in the form of 'outcomes' (as in the case of NVQ and GNVQ programmes) or they may be framed more loosely but in such a way as to help the teacher give a structure to the learning. On some programmes, it is possible, and often desirable, for the teacher and students to negotiate a set of objectives and for the negotiation itself to be regarded as a central part of the learning process.

So far, we have been talking about 'objectives' for teaching and learning and there has been some reference to 'outcomes'. Teachers also talk about 'aims' and 'goals'. Whilst there is little point in getting too pedantic about terminology, it might be helpful to separate these terms and use them to differentiate between the distinct elements of a teaching/learning situation. The following example is taken from a GNVQ Advanced course in business and focuses on Unit 4 of the GNVQ, *Human Resource Management.* This unit is broken down into elements, one of which, Element 4.3, is called *Evaluate Job Applications and Interviews.* The GNVQ course requirements for this element are that students be assessed according to the following performance criteria:

- recruitment procedures identified (application and selection methods);
- letters of application evaluated for clarity and quality of presentation;
- curriculum vitae evaluated for clarity and quality of presentation;
- interviewer techniques practised and appraised;
- interviewee techniques practised and appraised;
- legal and ethical obligations in recruitment explained (equal opportunities, contract of employment, concepts of honesty and objectivity).

The teacher knows in advance, therefore, what is expected in terms of learning outcomes, but in order to ensure that students achieve those outcomes, the teacher has to construct a teaching plan. This is where aims and objectives come in. We asked a trainee FE teacher to devise a plan for the teaching of this

GNVQ element and he began by setting down an overall aim, followed by a set of objectives:

Aim: To understand the process involved and the skills required when applying for a job.

Objectives:
1 To understand the recruitment procedures when applying for a job.
2 To respond to a job advertisement.
3 To complete an application form in a clear, accurate and professional manner.
4 To produce a covering letter to accompany the application form.
5 To complete an employer aptitude test.
6 To attend an interview with a personnel officer.

We can see from this that the aim encompasses the element as a whole whereas the objectives indicate the separate components which the student needs to master in order to fulfil the element. As this example is taken from a GNVQ course, the student would also be expected to demonstrate his or her ability in a number of core skills in communication which are laid down by the GNVQ awarding body. In addition, the teacher may want to extend the prescribed learning outcomes in order to reflect the needs of the students. Additional outcomes might include, for example:

- developing the students' confidence outside the classroom;
- developing the students' independent research skills;
- improving the level of written work amongst the students in general.

In defining these additional outcomes, the teacher would place this particular element within the context of the course as a whole. An outcome related to the students' research skills would, therefore, be associated with more than one element. Other outcomes might appear as a result of the teacher (or students) identifying a particular weakness in a previous session which requires attention.

In planning how to take the students through this element, the teacher might set 'goals'. For example, objectives 1 to 3 will be covered in three weeks; or one of the objectives will involve a group discussion or activity. And it is in the planning where the teacher can be creative, despite the prescriptive nature of the GNVQ framework. Our trainee teacher decided to divide the content of the element into seven sections and to employ a range of teaching strategies (TS) as follows:

Section 1: general overview
In this section, students are asked to discuss their attitudes to unemployment and the different ways in which people can apply for jobs.

TS: brainstorm as a group to get initial views; ask students to consider a set of case studies of people seeking work; ask students to choose two job vacancies from the local newspaper and obtain the necessary application forms (use telephone, letters and visit to job centre).

Section 2: the recruitment process
Students learn about how a typical company sets out to recruit staff.

TS: Teacher uses information from an actual company (e.g. Royal Mail) to explain the recruitment process. Teaching aids include OHTs and wipeboard.

Section 3: letters and job specifications
Students learn how to construct a letter of application and interpret job advertisements.

TS: Students have been asked to bring in copies of job advertisements from local newspapers and to select three jobs they could realistically apply for; the students work in pairs to assess the quality of a sample of specimen letters of application; the teacher goes through the key requirements in writing a letter of application; the students work on their own to produce a letter of application for one of the jobs they selected earlier. (These individual letters might be set for homework.)

Section 4: application forms and curriculum vitae
Students learn how to complete an application form and construct a CV.

TS: students work in groups to assess quality of specimen completed application forms; group discussion about what the applicant needs to do when completing a form; teacher reinforces the requirements by presenting a list on an OHT. The process is repeated for CVs and students use word processors, thereby covering some IT core skills associated with the element.

Section 5: equal opportunities and contracts of employment
Students learn about the legal obligations employers have to adhere to when recruiting staff.

TS: role play between teacher and student to demonstrate how certain questions could contravene equal opportunities legislation; group discussion of why equal opportunity matters in recruitment; students work in small groups to analyse a sample of contracts of employment; teacher reinforces legal knowledge with handouts.

Section 6: preparing for interviews
Students learn how to prepare for an interview and how to conduct themselves in an interview.

TS: teacher shows a video of good and bad interviews and students take notes; group discussion of video; teacher reinforces points related to how to prepare for an interview and how to behave as an interviewee.

Section 7: being interviewed

Students take part in mock interviews, acting as both interviewees and interviewers.

TS: mock interviews held using video cameras and external interviewers brought in; students watch the videos and analyse their strengths and weaknesses; teacher draws together all aspects of the element.

In devising his teaching plan, the trainee teacher was determined to provide his students with a lively and varied learning opportunity; hence he has deliberately chosen a range of teaching and learning strategies.

ASSIGNMENTS

The use of assignments as vehicles for encouraging participative, student-centred learning has been a central feature of college life for many years. Assignments can enable students to see their programme of study as a coherent whole in which all the parts are related to each other and through which they are encouraged to apply their knowledge, understanding and skills. In this way, assignments are an important means for enabling students to engage in *learning by doing* and for emphasising the integrated nature of their courses. The student-centred nature of assignments and their facility for including both individual and group tasks means that they highlight the process of learning as well as being agents for delivering outcomes of learning. When assignment work is assessed (either by teachers or through student peer assessment, or both), valuable lessons can be learned through a review of the process of learning which took place (see Chapter 6). The common features of assignments are:

- they include an element of independent student activity to be carried out individually or in groups;
- they are based on a realistic scenario;
- they can be of varying length;
- they encourage students to apply knowledge, understanding and skills to meaningful tasks in a realistic situation;
- they allow core skills to be integrated into the learning process and assessed as part of the overall learning outcomes.

Assignments can be created by individual teachers or by course teams who wish to create greater coherence between the modules, units and so on which comprise the distinctive parts of a course of study. Designing assignments can be divided into three areas:

1 Task – what a student does, often resulting in a product or outcome.
2 Activities – the process used in order to achieve the task.
3 Assessment – the benchmarks or criteria for the product and the process.

For example, if an assignment was built around the design and use of questionnaires, the three areas listed above would translate as follows:

Task　　　　　– devise and use a questionnaire.

Activities　　　– select sources and obtain information about questionnaire design; plan the questionnaire; pilot it; amend as necessary; use the amended questionnaire; collect data; evaluate and present data.

Assessment　　– range of methods used in obtaining information; fitness of resulting questionnaire for purpose – language, tone, degree of complexity, etc.; depth of analysis; clarity of presentation; adequacy of evaluation.

There is enormous scope when identifying scenarios for assignments for teachers to be creative and to utilise the expertise and ideas of a range of people. When designing an assignment, the following stages should be followed:

1 Choose the unit, element, etc., you wish to cover.
2 Formulate a scenario, exercise or brief for the students to work within. (Be realistic about the amount of time available to students to cover the work involved.)
3 Correlate possible tasks with criteria that will have to be fulfilled and take note of the range expected.
4 Identify the core skills which will be assessed through the assignment.
5 Decide if this will be a graded assignment.
6 Write the assignment as a series of tasks with guidance for students.
7 Write assessment guidance (including grading criteria if applicable), indicating the nature of the evidence to be obtained.
8 Design any necessary documentation for assessment purposes, for example grids, question sheets, logs, etc.

By evaluating the implementation of an assignment, the teacher (and or course team) can refine the different elements in order to improve the assignment and ensure its continued applicability and viability. Once a set of effective assignments have been created, the pressure on the teacher to produce teaching materials is reduced and more time can be spent supervising the actual learning process.

Being creative

As early as 1991, the FEU remarked:

In some colleges a new hybrid of staff (neither conventional lecturer nor support staff job specification) is emerging to take the new roles associated with flexible access to learning and accreditation.

(FEU, 1991, p.28)

As we discussed in Chapter 5, teachers have to be aware of the different ways in which their students approach learning and try to create a learning environment in which those different approaches can be accommodated. But creativity in teaching involves risk.

The following question and answer section examines the implications for teachers inherent in an outcome-based, student-centred programme such as GNVQ.

What teaching will I need to devise and deliver?

The teaching will have to be designed to contribute to the assignments, in other words, to provide the underpinning knowledge which students will require in order to complete the assignments. This will not always be provided by the teacher but the teacher may act as a facilitator in pointing the students in the direction of suitable learning resources. Teachers need to ask themselves: what do students need to know in order to fulfil the performance criteria for this unit/element?

A supplementary question will then be as follows:

Where or from whom can this knowledge be accessed?

The important point here is that there are a wide range of resources and sources from which knowledge can be accessed and the teacher should exploit the interdisciplinary nature of the college environment as well as drawing on resources available through the college's external networks.

How and where will the learning take place?

The answer to this question could be as wide as individual teaching staff wish to make it. If it is accepted that the opportunities for learning are constrained neither by the time nor the place at which it occurs, nor by the age of the candidate, then the opportunities presented by a wide range of diverse contexts and experiences are limitless. However, if teachers subscribe to the view that learning can only take place in classrooms where the teacher stands at the front and talks then it will be extremely difficult to deliver GNVQ or similar programmes effectively.

Examples of work-based learning activities include:

- Work experience placements
- Work shadowing
- Projects undertaken in companies specifically for those companies
- Simulations
- Organising and running events in the college, for example open days, careers fairs, catering and general reception duties.

A 1995 FEFC report indicated that within 75 per cent of GNVQ programmes, supervised work experience on employers' premises was available for students to provide them with the necessary vocational experience. (FEFC, 1995a) There was some variation in provision across the programme areas, but in the best developed examples assignments had been designed in conjunction with employers. Well-planned work placements allowed students to collect assessment evidence from their experience. In some cases assessments were undertaken by workplace supervisors and later verified by college staff.

There are obvious implications for quality control when parts of the programme are, in effect, being devolved to employers. Issues about the standardisation of assessment are still being resolved. Some colleges have been able to develop effective partnerships with companies by arranging for staff teaching on GNVQ programmes to have work placements in business and industry. The case study at the end of this chapter illustrates a well-developed partnership model for GNVQ delivery.

What sort of students will be involved?

The current profile for GNVQ students is a 16–19 year old in full-time education. It was not envisaged that this would be the main target group when the qualification was introduced but so far take-up of the qualification by part-time adults has been low. The government is currently looking at ways of making the qualification more accessible to adults who are studying on a part-time basis (DfEE/The Scottish Office/The Welsh Office, 1995).

How will assessment be organised and carried out?

Assessment is continuous throughout the programme and is based on a series of assignments which are completed during the programme plus a series of end of unit externally set and marked tests. Initially the tests were not included in the design but were later added in response to criticisms about rigour and in an attempt to confer parity of esteem with A levels. The outcome-based nature of the GNVQ should not, however, be forgotten:

> One characteristic of GNVQ assessment, which distinguishes it from assessment in most academic qualifications, is that it covers the curriculum outcomes far more comprehensively. All the outcomes reflected in the units must be achieved . . . doing well in one component cannot compensate for a poor result in another . . . and the primary component is the internal assessment which runs throughout a GNVQ.
>
> (Jessup, 1994, p.2)

Evidence for assessment is collected in the student's portfolio. The student has to satisfy the assessment criteria for each unit of the course and has to provide sufficient evidence that the mandatory key skills units have been achieved. The portfolio is graded according to a number of 'grading themes'; those relating to process include: planning, information seeking and information handling, and evaluation. The quality of outcomes is also graded within the overall assessment of the portfolio.

Choosing a strategy

It is clear from the GNVQ example above that teaching strategies are chosen for reasons which go beyond being a mechanism for ensuring that the students achieve the subject-specific outcomes. Certainly achievement of those outcomes is vitally important but the teacher also has to ensure that students develop their abilities as learners and build relationships with each other which contribute to an effective learning environment. We can portray this (Figure 5.3) as a model for effective learning.

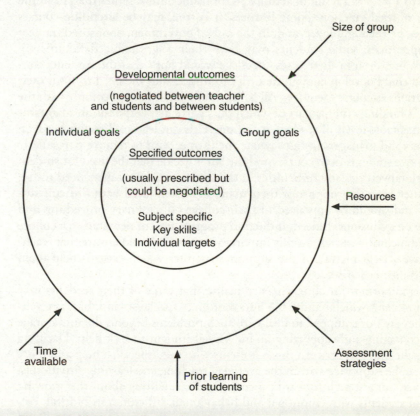

Figure 5.3 Model for effective learning

Once you are clear about the outcomes to be achieved in a session, and have taken account of any constraining factors, you can select one or more teaching strategies. As we noted earlier, those strategies will obviously reflect your preferences as a teacher but you may want to try out different approaches, albeit on a small scale to begin with until you gain confidence in using them. In the following section, we identify the characteristics of a range of teaching strategies and suggest tasks which students can be asked to perform in order to ensure that they participate as fully as possible in the learning situation.

MANAGING LEARNING: HANDLING 'DIFFICULT' STUDENTS

In the opening chapters of this book, we stressed the diversity of college life and, in particular, the need for FE teachers to appreciate that their students will reflect a range of abilities, needs and levels of motivation. Unlike schools, where all the students are legally required to attend, colleges expect their students to attend as a result of acting as responsible adults, rather than from the threat of legal sanction. Some learners, it is true, may be attending courses selected by their employers and, in the case of government-sponsored trainees or apprentices, some students may have their wages reduced for missing classes, but, even in these cases, a college would hope that the students concerned could develop enough maturity to understand the need to fulfil their obligations as course members. All colleges, of course, have to comply with the FEFC's funding criteria, part of which puts particular emphasis on maintaining acceptable levels of student retention. This can lead to disputes between teachers and managers in cases where the former wish to remove particularly disruptive students from courses and the latter decide that the need for student retention overrides any difficulties in the classroom. All teachers need to feel that they have the support of their managers when faced with difficult students and should be appraised of their college's disciplinary procedures and policy on exclusions. Indeed, induction programmes for new staff to a college should include a session on this important area and should ensure that teachers have a clear picture of the support structures which exist to help them should the need arise.

It is important for all teachers to realise that some of their students may have problems which require the intervention of specialists and that, as teachers, they are not equipped to deal with such problems beyond the initial stage of encouraging and supporting an individual student to seek help. Deciding where the line falls between those students who need specialist help and those who can be supported within the everyday teaching and learning situation is, however, not a straightforward process. Sue Rees, writing about the 'growing tide' of students with emotional and behavioural difficulties in Norfolk colleges, distinguishes between those students who can be said to be 'sad' and those who are thought of as 'bad':

The former ('sad') sub-group consists of students who are emotionally disturbed in some way. They may be lonely, isolated and have difficulties making relationships, but do not necessarily come to lecturers' attention because they do not cause obvious problems of discipline etc., during the educational process. The latter ('bad') group may be termed as 'disturbing' rather than 'disturbed'. Their emotional state manifests itself in behavioural problems and they are frequently aggressive and disruptive within the learning environment.

(Rees, 1995, p.93)

The more experience one gains as a teacher, the more adept one becomes at managing the learning process and spotting potential flashpoints. As we discussed in Chapter 4, if teachers demonstrate that they have empathy with their students, they are much more likely to create conditions which are conducive to co-operation with and between their students and in which all parties trust and respect each other. We also noted, however, that the pressures on students in terms of the lives they lead outside college can cause them to display behavioural patterns which appear disruptive in the classroom or workshop. But that pressure may also come from within the college if, for example, a student is struggling to keep up with their written work or if they are being bullied. And, of course, disruptive behaviour may be the students' way of telling a teacher that the sessions are boring, poorly organised or pitched at an inappropriate level. Changes in behaviour can usually be seen as signals of stress or anxiety and the teacher must be able to recognise those signals and act appropriately before the situation gets out of hand.

A key factor in the effective management of any learning situation is for the teacher to involve the students in the whole process. This involves the teacher in an exercise in sharing with students as follows:

1 Discuss with students your expectations (as a teacher) of them and identify their expectations (as students) of you – for example, try to establish a code of practice regarding lateness, the handing in of work, eating/drinking in class, dress codes, etc.
2 Explain to students the nature of what is to be covered in a particular session and how this relates to the rest of their course.
3 Explain clearly (and review at intervals) the assessment procedure you will operate – this includes both the informal (criteria you use to monitor student progress) and the formal (externally imposed criteria for summative assessment) criteria you will employ.
4 Discuss with students the constraints under which you and they must work – for example, presentation of work to satisfy external examiners, coverage of certain elements of a curriculum, the lack of sufficient computers or textbooks, etc.
5 Review your working arrangements as a group, giving students the chance to discuss whether they should be given more time to hand in work or to

receive more support with a particular part of the course – this may require you to recognise any inadequacies in your initial preparation for a course or to accept that you have made mistakes.

By sharing the necessary ingredients of the learning process with students, they are given the opportunity to act responsibly and with the same degree of professionalism as the teacher. At the same time, the teacher has to be prepared to show the same degree of respect to the students and to try not to retreat into a position of isolated superiority when challenged. Working with students does not necessitate a blurring of roles to the point where teacher and student become indistinguishable. Both teacher and students have to recognise the demands of each other's roles and that the teacher, like any manager, has to take responsibility for ensuring that the collective goals of the group are achieved.

The difficulties involved in creating a supportive atmosphere within colleges are illustrated by this extract from a 1996 inspection report:

> Students speak warmly of the helpfulness of teaching staff. A tutorial structure has existed in most parts of the college for some time, but it varies widely in its effectiveness. Some students are unaware that they have personal tutors in addition to their teachers. The college has prepared guidance on the role and responsibilities of personal tutors. Some good practice exists, particularly on access courses. However, on many courses, personal tutors wait for students to present issues to them, and some do not understand their responsibility for guidance. A range of student services, including welfare and counselling, complements the work of personal tutors. The demands for these services are increasing. Staff help students with personal and social problems which interfere with their ability to study effectively, while the welfare service's primary focus is on financial matters.
>
> (FEFC, Inspection Report January 1996)

In her Norfolk study, Rees concludes that strategic planning is required to help teaching and support staff tackle the problem of 'disturbing', 'emotionally disturbed' and 'disruptive' students and suggests that staff development, particularly in 'group management', is a key feature:

> staff will require techniques for dealing with confrontation: for example non-verbal communication methods for use with aggressive students. Personal and social skills are also important, and if these are imparted effectively to staff it is likely that they will find their way successfully into the curriculum. Support groups are desirable, to provide staff with a focus and to maximise communication. By such means it will be possible to generate a positive ethos, to shape staff expectations of behaviour and to manage the general level of discipline in a constructive, staff-oriented way.
>
> (Rees, 1995, p.96)

Team teaching

One of the most stimulating and rewarding ways to teach is to work with a colleague or team of colleagues. Forms of team teaching range from two people taking it in turns to address the class, to larger groups of teachers adopting a variety of roles including facilitating small-group discussion, working on a one-to-one basis with students and co-ordinating project-based activities. Such teaching can be used to counter prejudice along gender and racial lines, and to overcome the difficulties in mixed-ability classes. It can also help stimulate greater responsibility on the part of students who have to learn to co-operate with teachers who display different pedagogical approaches and styles.

A particularly useful role for team teaching is during induction periods when 'ice-breaking' activities can help cement a sense of group identity and community among students and teachers. In their classic text, the *Gamesters' Handbook*, Brandes and Phillips (1985) describe a number of activities, games and strategies which can be used to promote personal development and social cohesion.

Open, flexible and distance learning

Distance learning has been available in the UK and throughout the world for much of the twentieth century, beginning with correspondence courses in which there was no contact between tutor and student other than by post. The establishment of the British Open University (OU) in 1969 led to a number of similar institutions being set up around the world. The OU was notable for allowing people to study for undergraduate degrees without any entrance requirements and for combining distance learning via multi-media materials with attendance at residential summer schools. Many FE colleges are designated as study centres for OU students who attend a limited number of face-to-face tutorial sessions in their local areas and some colleges provide courses on study skills (sometimes called 'return to learn') for adults who are considering enrolling with the OU.

The term distance learning has joined a lengthy list of other terms, some of which are used interchangeably. These terms include: flexible learning; flexistudy; resource-based learning; and independent study. Although the expansion of distance learning has been largely aimed at adult learners, some of the techniques involved in the preparation of study materials have been used in schools and the learner-centred approach which drives many (though not all) distance learning programmes has influenced classroom-based and work-based teaching and learning.

Distance learning (and other associated terms, e.g. open, flexible, independent) has been and still is promoted in terms of its ability to provide access to learning to large numbers of people who need the flexibility of being able to study when and where they choose. The European Commission (EC), in particular, and some national governments have extolled the virtues of distance learning for some time. Most distance learning courses are modular and allow a level of learner choice which, though it is increasingly available on more traditional courses, gives people the chance to tailor-make a course to suit their specific needs. Some critics argue, however, that these newer forms of learning have grown in stature and availability as a result of the reduction in spending on staff development, training and adult education in general. Edwards (1993a) takes these arguments a stage further and suggests that the growth of open learning (which he uses as a generic term) reflects the wider societal change which is witnessing organisations shifting from Fordist (mass production lines, labour intensive) to post-Fordist (part-time working, flexible work patterns) structures. He is particularly concerned with the way in which open learning, as used in some industries, can separate employees from each other thus reducing opportunity for critical discussion of shared concerns. Many teachers, in common with managers and other professionals, now gain their professional development through open and distance learning courses which include Masters degrees and even taught Doctorates. Whilst Edwards's fears deserve constant attention, flexible approaches to course provision and learning are proving to be very popular, particularly with people whose professional and domestic lives allow them little time to study in conventional ways. Well-structured open and distance learning programmes include opportunities, often through residential weekends, for students to come together to share ideas and enjoy the experience of being 'real' students.

If you are involved in teaching on courses which have an open or distance format, you may have the opportunity to prepare learning materials in the form of written, self-study texts, audio cassettes, instructional videos, video-conferencing and interactive computer programmes (see Rowntree, 1990 for a useful handbook). The extent to which you can become proficient in these media will be determined by the amount of training available and the level of resources devoted to this mode of teaching. The development of electronic methods of communication is bound to have a profound effect on the types of media available in colleges and, although one should not get too carried away by the hype surrounding such developments, it is clear that both teachers and students will need to keep abreast of the electronic revolution. For example, in 1995, four colleges in East Anglia joined together to create an 'open systems information superhighway further education network' through which staff at each college can talk to each other and share ideas and materials, and students can access a wider range of courses (Furthering Education, 1996, p.25).

Chapter 6

Assessment and recording achievement

THE ROLE OF ASSESSMENT

An important and integral aspect of your work in teaching will be the assessment of your students. This is not only a mandatory requirement of examining and validating bodies, for whose qualifications you are preparing students, but you will want to do it in order to maintain a record of students' progress and to assist them in planning their own learning. Brown (1994) suggests that:

> Assessment, therefore, now has several functions including the diagnosis of causes of young people's success or failure, the motivation of them to learn, the provision of valid and meaningful accounts of what has been achieved and the evaluation of courses and teaching.

> (Brown, 1994, p.271)

When asked 'Why do we assess students?', a group of trainee teachers gave the following responses:

It's a measure of feedback for students.

We do it to grade students.

Assessment is formative.

It's for selection.

To empower the student and teacher to move forward.

The variety of responses indicates the multi-faceted nature of the assessment process. Assessment is now not so much something which is 'done unto' students but which often involves negotiations with students and sometimes with employers as well. Both its purposes and practice have changed during recent years. Some of these changes are associated with changes to the structure of courses and programmes. The introduction of compulsory assessment within the National Curriculum in the compulsory phase of schooling is mirrored by similar changes in the post-compulsory sector.

Throughout life, we are both being assessed by and assessing other people, whether it is formally as in the case of a teacher, magistrate, employer or parent, or informally as when we meet someone for the first time or attend a concert. In education and training, assessment is a powerful process which can both empower people as well as damage them. There are many adults who carry the scars of their encounters with assessment throughout their lives. Some, for example, remember failing the 11+ examination for entry to grammar school, whilst others may never forget the agonies of oral spelling tests or being made to write their answer to an arithmetic question on the blackboard in front of the whole class. Smith (1989) asserts that both the assessor and the person being assessed need to understand the nature of the assessment process and that:

> The more aware both assessors and assessed become of the relationship between the outcomes of the judgement process and the sources of evidence from which they derive, and the more honest assessors become about the sources of evidence from which their judgements derive, the more equitable and generally acceptable they are likely to be.
>
> (Smith, 1989, p.119)

As we saw in Chapter 3, the introduction of an outcome-based model of vocational qualifications has resulted in the measurement of achievement in terms of outcomes, that is through the demonstration of competence, usually within the workplace. Here there is a danger of the assessment dominating the learning process if achievement is measured in terms of outcome and bears scant regard to the process by which these skills are acquired. Assessment for assessment's sake is unhelpful and does little to enhance the learning process. Assessment should be an integral part of learning and should help to identify evidence of achievement as well as inform the design or redesign of learning programmes.

There are a wide array of assessment techniques which will be discussed in more detail in this chapter. Whichever method is selected it is important to recognise the purposes of the assessment and what it is designed to measure. Different methods of assessment will be necessary to assess practical skills from those designed to assess a student's ability to engage with a theoretical concept. A catering student's ability to make a soufflé will ultimately have to be assessed by the production of the finished product, not by writing about it. Nevertheless, a written assignment may be used to assess the student's knowledge of the underlying food science theory. Or this could be assessed by means of oral questioning. Similarly, intending teachers are assessed on their ability to convert lesson plans into practical teaching activities. Subject knowledge and classroom practice have to be assessed equally but using different techniques.

The focus of assessment should be on the student and the measurement of his or her achievement. Testing as a means of 'catching people out' does little to develop confidence or to identify real learning. Similarly, 'teaching to the test' may simply identify those with good memories or reflect a teacher's ability to spot questions. Most of us will probably remember our attempts to revise only seven out of the ten available topics, in the hope that some of them would 'come up'.

One teacher recently remarked: 'Our business is to help students achieve.' This should be a guiding principle in the design of assessment procedures. Such procedures should be formative and motivational and appropriate in their design for the purpose for which they are intended. Whilst assessment will be used for the purposes of selection it should always have a strong emphasis on the recognition of achievement. It may now be useful to consider the different types of assessment.

FORMATIVE ASSESSMENT

The purpose of formative assessment is to provide a continuous process which charts achievement, identifies areas for development and indicates next steps. It can be either formal or informal, or a combination of both. Most colleges now have continuous assessment procedures in place. GNVQ programmes require students to complete portfolios of evidence which testify to the students' achievement of the units and elements of the qualification. In this way they provide a record of achievement but they provide no real feedback on how the student is progressing. They simply record the steps along the way to achieving the full award. The same is true of NVQs. Here individual elements of competence are checked against performance criteria. The emphasis is on the 'can do' rather than the 'will do'.

A formative assessment should consider the 'will do' in that it should help to inform the next steps of the student's development. As teachers we are constantly involved in formative assessment through informal means, for example the chance remark: 'That's very good but next time why don't you think about including some conclusions at the end of your report?' We should also encourage our students to reflect upon their performance. We may ask them to consider such questions as:

- 'In which parts of this assignment did I do well?'
- 'In which parts of this assignment did I not do so well?'
- 'How did I manage my time?'
- 'Are there areas which I would wish to improve?'
- 'Do I need to access the Learning Resources Centre?'
- 'Did I work effectively with other members of my team in completing this assignment?'

Ideally, any formative assessment should involve a dialogue between student and teacher. Sometimes this may take the form of a record which may be signed by both parties. Overleaf is an extract from a student's profile which is designed to provide formative assessment for the student.

STUDENT PROFILE

Name:

Programme:

Group:

Date:

Date of last tutorial:

What assessed work has been completed since the last tutorial? (List)

What grades/marks were received? (List)

Do these marks reflect a fair assessment of my performance?

In which assignments do I feel I did particularly well? (You should consider not just the overall grade but if you believe you made a significant improvement on previous work or if you succeeded in spite of some practical difficulties.)

In which assignments do I feel I did not do well? (You should consider the possible reasons for this.)

Are there any areas in which I require help?

What are they?

What do I intend to do about this?

What do I want to achieve by the time of the next tutorial?

How shall I achieve this?

Signed. . . . . STUDENT
        . . . . TUTOR

The emphasis of the student's profile is on what has been learned and on what needs to be learned in the future. The purpose of the assessment should be to improve the learning. Placing a tick or simply writing 'well done' at the end of a piece of work gives little indication of how the piece might be improved further. Tests may be useful in identifying what students know or do not know but unless accompanied by some feedback may provide no diagnosis as to the reasons why students do not know. There is always a danger too that some of the correct answers may have been arrived at through guesswork.

One of the most important uses of formative assessment is to establish a student's level of ability in the basic skills of literacy and numeracy. Research by Steve Harris, a lecturer in a college in the West Midlands, found that students on a BTEC National Diploma in Computer Studies had problems with both their written communication and basic numeracy (see Harris and Hyland, 1995). Harris followed up this research by asking delegates to a national conference on BTEC Computer Studies whether his findings were common and found that:

> Managerial and financial pressures were forcing tutors to enrol students on the BTEC Computer Studies course who, without the basic grounding, were likely to experience considerable difficulty with parts of the programme.
>
> (ibid., p.45)

On the basis of his research, Harris's college decided to screen all new full-time students using an ALBSU test and to offer, through its School of Learning Support, a range of support measures including courses for students with learning difficulties and basic skills' drop-in facilities (ibid., pp.46–7).

SUMMATIVE ASSESSMENT

Summative assessment is used to judge if the aims of a course or programme have been achieved, for example through the setting of a final examination. Examinations often have an important role in selecting or de-selecting those for the next phase of education, for example from FE into HE or from a BTEC National programme to a Higher National programme. Within competence-based qualifications, summative assessment is made to ensure that all units and elements of the qualification have been achieved. Here are the mandatory units for GNVQ (Advanced) in Engineering. Each unit is divided into a number of elements, and evidence must be provided to ensure that all units and elements have been covered. These are checked by an internal verifier and an external verifier.

GNVQ ENGINEERING (ADVANCED)

MANDATORY UNITS

UNIT 1   Engineering and Commercial Functions in Business
Element
1.1   Investigate business functions which involve engineers
1.2   Investigate engineering and commercial functions in business
1.3   Calculate the cost of engineered products and engineering services

UNIT 2   Engineering Systems
Element
2.1   Investigate engineering systems in terms of their inputs and outputs
2.2   Investigate the operation of engineering systems

UNIT 3   Engineering Processes
Element
3.1   Select processes to make electro-mechanical engineered products
3.2   Make an electro-mechanical product to specification
3.3   Perform engineering services to specification

UNIT 4   Engineering Materials
Element
4.1   Characterise materials in terms of their properties
4.2   Relate materials' characteristics to processing methods
4.3   Select materials for engineered products

UNIT 5   Design and Development
Element
5.1   Produce a design brief for an engineered product and an engineering service
5.2   Produce and evaluate design solutions for an electro-mechanical engineered product and an engineering service
5.3   Use technical drawings to communicate designs for engineered products and engineering services

UNIT 6   Engineering in Society and the Environment
Element
6.1   Investigate the effects of engineering on society
6.2   Investigate the effects of engineering on the working environment
6.3   Investigate the effects of engineering activities on the physical environment

UNIT 7   Science for Engineering

Element
7.1   Describe physical systems in engineering in terms of scientific laws and principles
7.2   Calculate the response of physical systems in engineering to changes in variables
7.3   Determine the response of physical systems in engineering to changes in parameters

UNIT 8   Mathematics for Engineering

Element
8.1   Use number and algebra to solve engineering problems
8.2   Use trigonometry to solve engineering problems
8.3   Use functions and graphs to model engineering situations and solve engineering problems

(*Source:* BTEC)

A more detailed discussion on competence-based qualifications will follow later in the chapter. The important point to note here is that although the GNVQ is a programme which is based on a process of continuous assessment, the mechanism by which this is achieved is through a series of summative assessments. This is even more pertinent in the case of NVQs where candidates will present themselves for summative assessment whenever they consider they can demonstrate competence; that is, through the production of evidence. Such evidence may take a variety of forms, for example:

- copies of documents appropriately word processed;
- artefacts produced in practical classes;
- log books signed by supervisors testifying that certain procedures have been undertaken, such as, for example in retailing, *stock rotation*.

Essentially the assessment is to verify that the candidate 'can do' what is described in the element.

Whilst summative assessment plays an important part in assessing students and, it could be argued, is the only means of assessment in competence-based qualifications, ideally this type of assessment should always be underpinned by a diagnostic process which will help students identify how they can improve their performance. Competence-based qualifications attest to candidates' abilities through a series of 'can do' statements; however, there is little scope for indicating how well a candidate 'can do' something over a period of time. As individuals we all know that we can perform a whole range of activities but some of them we will perform much better on some days than on other days and under different sets of conditions and circumstances.

As teachers we need to be aware of the range of assessment techniques available to us and to select those most appropriate for the piece of work we are trying to assess. In practice we are likely to adopt a range of approaches within our teaching programmes. Let us now consider some of these different approaches.

ESSAYS

There has been a considerable shift away from essay-type assessment during recent years, particularly within vocational programmes. However, GCSE assessment, which initially included a fair proportion of coursework assessment (up to 50 per cent), has now reverted to a more examination-based assessment. The problems associated with essay-type tests are that, as Cohen and Manion note, they 'are more difficult to assess reliably. With only one assessor a considerable degree of subjectivity can creep in' (Cohen and Manion, 1989, p.286). In an examination constructed around essays, within a tightly regulated time frame, there is only a limited capacity to cover all the syllabus. This may result in some candidates being unable to show their real ability if they have 'spotted' the wrong question. Those who favour the competence-based approach would argue that this method of assessment ensures complete coverage in that the achievement of every element of every unit must be demonstrated. The essay, on the other hand, gives only partial coverage. Nevertheless, the essay does test students' abilities to organise material, present arguments and to interpret the question in the student's own way. It allows for a degree of creativity and individuality, though this individuality can create problems in the marking. Since no two essays will be alike, it is important to establish clear criteria, in advance, by which the resulting essays can be reliably assessed. In public examinations, the number of candidates can be enormous. It is, therefore, essential that marking is standardised and that it is subject to checks and double-checks.

One approach is to consider what an ideal answer might look like. In setting an essay question you should ask yourself: 'What is it that I want students to be able to demonstrate?' You should also decide what marks you would want to allocate for the style, grammar and syntax. Two illuminating examples spring to mind from a career in FE teaching. One chemistry candidate was referred by the external examiner because of the poor presentation of the written work, including weak spelling and punctuation. The chemistry content, when it could be disentangled from the unstructured answer, was perfectly adequate. The second example occurred during a programme review board. An HND catering student was presented as a fail, but the head of department leapt to his defence stating: 'the boy writes beautifully . . . he's a poet'. The fact that there was very little catering theory included in the answer appeared to have escaped the head's attention. These may be extreme cases but they serve to highlight the importance of setting a fixed analytic grading scheme in advance and of having a clear view of what is expected in the answer. This will avoid some of the pitfalls of impressionistic marking. It is often helpful to indicate a numerical marking scheme for students alongside the question. This will indicate the relative importance of different sections of a question.

You will notice that some assessments are given a numerical rating whilst others may receive a literal grade. The public examination results for GCSE and A level are expressed in literal terms. There is a further element of potential confusion here since what might be a B grade to one marker may be a C to another. It is necessary to have some correlation between a possible numerical score and its literal counterpart, for example 50 to 55 may equate with C. This has to be clearly stated in advance.

In all externally set and marked examinations there is usually some process of moderation. That is, an external examiner or moderator will check a sample of scripts to ensure that marking is consistent across the range of candidates and markers. One useful way of doing this for beginning teachers is to sample a range of scripts and to mark them according to the stated criteria, and then cross-check the results against those of the experienced teacher. Try to identify why differences have occurred.

WRITTEN TESTS

There are many other ways of assessing students than through essay writing. These can range from simple questions requiring tick-box answers to those questions which are more unstructured or open ended and require a student to think more deeply about a topic, to analyse, reflect and present arguments. Obviously this form of questioning is far more suitable for some topics than for others. In mathematics, answers will be either right or wrong. Here are some questions suitable for GNVQ (Intermediate) Key Skills:

Application of Number

Element 2.2:

Represent and tackle problems at Key Skill Level 2.
Solve whole number problems involving addition and subtraction.

Question: Here are the figures for 'Krazy Kuts' hair salon during the last week.

	Mon	Tue	Wed	Thur	Fri	Sat
Cut & Blow-dry	6	10	8	16	25	20
Shampoo & Set	5	8	7	13	21	20
Perm	2	3	2	5	7	10
Tints	4	2	0	4	5	16

(a) How many more perms were sold on Saturday than on Tuesday?
(b) How many 'cut & blow-dry' appointments were made during the week?

(c) On which day were most 'shampoo & sets' carried out?
(d) Which is the least popular treatment?
(e) If the salon decided to close on one day of the week which day should it be? Why?

In designing questions like this it is helpful to place them within the context of the students' learning. This is particularly important in the case of vocational programmes where students often find difficulty in relating the theoretical applications of topics to practical situations.

Within GNVQ the mandatory key skills are:

● Application of number
● Communication
● Information technology

Notice the terminology: the areas are not described as mathematics or English. As a lecturer beginning your work in FE you will need to make these connections in designing your assignments for students. You may have a background in academic mathematics or English and, therefore, you will need to consider the application of your subject knowledge to new contexts.

Highly structured questions are, obviously, much easier to mark than unstructured questions. Multiple choice questions are used by some examination boards and the answers can be pre-coded for ease of marking. In designing such tests care has to be taken in eliminating ambiguity from the possible answers offered since there must only be one 'right' answer. This method of testing purports to offer wide coverage of a syllabus but it offers nothing in the way of analysis or interpretation, dealing primarily with recall. Minton (1991) suggests that 'Multi-choice objective tests of the kind used by examining boards are best left to experts to compile. Few people have the skills to write them' (Minton, 1991, p.194).

Short-answer tests are relatively easy to write and can provide a useful means of checking from time to time on students' learning. They can identify any misunderstandings which might have occurred. However, a balance has to be struck between the amount of time given to testing and that given to real learning. If too much time is spent preparing for tests, including teaching to the test, then this will impede the overall learning process. It can also be demotivating for students. Testing should be seen as part of an overall learning strategy in which there are a variety of assessment methods.

In writing short-answer questions, it is important that the teacher makes absolutely clear what is required; questions should be unambiguous. It is useful to include guidance on marks awarded for each question so that a student can see the relative importance of the questions and plan the timing accordingly.

Here is a short-answer question suitable for NVQ 2 Business Administration. This covers the topic of Reception Duties.

NVQ 2 Business Administration

Unit 15

Element 15.1   Receive and direct visitors

1. List 3 skills/qualities required by a good receptionist
    i)
    ii)
    iii)

                                                    (3 marks)

2. What procedures should be followed when a visitor with an appoint-
    ment arrives at your company?

                                                    (5 marks)

3. What information should be included when leaving messages for
    members of your company which have been left on the reception
    answerphone?

                                                    (5 marks)

4. Where would you find the following information?
    (a) a copy of the company's Annual Report
    (b) the telephone extension of the Personnel Director
    (c) the nearest first aid box
    (d) the telephone number of a local taxi company
    (e) a brochure of the company's product range

                                                    (5 marks)

Objective tests require very little judgement on the part of the marker because
there may be only one correct answer. Students may be required to fill in
missing words from a sentence, for example, or identify places on a map. They
are reasonably easy to write and simple to do. Again they should not be used
as the only means of assessment because they do not allow for creativity.

Here is an example of an objective test which might be used with some
NVQ Level 1 Catering students:

Matching pairs

Draw lines to link the type of pastry with the correct dish

Hot water crust   Apple dumplings
Choux pastry   Sausage rolls
Short crust pastry   Pork pie
Suet pastry   Eclairs
Puff pastry   Plum tart
                         Peach crumble
                         Yorkshire pudding
                         Fruit cobbler

ORAL TESTS

Oral tests now form part of many students' assessments. GNVQ programmes often include some form of presentation to a variety of audiences. Presentation skills are included within the specifications for Communication – Key Skills. Here is an example:

Element 3.1: Take part in discussion:

You must:

1. make contributions which are relevant to the subject and purpose
2. make contributions in a way that is suited to the audience and situation
3. confirm that you have understood the contribution of others
4. make contributions which take forward the discussion
5. create opportunities for others to contribute.

(Adapted from Core Skills Log Book Level 3 BTEC – Issue 1 – December 1995)

The assessment of such skills is complex and can, of course, be highly subjective. The assessor has to be very clear about what is being tested and has to make this known to the candidates. There should be a marksheet available and it is helpful to have another marker or moderator present in the audience. This can help to eliminate tutor bias. A sample marksheet might look like this:

	Marks awarded	Max. mark allowed
Content:		20
Structure:		15
Suitability of language for purpose:		10
Clarity of exposition:		15
Accuracy of information:		20
Use of visual aids:		5
Ability to handle questions:		10
Appearance:		5
		100

The relative weightings of the marks can be adjusted according to the purpose of the assignment. Were one judging students' abilities in public speaking, for example, one might want to include marks for diction or, in the case of a poem, a mark for interpretation.

As with all assessment, feedback is extremely important in this type of activity and it has to be handled with great sensitivity. It is often less threatening to students if they begin by making short group presentations in which each can play a small part before asking them to embark on individual presentations.

ASSIGNMENTS

As we saw in Chapter 5, these are much longer pieces of assessed work and form a very important element in the assessment strategy of vocational education qualifications. The assignment is central to the learning process and should bring together and integrate different components of the programme. Designing and writing assignments is a complex task and is very different from writing essay questions or short-answer tests. In Chapter 5 we looked at the design of assignments. Every assignment should carry with it a set of grading criteria and students should be absolutely clear as to what is required.

Within GNVQ programmes there are two broad grading themes:

1 Those concerned with *process* which include planning, information seeking and information handling and evaluation.
2 That concerned with *outcome*, namely the quality of the outcomes.

On all assignments, each theme will be awarded a pass, merit or distinction grade.

Full details on GNVQ assessment procedures are available from the awarding bodies and, because they are subject to revision from time to time, readers are advised to ensure that they have the latest available guidance.

The marking of assignments requires co-operation amongst different staff teaching on the programme. If the assignment is to be truly integrative, then it should be jointly designed and written by the course team as well as assessed by them. Coverage of the various units and elements will be cross-checked against the evidence provided in the assignment.

This evidence may take a variety of forms. Within the same assignment a student may be required to:

● produce some written work, for example to write a report;
● undertake some practical activity, for example strip down an engine;
● give a short oral presentation;
● produce a set of drawings.

Within this the demonstration of key skills will also be assessed.

The teaching and assessing of key skills has proved particularly problematic within GNVQ programmes causing the FEFC to report that 'The development and assessment of key skills give cause for concern in the majority of colleges inspected' (FEFC, 1995b, p.2). The Inspectorate points to the lack of integration of core skills within the vocational area of programmes; core skills require contextualisation. For this reason key skills should be taught within vocational areas and not as 'bolt-on' separate subjects. Staff development may be required in order to familiarise teachers with current commercial practices within the vocational areas concerned.

Assessment of GNVQ students may involve using a variety of evidence and need not be done on the basis of paper-based evidence alone. Teachers have sometimes been reluctant to design assignments which will allow students to present evidence in different forms, for example using tape-recordings, photographs, log books. This may in part reflect the culture of academic teaching where the only acceptable evidence is the production of written work, often under examination conditions. Group work may be seen as tantamount to 'cheating'. There is a further concern which relates to the difficulty of providing valid and reliable methods of assessing work which is not written.

In designing practical assignments it is necessary to strike a balance between the assessment of the finished product/design/result and the skills and knowledge used in achieving that result. For example, what percentage of the marks should be given to manual skills, to the selection of appropriate tools or materials and what percentage to the final product? If a student worked with little regard to health and safety procedures should this invalidate the finished result? All these considerations need to be taken into account in drawing up the grading criteria for an assignment.

One Midlands college has designed an assessment procedure for NVQ Catering which involved the production of a set of photographs indicating 'standard' dishes. Students' practical outputs are judged against the 'photographic standards'. This also helps students to identify what they are aiming for in the finished product.

It is often a useful strategy to show students' pieces of work which have been completed by former students, subject, of course, to those students' agreement. With a teacher's help, students can be encouraged to identify the strengths and weaknesses of different approaches. This is particularly helpful in the case of adult students who may be returning to learning after a considerable break and who may be anxious about the production of assignments. You have already met some of these students in Chapter 2.

You will gather from all of this that the process of assessment and recording achievement is an extremely complex one. The teacher is required to act in a number of different roles, ranging from being purely a marker to being a guide, counsellor and mentor. Some of these roles are potentially conflicting. As a tutor you may know that a student is undergoing a series of personal difficulties which you feel may have impinged upon the production of a good piece of work. How then are you to assess the work? In terms of a strict 'standards' methodology the work does not meet the criteria. As tutor, you are aware of the reasons why this work may not meet the standards. This brings us back to the fundamental purposes of assessment and the balance between the formative and summative elements.

The FEFC Inspectorate's advice concerning group assessment may well be applied to all forms of assessment:

A strategy is needed to support teachers in balancing the formative, diagnostic role of assessment with its summative function of accumulating evidence and certifying achievement.

(ibid., p.25)

The tutor has to strike a balance between directing the students and 'letting the students go'. In her book, *Adults Learning*, Jenny Rogers writes:

Some teachers who rightly pride themselves on the standard of their own work, sometimes find their students' mistakes too painful to contemplate, and will often seize the work and do the difficult bits themselves, sometimes under the impression that students are grateful for such professional additions. There may be occasional students too placid to object, but most people feel cheated if someone else does all the hard work for them. They want the satisfaction and sense of achievement of learning to cope for themselves.

(Rogers, 1992, p.63)

ALBSU (1991) highlights the role of the tutor as the facilitator of learning particularly with adults on open learning programmes. Here a distinction between formative and summative evaluation is a particularly difficult one to draw.

Students may be encouraged to involve themselves in both peer and self-assessment. Peer assessment needs to be handled very sensitively and should not be embarked upon until the teacher has a good knowledge of the group. Guidance should also be provided on the criteria to be applied in making peer assessments. Comments such as 'That was great' or 'That was rubbish' are to be avoided. On the other hand, self-evaluation is an important part of the learning process because only the individual knows his or her objectives in undertaking the programme and should, therefore, be best able to judge whether or not such objectives are being achieved. This may be a new idea to some of your students and they will require guidance in developing techniques of reflection and self-evaluation. You may wish to provide some standard form on which students can record their own evaluation or you may prefer to provide some prompts. As students become more practised they will probably be able to write a short evaluation for each assignment undertaken.

Marshall and Rowland (1993) have drawn attention to the importance of self-evaluation in the learning process and of its role in helping to provide student independence. Students should also be encouraged to discuss their assessments with tutors and there may well be a case for involving students in joint marking with tutors. This can be highly motivational.

COMPETENCE-BASED ASSESSMENT

As we saw in Chapter 3, in competence-based assessment the assessor must make judgements concerning the sufficiency of evidence supplied by the candidate. Evidence can take a variety of forms but the assessor needs to be assured of its validity. The assessor will want to make sure he or she has satisfactory answers to the following questions:

- Is this the candidate's own work?
- On how many occasions was this task performed?
- If a 'real-life' situation is unavailable how reliable are those results achieved through a simulation?

The following all provide legitimate forms of evidence. You may wish to consider how you would reliably assess them.

- Displays and presentations
- Practical demonstrations
- Planning and organising events
- Creative use of photographs
- Making and producing models/drawings/paintings
- Group work
- Designing products and services
- Projects undertaken by individuals or groups
- Role-play work

BTEC (1993) suggests that evidence can be divided into two types: performance evidence and supplementary evidence. Performance evidence is required for each element of competence within each unit and should be derived as far as possible from a 'real' environment. For example, a candidate could be observed welding metal within a workshop situation. The candidate could also be assessed on a finished product. If processes cannot be directly observed by the assessor then evidence from videotape or audiotape may also be used providing it can be authenticated. Evidence might also be collected by questioning the candidate. There must be sufficient evidence to meet all the performance criteria for an element.

Often evidence collected to fulfil the performance of one element may be relevant to and provide evidence for the achievement of other elements within the full qualification. It is not necessary to generate a separate piece of evidence for every performance criterion; the role of the teacher is to help students identify what evidence may count towards the achievement of the performance criteria.

Let us consider an example. Here is a unit from NVQ4 Engineering. The title of the unit is: **Selecting Design Options**. This unit is broken down into three elements. Each element has a set of performance criteria which must be met in order to achieve the element. For each element a range is identified which indicates the depth and extent of the coverage required by the candidate to meet the requirements of the element.

QUALIFICATION	NVQ4 ENGINEERING
UNIT TITLE	SELECTING DESIGN OPTIONS

ELEMENTS	1. Produce engineering analysis of compliance and development potential. 2. Produce cost analysis for each option. 3. Liaise with all interested parties.

PERFORMANCE CRITERIA	For example for Element 2, there are 2 performance criteria: 2.1 For each design option estimates are made for any non-recurring costs which may be incurred during development or set up such as materials, capital equipment and labour. 2.2 For each design option estimates are made for all production costs.

RANGE	Non-recurring costs: materials, capital equipment, labour. Production costs: materials, capital equipment, labour, overheads, outside the established norm.

(EnTra. Copyright, Training Publications Limited. Engineering Training Authority. Industrial Standards of Competence, with permission.)

Assessment involves making judgements about the evidence which the candidate provides. This assessment may involve observing a candidate's performance in the workplace, that is watching the candidate in action. Where performance evidence cannot be assessed, supplementary evidence may be used to infer performance. For example, you may want to question a candidate about certain activities or set some form of written test. However, it should be remembered, when considering performance and supplementary evidence, that:

The two sorts of evidence complement each other. Activities which provide supplementary evidence do not exist in a vacuum. They are designed to support the performance evidence you have collected by confirming the knowledge and understanding of the candidate.

(Huddleston *et al.*, 1995, p.39)

Competence-based assessment is generally carried out by college staff within the college even for candidates who are in employment, though sometimes college staff may go to the employers' premises to carry out assessment. The lack of employer involvement in the assessment of those employees who attend college as part of their NVQ programme raises questions as to what extent competence-based assessment is taking place in the workplace as opposed to a simulated environment. One of the barriers appears to be the lack of trained and accredited workplace assessors. NVQs require competence to be demonstrated in a 'realistic environment'; that is, as far as possible under the normal conditions and pressures of the workplace and with the use of appropriate equipment and facilities. Where this is not possible simulated working environments have to be provided. Within colleges, assessment may, therefore, be undertaken in college training restaurants, hairdressing salons or training offices, for example.

For full-time students working towards NVQ accreditation, work placements have to be found in order for them to demonstrate competence to workplace standards. Here assessment may be problematic since it will depend upon the goodwill and co-operation of those employers willing to provide work place-ments. In some sectors it is extremely difficult to access sufficient placements and there are often competing demands on them. Consistency across work place-ments may be variable: whilst some may provide excellent opportunities for candidates to demonstrate competence others may be of a poor standard. The FEFC has drawn attention to the particular difficulties involved in attempting to provide sufficient placements within the care sector (FEFC, 1994a).

There are some key questions upon which you may wish to reflect con-cerning issues of assessment within the NVQ:

- Who is assessing?
- What is being assessed?
- How valid and reliable is the evidence?
- Is there a consistency of standards across different units/elements of the qualification?
- Where is the assessment being carried out?
- What is the balance between performance evidence and supplementary evidence?
- Do the candidates understand the assessment process?
- How is evidence being recorded?

We shall discuss the assessor awards and the process of internal and external verification later in this chapter. Before doing so it may be useful to consider assessment within GNVQ programmes which has much in common with the process described above for the NVQ.

Assessment within the GNVQ is based upon units so that each unit can be separately awarded. Like the NVQ, it is an outcome-based model and students have to provide sufficient evidence to demonstrate achievement. Evidence is collected in the student's portfolio which is derived from the student's coursework and will include assignments, projects and other forms of assessed work. There are also externally set and marked tests which are compulsory for the mandatory vocational units. These are short-answer or multiple-choice tests. There has been significant concern over the external tests and they are currently being reviewed.

The assessment process in GNVQ programmes involves students collecting evidence which can demonstrate that they have met the performance criteria and covered the range statements for the particular unit or elements of a unit. This is then checked by the assessor to ensure that the evidence meets the performance criteria and shows sufficient coverage of the range. The assessor will then provide feedback to the student, making recommendations as necessary and recording achievement. All this information has to be carefully recorded and colleges will have their own systems for doing so. Concern over the amount of time colleges have to spend in collecting and collating GNVQ assessment evidence has been expressed by the FEFC (1995a) and by an NCVQ task group chaired by Sir John Capey (1995). It is likely, therefore, that further modifications to the GNVQ assessment procedure will result and it is too early to predict any changes which may occur.

Despite the likelihood of such changes, however, it is essential that you familiarise yourself with the rationale and procedures of outcome-led models of assessment. You should also be familiar with the documentation produced by your college to record student achievement. Colleges have a range of tracking and record-keeping systems to monitor and record student achievement and some colleges are investigating the use of information technology to store such records.

Whatever form these documents take, they have to record the evidence to prove that all the elements of the qualification have been covered. The record will also include the grading achieved for assignments. Grading themes are indicated by the NCVQ in conjunction with the three GNVQ awarding bodies.

Students can receive a merit or distinction award for work which is above the basic GNVQ requirements. In this respect the GNVQ differs from the NVQ award. You will recall that we discussed earlier the notion of competence and that it was concerned with 'can do' statements. It is *not* concerned with how well a student 'can do'. The GNVQ records outcomes in terms of statements of achievement and, therefore, there is scope for indicating how well a student can do something.

ASSESSOR AND VERIFIER AWARDS

Those responsible for assessment within NVQ and GNVQ programmes are now required to become qualified to Training and Development Lead Body (TDLB) standards. Colleges are implementing staff development programmes to enable staff to collect evidence for the achievement of the assessor awards. The process through which staff acquire these awards is exactly the same as that undertaken by their students when compiling evidence for any other NVQ or GNVQ.

There are two units relating to assessment as shown below:

UNIT

D32 Assess candidate performance

ELEMENTS

D321 Agree and review a plan for assessing performance

D322 Collect and judge performance evidence against criteria

D323 Collect and judge knowledge evidence

D324 Make assessment decision and provide feedback

(Institute of Personnel Development: Assessor and Verifier Awards)

Unit D33 is the national standard for the assessor who has to collect and judge competence from a variety of sources. Such sources will include not only the candidate but the evidence provided by others about the candidate. Some of the evidence required to gain the D33 award may already have been provided in the accreditation of D32 and would not need to be covered again. Evidence from one unit may be counted towards another unit providing that there is sufficient and adequate evidence.

For unit D33 there are three elements:

UNIT

D33 Assess candidate using differing sources of evidence

ELEMENTS

D331 Agree and review an assessment plan

D332 Judge evidence and provide feedback

D333 Make assessment decisions using differing sources of evidence and provide feedback

(Institute of Personnel Development: Assessor and Verifier Awards)

The process of verification for NVQ and GNVQ programmes involves two parts: internal verification and external verification. Internal verifiers check internal assessments made by teachers and review student portfolios. In the best examples, colleges have developed rigorous quality assessment procedures through such measures as holding regular meetings to moderate each others' assessments. Grading standards exercises may be carried out annually. Common approaches to portfolio building may be adopted and cross-college systems have been designed to ensure that there is consistency in standards applied to NVQ/GNVQ programmes across an institution.

The internal verifier award, usually referred to as D34, qualifies an individual to monitor assessment within an approved centre. The role of the internal verifier also includes offering advice and support to assessors and acting as a link between assessors and the awarding bodies. There are three elements within the unit:

UNIT

D34 Internally verify the assessment process

ELEMENTS

D341 Advise and support assessors

D342 Maintain and monitor arrangements for processing
assessment information

D343 Verify assessment practice

(Institute of Personnel Development: Assessor and Verifier Awards)

External verifiers are appointed by the awarding bodies as part of quality assurance procedures. Their role is to monitor standards of assessment across centres and to ensure that internal assessment and verification procedures are being appropriately and consistently applied. They are responsible for reporting to the awarding bodies on the quality of assessment in centres. It is also intended that external verifiers should support centres and advise them on improvements which might be made to assessment procedures. Those acting in this capacity will hold the D35 – external verifier award. This unit contains three elements as shown below:

UNIT

D35 Externally verify the assessment process

ELEMENTS

D351 Provide information, advisory and support services to centres

D352 Verify assessment practice and centre procedure

D353 Maintain records of visits and provide feedback to awarding bodies

(Institute of Personnel Development: Assessor and Verifier Awards)

Although the focus of this section has been on the role of verifiers within the NVQ/GNVQ system, you should be aware that moderation, both internal and external, is a common feature of many assessment procedures.

CONCLUSION

You will have reflected that assessment is a complex and a time-consuming business. The nature and forms of assessment have changed considerably during the past ten years. The contexts in which assessment is undertaken have also changed. It is not just a matter for the examination hall but for the workplace too and many other settings as well.

The ways in which grades and marks are applied to assessment have also changed. There is greater emphasis on criterion referencing, that is on what and what has not has not been achieved, rather than on norm referencing. Norm referencing involves the measurement of an individual's achievement against the achievement of others taking the same test or exam. This is typified by the examination pass list with the marks and positions of candidates shown. You will recall the recent debate over alleged falling standards in GCSEs and A levels because too many candidates appeared to be gaining higher grades! The debate has now been transferred to the HE sector where too many graduates are allegedly gaining 'good' degrees (see Ainley, 1994). The process of assessment has become more transparent and more emphasis is placed upon the dialogue between the assessor and the assessed. Increasingly, assessment serves a variety of purposes. It helps to identify starting points, and in this sense it is diagnostic. It may help to identify previous learning for which a student may wish to claim credit, as in accreditation of prior learning (APL) procedures. This type of assessment can help to inform the learning plan and avoid unnecessary duplication.

Assessment, in its formative aspects, maintains a record of ongoing progress. This type of assessment aims to improve the quality of what is being achieved and helps to structure learning. On the other hand, summative assessment may be a summary of the formative assessments already carried out of what a student can do at a given time.

In designing assessment plans for our students we will need to ensure a balance of these different types of assessment. We can collect evidence in a variety of ways and over different time periods. We can also collect evidence provided in different contexts; we all know that our students may perform differently on employers' premises from the way they perform in our practical classes. We should also consider the motivational and personal development opportunities implicit in a negotiated record of achievement or profile.

We should not neglect the opportunities provided by assessment to review our curricula and their organisation, and to judge their suitability for the students for whom they are intended.

Part III

Professional development

Chapter 7

Evaluation, reflection and research

> The activity of reflection is so familiar, that as teachers or trainers, we often overlook it in formal learning settings . . . reflection is a vital element in any form of learning and teachers and trainers need to consider how they can incorporate some forms of reflection in their courses.
>
> (Boud *et al.*, 1985, p.8)

> Stimulated by surprise, they turn thought back on action and on the knowing which is implicit in action . . . it is this entire process of reflection-in-action which is central to the 'art' by which practitioners sometimes deal well with situations of uncertainty, instability, uniqueness and value conflict.
>
> (Schon, 1983, p.50)

In this chapter, we examine the benefits which teachers can gain from applying the concept of the 'reflective practitioner' as a means of evaluating and considering their own practice, and by helping their students use the same concept to reflect on their development as learners. Throughout this book, of course, we have been asking you to reflect on your own learning, on some of our ideas, and on your approach to teaching.

Reflection is a natural part of human life but for professionals and students, structured reflection can provide a framework within which they can examine their strengths and weaknesses and identify strategies for improvement. In addition, professionals can use reflection as a bridge to help span what is often regarded as a chasm between the reality of their practice as teachers and the theoretical models and concepts put forward by academics who research education.

Reflection can sometimes turn into 'navel gazing', a pleasant enough pastime for some but not one which will necessarily take the reflector any further forward or cause any changes to his or her practices! This is why we are advocating the need for reflection, whether by teachers or students, to be structured and fully incorporated within the formal framework of a course or teaching career.

Later in this chapter, we discuss ways in which teachers in colleges can build on the reflective process and begin actively to research their practice. By turning one's reflections into ideas for research projects, those reflections can be sharpened and scrutinised, and lead to real and worthwhile policies for improved practices (and policies) for both individuals and institutions.

REFLECTION FOR STUDENTS

In his book *The Enquiring Tutor*, Stephen Rowland, who has taught in both schools and HE, explains his commitment to student-centred learning:

> At the heart of this approach is the view that, both morally and practically, it is worth taking our students seriously. What they have to say about themselves provides us with the most significant information about their own learning, and thus our teaching. If we can give voice to our students' experience, we have come a long way towards understanding our own practice.
> (Rowland, 1993, p.6)

There are many ways in which teachers can and will encourage their students to reflect on their learning but, all too often, reflection becomes confused with assessment. As we saw in Chapter 6, constructive feedback which arises out of assessment can, of course, facilitate reflection, but students need to learn how to reflect and come to regard it as a natural process in its own right.

In order to reflect, you have to ask yourself questions, some of which might be difficult or awkward. The identification of those questions may be straightforward if, for example, you have been struggling to write an essay and cannot decide how the story ends, or you may have been cooking and discover that you have left out a key ingredient from the recipe. If, however, you are reflecting on why you find it so difficult to learn how to conjugate verbs in French or how to turn what you have read in a book into a summary using your own words, then the questions you need to ask become more complex. Students, therefore, will have to practise reflection and to do that they need some guidance.

One way of helping students to reflect would be to ask them to analyse themselves as learners. They could, for example, do the exercise at the beginning of Chapter 5 in which you were asked to consider whether you were a 'good' learner. They could use Honey and Mumford's *Learning Styles Inventory* (1982) to discover whether, by nature, they adopt one of the following learning styles:

Activist (rolls up sleeves and rushes into action)

Reflector (contemplates the problem and considers how to approach)

Theorist (consults 'experts', researches the issues before acting)

Pragmatist (selects the most appropriate form of action given the circumstances)

Whichever method is chosen, however, the student has to learn to reflect in a way which suits his or her own style and needs and the teacher has to create a supportive atmosphere in which this can take place:

The open teacher, like a good therapist, establishes rapport and resonance, sensing unspoken needs, conflicts, hopes and fears. Respecting the learner's autonomy, the teacher spends more time helping to articulate the *urgent* questions than demanding *right* answers . . . . Just as you can't 'deliver' holistic health, which must start with the intention of the patient, the true teacher knows you can't impose learning. You can, as Galileo said, help the individual discover patterns and connections, foster openness to strange new possibilities, and is the midwife to ideas. The teacher is the steersman (*sic*), a catalyst, a facilitator – an agent of learning but not the first cause.

(Ferguson, 1982, pp.320–1)

We asked a number of students in different colleges to reflect on a recent learning experience. In the first set of examples, three 16-year-old students (two full time and one part time) give their reactions to their tutors' assessments of a piece of work:

GNVQ Group Assignment: a student reflects on how the group worked together

I think the grade is fair because we all really put a lot of work into this. I mean just writing the letters and arranging the company interviews took ages. As usual, Angela did practically nothing, but I think Mrs Bennett [the tutor] knows this because she gave her a lower grade which is only fair anyway. I wasn't too happy about the marks for the oral presentation because I think we did as well as we could have done. I mean, we're not all bloomin' TV presenters! I don't see why we should have so many marks for oral presentation when it's all in the file anyway.

I think Kamal did a brilliant job with the accounts; it really helped our assignment. I am pleased he was given a higher mark for that because he really deserved it. What I especially liked about this assignment was that it really gave us a chance to get together out of college. I mean, in the evenings we used to meet up at someone's house and do all the planning – it was really great. Sharm's Dad gave us lots of help as well, like where we could find out things, and he even brought us some company brochures and reports.

I used to think people in our group were, well, sad until I got to know them through this assignment. Now I know they're OK.

An A level student reflects on the comments she received for an essay on *Hamlet*

I must say I am very disappointed with this mark. I put a lot of effort into this, practically regurgitating all the notes which we had been given. That always seemed to work at GCSE. English was my best subject. If the lecturer can't tell us the answer and give us a decent set of notes, what can he expect? He talks about critical reflection; I don't even know what he means. I don't see how he can expect me to go off and find the stuff when he hasn't told me what to look for. After all, he's paid to teach us and get us through the exam. I don't see why I should have to 'look things up'. Perhaps I should buy a set of those revision notes.

Perming hair: a hairdressing student reflects on an activity in the college's training salon

Well I think that the perm was all right. I mean, not brilliant but all right. Mrs Smith [the tutor] thought it was a pass but she said it wouldn't be fast enough in a real salon. Well it ain't a real salon anyway and the people who come here know that – that's why it's cheap. Anyway, I think Mrs Smith has got it in for me since she caught me using the mousse in the practice salon. I don't care because the gaffer [manager of the salon in which the student works when not at college] thinks I'm OK and that's what matters. He says the college don't know what they're talking about because they don't have to run a business. Anyway, college is a laugh. We have a great time and as long as I just get by that's OK. There was nothing wrong with the perm anyway.

These reflections capture the emotional tensions which formal assessment can engender. In the first example, the experience of learning within a group structure has enabled the student to recognise the strengths and weaknesses of individual group members and to celebrate the social enjoyment to be found in working closely with colleagues. In the second and third examples, we see the students struggling to accept criticism of their work and behaviour. These students instinctively blame the tutor rather than examining their own weaknesses. They may have legitimate reasons for criticising their tutors but unless they are given opportunities to discuss the thinking behind the assessments, they may have difficulty in demonstrating their true abilities. When tutors and learners reflect together about the learning process, both parties can confront each other's level of contribution, thus identifying ways in which that process can be improved.

In the second set of examples, three mature students (one full time and two part time) reflect on their individual progress after six months on a course:

Adult basic skills student: 45-year-old Jack has been unemployed for three years

I finally started to understand where I'd been going wrong with maths when I stopped blaming myself for having failed at school. It was this week the penny dropped and I've been here nearly six months. I just sat in class on Tuesday and I heard Brenda [a fellow student] shout at our tutor. She said, 'I'm really good at some things you know. I might not be any good at these sums you give us but I used to get good marks at school for my writing.' I thought, she's right; just because we're not much cop at maths doesn't mean we're stupid, and then I seemed to lose my fear about what Brenda calls 'sums'.

Information technology student: Frances is a 33-year-old secretary

I still don't really like coming here. I'd rather be at work but my boss wants me to learn about this stuff and I know I need to really. It's not the tutors, they're smashing. Well, I suppose it's the effort of having to concentrate on learning new things when at work I seem to get by so easily and I feel in control. When there's a test I just go to pieces and my husband says he can tell I'm worried about college because I take it out on everyone at home. I'll be glad when its finished . . . awful isn't it? I should be grateful for the chance really.

Catering student: Edward is a 27-year-old former policeman who is now training to be a chef

If only I'd done this years ago, I would have been much happier. The course is going well but then I know I've got a good attitude, better than some of the others who are a bit up and down about the whole thing. I can't wait to get into the kitchen and the pressure doesn't bother me at all. I'm much more motivated about this than anything else I've been on and it really makes a difference to your standard of work. I never knew I could learn so fast.

In these examples, their maturity helps the students reflect more deeply on their learning experience and they can relate back to earlier experiences to gain insights into their problems and successes.

CONSTRUCTING A REFLECTIVE DIARY

A 'reflective diary' can take many forms and should be a very personal record so you can be as creative as you wish. You might decide to use a typical diary format, making entries for each day or week in a notebook. You might keep a boxfile or shoebox in which you can store any jottings, cuttings from newspapers, cartoons, photographs and so on. Or, you might keep a very visual record using diagrams or pictures to illustrate your journey through the teaching year. If you feel happier with a more formal structure for the diary, here are some suggestions for dividing the diary into sections to include:

- a record of newly acquired knowledge, understanding and skills which are important to you;
- a commentary on your personal/professional development as you progress through the year;
- a commentary on the interesting (and perhaps contentious) issues and concepts which arise out of your professional experience;
- responses to critical incidents.

Here are two extracts from reflective diaries which show how experienced college teachers record their concerns and queries about their students. The first extract records a teacher's thoughts after an induction meeting with a group of adult students on a 'two plus two' degree course:

> This seems a pleasant enough group. It's a real 'mixed-bag' though. One or two obviously have the impression that they know it all and tend to dominate the rest, mainly through their attempts to monopolise the discussion and to 'name drop' one or two key texts. Mrs Baker is a bit of a worry because she obviously knows quite a lot but is anxious about expressing her opinions. I must remember to let her take a more active role next time. Perhaps I should let her act as a rapporteur for feedback on group work.
>
> Greg seems particularly anxious. I notice he was hovering at the back afterwards waiting to catch me on my way out. Did he really need to check the time of the next class or was there something more important that he wanted to discuss? I noticed that he moved away very quickly when Tony came up.
>
> I must remember that Winifred is repeating this year; I need to keep her interest. I must draw on her knowledge and expertise to help me and the group. It's going to be tough for her because her son is in hospital again. I think I might suggest we plan a group get-together at the local pub or bowling alley to help establish a real group identity.

The second extract is from a catering tutor's diary written after she assessed a group of students working in the college restaurant:

> On the whole, the group performed well with one or two notable exceptions. Ros was late and Chris didn't have his white jacket. Nevertheless, Ranjit, who was maitre d'hotel for the evening, handled the situation very well. I must remember to enter his performance under core skills in his portfolio. His communication skills were particularly appropriate.
>
> The main courses were well presented and service was competently handled. Must remember to tell Gill about her mistake with the cutlery although I don't think she was the only one. Lee should have noticed that the water jugs were empty before the customer had to ask. The dessert trolley was the least well handled. This group are very poor at describing the individual dishes to customers. It's not that they don't know, I think they are too scared to say. I must speak to their communications lecturer. We need to develop some role play situations so that students can practise before they meet real customers.

It may seem daunting to try and find the time to record observations and ideas in this way, but the two extracts above show how a number of important details can be logged by teachers in a relatively short diary-style account.

In the next extract, from a trainee teacher's record of a session with a GNVQ Intermediate class which was being observed by the teacher's tutor, we see an example of how a teacher can reflect on a critical incident:

It was a disaster, I just totally lost it. I thought I had it all planned and organised and it all went dreadfully wrong. There are some real trouble-makers in this group. I should have realised that, I just wasn't prepared for it. I should have realised that the trouble was starting once the two at the front began banging the cupboard doors. I should have separated them. I can't think why I let them sit together, the whole thing just became worse and there was nothing I could do about it.

I realise that while my attention was being taken by the trouble-makers others were starting to become restless. Then those who were working well were not being given any attention. I really need to think about everyone in the group and not just concentrate on those who are causing trouble. I couldn't believe it when they started throwing the paper darts. Obviously I was an easy target. I knew then I had lost it. My real worry is how I am going to face them next week.

The trainee teacher's tutor also recorded her own reflections on the session she had observed and provided her student with these comments:

A. Opening
Try to be on time and establish control before taking the register. What about the young lady loitering at the door, was she supposed to be in or out of the class? Close the door to show that the class has begun.

B. Introduction
You need to recap on previous class. Make sure everyone is attending before you start. What was that boy doing wandering around? You must ensure that: i) everyone understands the task and is fully prepared and ii) everyone is working through the task. Try to deal with one question at a time. You broke off in the middle of answering one boy's question to answer another. It gives the impression to the group that you are not fully in control. You must deal with the boy at the back who kept shouting. There was a lot of constructive work going on in some parts of the class, try to capitalise on this. Class eventually settled down well to the task.

C. During lesson
Make sure that the troublesome elements are also on the task. Don't leave people too long before checking up on them . . . the boy next to me was drawing cartoons.

D. Feedback from activity
Make sure all the class is ready to engage in the activity, people were still writing, others talking amongst themselves. You must draw the whole group together before attempting a de-brief from the exercise. How should you deal with the paper darts incident? The disruption with the cupboard was very unfortunate – one strategy would have been to move the boy away from the cupboard rather than have the confrontation. The class was

aware that you were losing control. It is a great pity that those who were working on the task and who had some good ideas were not used more; the disruptive students were really dominating the class. In fact if you notice there are only 5, at the most, disruptive students, the rest of the class is fine so capitalise on them.

E. Rounding off
Keep your eye on the time so that you allow sufficient time to draw everything together and reinforce any key points. The lesson didn't have a proper ending but just stumbled to a close.

F. Reflection
What do you feel the students learned from this class?
How would you sum up your classroom management?
What went well?
What did not go well?

Put together, the two sets of reflective notes create a much more meaningful critique of the lesson than if one simply had access to just one person's account. Clearly, the trainee teacher has written his notes from a fairly acute sense of failure and, to some extent, foreboding, given that he will have to meet this same group again. His account gives the impression that the majority of students in the group were behaving badly, that the noise level was high and that he lurched from one crisis to the next. His tutor's notes provide a more coherent account (having been written from the relative calm of the back of the room) by breaking the lesson down into a chronology of pedagogical principles. We learn from this that the trainee teacher apparently arrived a little late for the lesson and so may have created the wrong impression with some students. In addition, we learn that a very small number of students caused the disruptions whereas, for the trainee teacher, it was as if they had completely taken over the proceedings. Finally, the general lack of organisation in the classroom is obviously something which the trainee teacher cannot blame entirely on five so-called 'troublemakers'.

We are, of course, surrounded by examples of people learning, whether at home, at work, in the street, in the pub, or at the football ground. The list is endless. Try to observe your friends, relatives, colleagues and even strangers if you see them in a learning situation and record your observations in your 'reflective diary'. In fact, treat the everyday world as your research laboratory and don't forget to include yourself too!

In Chapters 4 and 5, we discussed some of the theoretical literature related to teaching and learning and tried to show how theory can inform and illuminate the teacher's role. The individual teacher should have the opportunity to contribute to and engage with the theory, and this is where the process of reflection can have real meaning and purpose. For Quicke (1996), theory needs to be balanced with reflective practice, otherwise it is in danger of putting a 'straight-jacket on teacher thought' (Quicke, 1996, p.21). He gives three reasons for this:

> First, they (theories) may no longer be relevant. Although conceived orig-inally as a way of clarifying and helping to resolve problems with which common-sense knowledge was no longer adequate to deal, they now address problems which are no longer salient. There may be new agendas in place in relation to which old theories may be obsolete. Second, theories may become reified. This problem is not so much to do with the content of a theory as with the manner in which the theory is held . . . . Thirdly, theories are not so much irrelevant in terms of the issues they address but are irrelevant as theories. There may be other theories which address the same problems 'better' by constituting them differently or it's possible that common sense has already been informed by such theories. What is required is reflection on existing common sense using ideas from other aspects of common-sense knowledge.
>
> (ibid.)

TEACHER AS RESEARCHER

The concept of the 'teacher as researcher' has been promoted for some con-siderable time, certainly since the 1970s when the work of Lawrence Stenhouse advocated the need for practitioners to become researchers in their own right (see Stenhouse, 1975). In the current climate of change which has swept through FE colleges during the 1990s, the concept is being re-examined for it has the potential to act as a vehicle for enabling college staff to investi-gate collaboratively the key questions and problems which concern them. Schon, as part of his advocacy of the 'reflective practitioner', insists that there needs to be a shift away from the type of educational research which appears unconcerned with the realities of practice to research which is grounded in that practice:

> In the varied topography of professional practice, there is the high ground overlooking a swamp. On the high ground, manageable problems lend themselves to solution through the application of research-based theory and technique. In the swampy lowland, messy, confusing problems defy tech-nical solution. The irony of this situation is that the problems of the high ground tend to be relatively unimportant to individuals or society at large, however great their technical interest may be, while in the swamp lie the problems of greatest human concern. The practitioner must choose. Shall he remain on the high ground where he can solve relatively unimportant problems according to prevailing standards of rigour, or shall he descend to the swamp of important problems and nonrigorous inquiry?
>
> (Schon, 1987, p.3)

FE teachers are familiar with researchers, evaluators and representatives of management consultants who visit their colleges to interview students and staff, collect statistical data and observe teaching and learning. Ironically, however, the concerns of the FE teachers themselves may – though this will be rare – form the focus of this externally generated and externally led research activity. In the main, the teachers are left with their concerns and the external researchers move on to another set of problems. Academics in HE have, of course, their own legitimate reasons for carrying out research and play a crucial role in helping practitioners tackle the theoretical underpinning they need in furthering their understanding of and ability to examine critically the educational context in which they practise. But this relationship can be limited and much of the important work that it generates is hidden from view. There is a need, therefore, for the two communities to work much more collaboratively to ensure the following:

- that research outcomes are disseminated widely and acted upon;
- that teachers and other professionals play a more pro-active part in determining the research questions to be addressed;
- that teachers contribute their professional experience and expertise to the whole of the research process rather than just a small part of it;
- that researchers are made to challenge their research practices and findings through collaborative enquiry and ongoing dialogue;
- that researchers pass on their skills to others and demystify the process of research.

This new relationship cannot, of course, be simply formed in order to meet the needs of one of the partners. It has to be recognised that university education departments are struggling to maintain adequate student numbers at postgraduate level. Gone are the days when the local education authorities and institutions would pay teachers to attend courses and give them time to study. Teachers and other professionals are having to pay their own fees and may, in some cases, be actively discouraged from attending certain courses by their managers. The pressure for college staff to gain the assessor awards linked to the delivery of NVQs and GNVQs has meant less time to attend HE courses.

From the colleges' point of view, a collaborative relationship with HE should not be driven solely by management priorities or imposed on staff as yet another workload clause in their contracts. Staff who are told on a Monday morning by the college chief executive that they are all to become 'researchers' are unlikely to react positively when a group of academics arrives to begin work. The considerable amount of pedagogical, curricular and policy change which has affected colleges in recent years and the increased emphasis on the role of FE in terms of rising post-compulsory participation rates have presented college staff with a plethora of problems and concerns to be investigated. Given the pressures of workload affecting all staff and the demands of external bodies such as the FEFC and NACETT for information about individual college performance, it will be necessary to ensure that institutions separate routine data gathering and monitoring from a more searching research programme which combines quantitative and qualitative methods and draws on a range of different research traditions and methodologies. At the same time, college staff will need to be supported over a realistic time span in their research activity by both their managers and the academics with whom they are to collaborate.

There are exciting possibilities in this area. University departments are seeking to accredit teacher-led research projects within their award-bearing programmes and there are opportunities for colleges and universities to apply jointly for research funding.

Chapter 8

Professional development

INTRODUCTION

In previous chapters, we have emphasised the multi-skilled nature of the FE teacher. Given the diversity of FE life and the volatility of curricula within colleges, every FE teacher has to make plans to ensure he or she has access to relevant and appropriate professional development opportunities. Given also that teachers in FE stretch from those who concentrate on basic skills through to those teaching at undergraduate and postgraduate level, the scope of professional development must, necessarily, be broad enough to encompass the wide range of professional needs.

In recent years, two phrases have tended to dominate policy documents, theoretical literature, organisational mission statements and speeches which discuss the concept of professional development. Those phrases are:

Lifelong learning

The learning organisation

Both phrases act as clarion calls for people to rise up and pledge themselves to the altar of human resource development (HRD). The language of HRD now permeates colleges where once it was restricted to the worlds of industry, business and commerce. Colleges are appointing human resource managers instead of the once familiar personnel or training manager. This is not to argue against the need for people to carry on learning throughout their lives or for organisations to be led by a philosophy which recognises that everyone in the organisation should be encouraged to contribute to its development and renewal. We are, however, sceptical about the rhetorical flourishes which surround the HRD bandwagon. In addition, we prefer to see teachers and support staff in colleges as people rather than as a human resource, as the latter terminology, ironically, sits uncomfortably with the inclusive and democratic notions underpinning a true learning organisation.

In Chapter 7, we discussed the role that theory plays in developing our understanding of teaching and learning. Whilst the initial teacher education programmes, referred to later in this chapter, will provide opportunities to engage with a range of theoretical literature and ideas, it is important to maintain an interest in educational developments. In addition, you will also need to ensure your specific professional area of expertise is kept up to date. Michael Eraut, who has made a key contribution to our understanding of professional knowledge and competence, sees the 'disposition to theorise' as the 'most important quality of the professional teacher' as once they gain this, teachers will:

> go on developing their theorising capacities throughout their teaching careers, they will be genuinely self-evaluative and they will continue to search for, invent and implement new ideas. Without it they will become prisoners of their early . . . experience, perhaps the competent teachers of today, almost certainly the ossified teachers of tomorrow.
>
> (Eraut, 1994, p.71)

For Michael Tedder, writing from his experience of teaching in colleges, the concept of professionalism has many meanings in FE:

> Many of us use the term 'professional' regularly to convey a range of meanings among which might be identified the possession of a body of knowledge and expertise, normally accredited with academic or vocational qualifications, and the awareness of a set of values or a code of conduct that governs our relationship with 'clients', the ethics of our profession. Professionalism also implies a relationship with colleagues that includes responsibility for monitoring the standards in our practice and an acceptance of responsibility or a sense of accountability to the community we serve.
>
> (Tedder, 1994, p.74)

Professional development is itself a concept in need of some clarification. A more familiar term might be staff development, but often, this will tend to refer to largely in-house, short and management-led initiatives rather than activity which is determined by the individual teacher to fulfil personal development goals. Prior to incorporation, staff development in colleges had had a mixed history. As Castling (1996) has shown, the 1970s were a period in which staff development probably meant being sent on an external course for updating related to one's teaching area, whereas in the 1980s, more emphasis was placed on colleges creating internal staff development programmes, often using ideas generated by the FEU. Local education authorities (LEAs) also played a key role in the 1980s as they managed government funding targeted at staff development, whilst Her Majesty's Inspectorate (HMI) ran national conferences for staff development officers. The levels of nationally available funding gradually decreased, however, and post-incorporation, staff development is very much seen as a cost to be borne by colleges themselves. It is perhaps worth recording that in its last year (1992), the Grant for Educational Support and Training

(GEST) provided £20 million to FE colleges to fund staff development (see Betts, 1996, p.100).

The FEFC requires colleges in England to specify their arrangements for the development of their 'human resources' in their strategic plans under the heading of quality assurance which itself relates to the FEFC's four-yearly cycle of college inspections. As Robson (1996) points out, this use of the term 'human resources' is a marked shift from the use of the term 'staff development':

> This change of terminology in official documentation with regard to planning is indicative of an approach which is more systematic and more related to institutional needs than has been common in the past. Although in its reports on colleges the FEFC inspectorate to date continues to comment on 'staff development', the expectation is nevertheless that human resources development will become more strategic and more directive. Staffing needs will be derived from analyses of the college's objectives and staff development activities will be determined less by perceived individual need than by the college's academic and strategic plan.
>
> (Robson, 1996, p.3)

Thus the majority of activity which falls under the umbrella of staff development tends to be related to servicing an immediate need (e.g. health and safety training, new assessment procedures, TDLB requirements, etc.) or, where it is seen as servicing a long-term goal, as Robson states above, it will be closely tied to the college's strategic plan. There is, of course, every likelihood that some of this activity will complement the professional development needs of some teaching staff. And where a college is prepared to invest large amounts of money, perhaps to retrain teachers or help them develop their professional competence in order to run courses at higher levels, then so-called staff development becomes indistinguishable from professional development.

Staff development tends to take place within the college's own campus and involve only college staff, though an outside speaker might be called upon. Whilst there are clearly times when a purely internal arrangement is sufficient, there is a real danger that staff and management become too insular if all their staff development is conducted in this way. Castling warns:

> There is the risk of staff becoming bogged down in institutional problems which can obstruct progress, and there may be a lack of fresh ideas which would normally come from working with colleagues elsewhere. There might be a reluctance to resource the input by college staff as fully as that by outside experts, and indeed college staff might not command the respect which would have been accorded to visitors purely because they were from outside. The chief danger is probably insularity. The staff developer managing the programme will need to import wider views, either from their own research or by selecting colleague contributions carefully.
>
> (Castling, 1996, p.80)

Perhaps then staff development should come with a health warning or at least those 'being developed' should recognise that the fix they gain from participating in staff development activities may be less than satisfying.

Eraut reminds us that:

> Professionals continually learn on the job, because their work entails engagement in a succession of cases, problems or projects which they have to learn about. This case-specific learning, however, may not contribute a great deal to their general professional knowledge base unless the case is regarded as special rather than routine and time is set aside to deliberate upon its significance. Even then it may remain in memory as a special case without being integrated into any general theory of practice. Thus according to the disposition of individual professionals and the conditions under which they work, their knowledge base may be relatively static or developing quite rapidly. There is little research evidence to indicate the overall level of work-based learning in any profession, but individual examples of both extremes are frequently cited.
>
> (Eraut, 1994, p.10)

Depending upon the formal requirements of particular professional bodies, people will take different steps on the journey to becoming qualified to practise. As we noted in Chapter 1, there is no statutory requirement for FE teachers to hold a professional qualification, a dubious privilege they share with their colleagues in HE. However, many of those same teachers will hold qualifications related to their area of expertise. For example, lecturers in accountancy, engineering, catering, and law may all have engaged in some form of what Eraut calls initial professional education (IPE) and this may be being 'topped up' by bouts of continuing professional education (CPE) or continuing professional development (CPD). The stage at which these discipline-based professionals will add a qualification in teaching to their curriculum vitae will depend on the nature of their entry to FE. Norman Lucas has argued that this duality of professional role, that is of being at one and the same time a teacher and an expert in a professional or craft/trade area, has dogged the development of a statutory qualification structure:

> Management and staff associations have traditionally united against any statutory professional teaching qualification for further education. Historically lecturers in further education have seen their qualification or expertise in an academic or vocational area as sufficient for teaching. This has placed specialist knowledge of subject or trade above pedagogy. Thus the notion of lecturers being seen as, or seeing themselves as professional teachers with a coherent structure of initial training and professional development has been secondary to a concentration of delivering narrow specialist expertise.
>
> (Lucas, 1996, p.69)

Lucas notes that the number of full-time teachers in FE with a teacher quali-fication recognised by the DfEE was estimated to be around 60 per cent in 1995, whereas the figure for part-time staff was as low as between 20 per cent and 30 per cent (ibid.). The picture is further complicated by the question of what form of professional development should be required of and provided for support staff in colleges whose numbers are on the increase. Support staff often perform duties which straddle the boundaries between recognised sup-portive roles (e.g. technicians operating audio-visual equipment, librarians, etc.) and newer hybrid roles which have a pedagogic dimension (e.g. student counsellors, open learning centre instructors, etc.).

INITIAL PROFESSIONAL EDUCATION FOR FE TEACHERS

Although we have pointed out that FE teachers are not required by statute to be qualified as teachers, despite the fact that, in 1975, the Haycocks Report recommended that all staff, full and part time, should gain a minimum of a Certificate in Education. There are, however, a number of qualification routes which FE teachers can follow and they include:

1 Postgraduate Certificate in Education (PGCE): this is a one-year full-time course which leads to Qualified Teacher Status (QTS). This course is a statutory requirement for anyone wishing to teach in primary and sec-ondary schools, and is delivered by a local higher education institution (HEI) in partnership with a number of schools. Students spend up to 12 weeks in the HEI and the rest of the year in schools learning to teach 'on the job' supported by a mentor (an experienced teacher within the school) and visits from their HEI tutor. Some PGCEs allow students to carry out their teaching practice in FE colleges. Since 1994, the initial teacher education (ITE) for schools has been controlled by the Teacher Training Agency (TTA) who, in 1996, were charged by the DfEE with the responsibility for improving the standard of ITE which had been criticised by Ofsted, the school inspectorate.
2 Certificate in Education (FE): this course, which can be taken in one year full time or two years part time, is delivered by colleges in partnership with HEIs or by HEIs on their own, and is recognised by the DfEE. The major-ity of HEIs are the 'new' universities reflecting the historical link between the former polytechnics and FE colleges.
3 City and Guilds Teacher's Certificate (7307): this course is delivered by col-leges on an in-house basis and is recognised as Part One of the Certificate in Education by some HEIs. In 1990, City and Guilds began turning the 7307 into a competence-based certificate so there is now the competence-based 7306 (described below) running alongside the 7307. Originally known as the Technical Teacher's Certificate when it began life in the 1950s, the 7307 recruits some 10,000 FE teachers per year.

4 City and Guilds Teacher's Certificate (7306): this certificate is built on the competence standards identified by the Training and Development Lead Body (TDLB) and incorporates the assessor (D32 and D33) and verifier (D34) units described in Chapter 6.

5 Related awards: there are a number of other certificates and diplomas which FE teachers can take. These include, for example: the RSA's Diploma in Teaching and Learning in Adult Basic Education and Certificate for Vocational Preparation Tutors; BTEC's Certificate in Management Studies (Education Management); City and Guilds' 926 Adult Trainers' Award; and the Certificate for Teachers in Adult Education offered by regional FE bodies.

Young *et al.* have found that the different routes described above cater for different audiences so that the full-time PGCE courses tended to cater for younger people with more academic qualifications who intended teaching the humanities, English, foreign languages and sciences, whilst the part-time Certificate in Education route attracted older people with work experience in areas such as engineering, electronics, information technology, nursery nursing and careers guidance (Young *et al.*, 1995, p.12).

The most significant change to initial teacher training qualifications for FE reflects the change to the post-16 curriculum in general which those newly qualified teachers will themselves be delivering, that is the move to a competence-based approach. As we noted in Chapters 3 and 6, this approach is being subjected to intense scrutiny and criticism and is being reviewed by the DfEE. One of the concerns about the use of the TDLB standards as the basis of an FE teacher training qualification is that those standards were originally intended for workplace trainers. As such, the TDLB standards do not contain many of what Young *et al.* regard as 'the more traditional features of teacher education':

> For example, student motivation is assumed and there is no reference to giving examples and analogies, or to encouraging a student's conceptual development.
>
> (ibid., p.26)

In contrast to the non-competence-based Certificate in Education, the 7306 could be seen as a device for deskilling FE teachers. Last and Chown, who both tutor on teacher training programmes in an FE college, argue:

> Existing Certificate in Education (FE) programmes provide personal and professional development to the level of first degree study. In our view, teachers who are able to respond effectively to the needs of adult learners in a rapidly changing FE sector require coherent initial professional training to graduate level. Will the adoption of competence-based qualifications in the NCVQ mould help us towards the ambition? Will they at least maintain the current position? Or will they have the effect of removing FE

teacher training from HE altogether, with a consequent loss of professionalism to the detriment of the sector?

(Last and Chown, 1996, pp.31–2)

Despite the widespread concerns about the application of the competence-
based approach to teacher training and the training of professionals in general,
it is highly likely to remain in some form, albeit modified and expanded. As
we noted in Chapter 1, the Further Education Development Agency (FEDA)
has commissioned a 'mapping' of jobs in the FE sector using the concept of
functional analysis which underpins NVQs, with a view to identifying
national standards against which those who work in colleges will be appraised,
recruited and, presumably, 'developed'. This leads us to assert that anyone
teaching in FE or about to start their teaching career in a college should look
carefully at how well programmes such as the 7306 will prepare them. It is our
belief that they will need a far more substantial professional development
programme to meet their needs.

BARRIERS TO PROFESSIONAL DEVELOPMENT

As we write, FE teachers are faced with a number of problems when attempting to find the most appropriate vehicle for their professional development.
Firstly, some colleges are using most of the money in their professional development budgets to pay for their staff to gain the assessor and verifier awards
we discussed in Chapter 6. Whilst college staff must gain these awards if they
are involved in NVQ and GNVQ programmes, they only train people to
assess competence as defined under the NVQ framework. Such narrowness of
purpose hardly qualifies the TDLB units as key vehicles for the level of sophistication which professional development in today's FE colleges should reach.
In addition, the TDLB units are unsatisfactory if used as the only means of
training for assessment of GNVQs where evidence is collected through written assignments, projects and case studies and where students are expected to
demonstrate analytical and problem-solving skills.

Secondly, not all college managers are keen to support professional development if it means teachers have to take time off work to attend courses or if
it means paying fees on behalf of a teacher. Thirdly, the demands of working
in FE are such that, for many people, the thought of spending one's precious
free time reading yet more papers or discussing work-related issues is not that
attractive. Fourthly, the opportunities and encouragement afforded to you will
depend on the culture of the college in which you work. This latter point
deserves some discussion at this point.

Clearly all colleges have their own culture and ethos which may have grown
up over a number of years or which may reflect sudden changes introduced by
a new senior manager or management team. The level of importance attached
to the professional development needs of staff is dependent on that culture so

that in some colleges staff may have to fight quite hard to get their real needs met. Jackson *et al.* (1996), in their study *Managing Careers in 2000 and Beyond*, stress that individual employees cannot afford to wait for their organisations to take the lead in terms of their career development:

> The trend is clearly towards increased demand on people to be proactive in looking after their own careers using their own resourcefulness. This requires continuous information-gathering and analysis, self-assessment, planning ahead for the next few years, and social skills including negotiation and self-presentation.
>
> (Jackson *et al.*, 1996, p.52)

PATHWAYS TO PROFESSIONAL DEVELOPMENT

Throughout a career as a teacher in FE, you will probably want a mix of provision to satisfy your professional development needs. As we discussed earlier in this chapter, some of your immediate needs might be covered in staff development activities run within the college.

One of the key mechanisms through which you will be asked to try and identify your professional development needs will be through the college's appraisal system. At the time of writing, there is no statutory requirement for colleges to have appraisal systems though most are developing them.

If the appraisal system in your college is not satisfactory in terms of helping you identify and discuss your professional development needs, you will have to find other means for this. You may, for example, be assigned a mentor. This will most likely be an experienced member of staff who provides ongoing support, advice and guidance, but in some colleges, teachers provide each other with peer mentoring. The process of mentoring has to be nurtured, especially in colleges where individuals feel under pressure to compete with each other and feel at the mercy of externally imposed targets and inspections. From her research on the mentoring of student teachers by experienced staff in FE, Cox writes:

> There is an absence, in further education, of a culture which encourages or even allows open discussion of teaching. In order to have effective mentoring, the mentor and the student teacher must step outside the normal conventions of staffroom discourse and openly discuss, evaluate and reflect on practice. This can be difficult for both parties.
>
> (Cox, 1996, p.41)

She advocates peer or collaborative mentoring because:

> In this context, the imbalance of power is less of an issue and the tension generated by the assessment function of the mentor is absent. The discussion of one's own and a collaborative colleague's teaching can be developed in a supportive atmosphere, in a constructive, private dialogue.
>
> (ibid., p.42)

As well as helping you to identify and discuss your professional development needs, working with supportive colleagues will also provide tacit doses of professional development as well as enriching one's day-to-day life in college.

Another strategy for considering your professional development needs involves keeping a record of your professional experience in and outside college. This record could take the form of a portfolio, diary or log and could include a combination of examples of your work with students (e.g. teaching plans, assessments, photographs of students' work, etc.) and more discursive accounts of your development as a teacher (e.g. reflections on critical moments, ideas for new ways to teach, etc.). It might also include evidence of your activities related to your area of professional expertise or your links with the local community.

Linked to this notion of recording one's experience is the increasing use of autobiographical writing by teachers throughout all sectors of education. Here, a teacher constructs a narrative of his or her ongoing life as a teacher and uses it to reflect on the extent to which external as well as personal influences determine one's progress and development as a professional. As Bateson argues:

> These resonances between the personal and the professional are the source of both insight and error. You avoid mistakes and distortions not so much by trying to build a wall between the observer and the observed as by observing the observer – observing yourself – as well, and bringing the personal issues into consciousness.
>
> (Bateson, 1984, p.161)

By gaining a better understanding of the personal and the professional, we can then begin to 'map' out our career path and, hopefully, take more control over the nature and scope of the professional development on offer to us. In his highly creative book, *The Man Who Mistook His Wife for a Hat*, the neurologist Oliver Sacks describes a patient of his called Rebecca, a young woman whom he had known for some twelve years and who, after the death of her grandmother, appeared to emerge much more strongly as a person in her own right:

> 'I want no more classes, no more workshops,' she said. 'They do nothing for me. They do nothing to bring me together . . . I'm a sort of living carpet. I need a pattern, a design like you have on that carpet. I come apart, I unravel, unless there's a design.' I looked down at the carpet, as Rebecca said this, and found myself thinking of Sherrington's famous image, comparing the brain/mind to an 'enchanted loom', weaving patterns ever-dissolving, but always with meaning.
>
> (Sacks, 1986, p.175)

Some professional development courses now include biographical accounts and portfolios as part of the assessed work submitted by students. There can be problems when personal material of this nature is then used in a public context and Bloor and Butterworth (1996), in their study of the use of portfolios at the University of Greenwich, suggest that these concerns may lead to professionals being less inclined to commit themselves to paper. They stress that the ownership of portfolios must be clarified at the outset.

Clearly, if you are preparing an autobiographical account or portfolio for purely personal use, you will not have the problems of ownership. What you might want to do, however, is to use some of that material as the basis for discussions with friends or colleagues about how well you have managed to address your strengths and weaknesses. As Holloway points out, we need to have our personal constructs challenged, albeit in a gentle and supportive way:

> I know from paying close attention to myself giving accounts in a variety of different settings, that I have a stock of ready narratives to draw on which fit particular situations and which tell me nothing new unless the person I am talking to helps me produce something new.
>
> (Holloway quoted in Kehily, 1995, p.28)

Apart from the personal development aspect of building a portfolio or some kind of record of your professional experience, there are important pragmatic reasons for doing so. For example, the practice of the accreditation of prior learning (APL), which we discussed in Chapter 6, is used in a number of HEIs and by professional bodies to give exemption from parts of programmes leading to qualifications. Also, you may find that having some physical evidence of your work will come in useful at job interviews or for promotion panels.

Once you have a 'map' or, at least, some idea of your professional development needs, you may wish to pursue a postgraduate course leading to a diploma or Masters degree, or you may be a member of a professional body which itself provides professional development courses. All of these may be available within your own college (if it is linked in some way to an HEI) or you may have to find a course elsewhere. Many HEIs now offer flexible ways to gain a postgraduate qualification, for example by distance learning or residential weekend study, and, as we noted above, some have introduced APL procedures to allow experienced people to be exempted from taking the full set of course modules.

The most common postgraduate degrees are:

Masters in Education (MEd)

Master of Arts (MA)

Master of Science (MSc)

It is usual to find that these degrees are split into two components: the first part will consist of taught modules, on completion of which a student can gain a diploma; the second part consists of a dissertation or project, on completion of which, along with the taught component, the student will be awarded a Masters degree.

Some HEIs have also introduced a structured doctoral programme leading to the Doctorate in Education (or EdD). For this, students take a number of 'taught' modules, some of which will cover research methodology, and have to produce a substantial thesis. As we noted in Chapter 7, some HEIs are developing research links with FE colleges which go beyond the traditional professional development relationship in which FE staff are merely seen as students working towards an accredited qualification. To this end, Masters and EdD programmes often encourage students to conduct action research projects, empirical studies and other forms of analysis based within their professional context.

If you are interested in developing your research potential and feel motivated enough to dedicate some three to five years to one project, you could pursue a research degree (MPhil or PhD). In this case, you would be appointed to a supervisor who has a keen interest in your research ideas and who possibly also carries out research in a similar field. Although all HEIs offer research degrees, it is advisable to gain a good impression of an institution's research rating. All HEI departments are given a rating from 1 to 5, with 5 being the highest and denoting that the department has academics conducting research of national and international excellence. In addition, you should also try to find out which academics are based in the department in which you would be based as there may be someone who has published articles and books related to your research interests. Departments differ, too, in their provision for part-time research students in that some bring students together for seminars and social events and may provide access to information technology. A useful way to begin your investigation of an academic department in an HEI is to visit the institution's library which will house copies of all Masters dissertations and research degree theses. By looking at a sample of this research output for the department you are interested in, you will gain some idea of the nature and scope of projects the department is able to supervise.

Although we noted earlier in this chapter that many colleges seem to be using the majority of their staff development funds on the TDLB awards, there are cases where individual staff may get support to pursue a Masters or research degree. In 1987, Suffolk College set itself the target of creating an all-graduate teaching staff from a baseline of 65 per cent. By 1996, that baseline had risen to 95 per cent and stimulated a demand from staff to progress to Masters level. College management, therefore, agreed to second staff to gain Masters degrees and hope that by the year 2000, 50 per cent of the teaching staff will have reached that level. Writing about the Suffolk model, which is linked to the desire to build a research culture in the college, five senior managers report:

> Implicit in this significant commitment to staff development is a drive towards a quality-led learning organisation. Explicit are the opportunities offered to teaching staff to enhance their professional skills and knowledge base in order to contribute more widely to an expanding economy organisation.
>
> (Robinson *et al.*, 1996, p.24)

Here we see that the strategic goals of the college are a major driving force behind the decision to invest in long-term professional development programmes but, at the same time, the college has chosen to reach those goals by recognising the individual needs of staff who, in gaining externally accredited qualifications, can enhance their own profiles and have access to high-quality learning which takes them out of their immediate work environment.

If you are a member of a trade union, you should keep in touch with the professional development programmes it offers as well as conferences and discussion group meetings.

Reflection

The following questions and instructions are designed to help you evaluate and identify your professional development needs. You may find them useful during initial training as well as at different stages during your teaching career:

1 Make a list of the skills you would like to gain (or improve) in order to be a more effective teacher. Can you acquire those skills on an in-house staff development programme? If you are on an initial teacher training course, does the course help you develop these skills?

2 Are you comfortable with the curriculum demands imposed on you? Would you feel happier if you could update your skills and knowledge in a particular area of your professional expertise? Have there been recent changes to your professional area (e.g. new legislation, new inventions, changes in information technology, etc.)? Can you cope with these changes?

3 Are you aware of the different organisations which could supply you with information and ideas to support and enrich your teaching? Would you gain by joining a professional body? Are there people in neighbouring colleges, schools, HEIs, companies, TECs and other organisations with whom you should be in contact or with whom you might work in partnership?

4 Will your management support your professional development plans? What will they expect in the form of a proposal (e.g. a written proposal with costings?) and who is the best person to approach first?

5 Have you considered changing direction? There may be opportunities within the college to try a completely new field (e.g. move from teaching into student services) or to set up a new course in a related discipline, or a multi-disciplinary programme.

6 Where do you want to be in five years in terms of your career? Can you identify any professional development issues now so that you can plan your career in advance?

Chapter 9

Networks and support agencies

INTRODUCTION

FE colleges play a significant role in the life of their local communities and beyond; indeed some which specialise in certain courses attract students on a national basis. The range of people who come through the college doors, as we saw in Chapter 2, represents the diversity of the college's geographical, socio-economic and cultural location. Reaching out from the college, the links into the community will include outreach centres for teaching and access-related services, partnerships with local schools and HEIs, and a range of mechanisms for relating to the world of business and industry. As a college lecturer, there-fore, you will be constantly aware of the wider world beyond your immediate teaching room.

Part of your duties and responsibilities as a lecturer may include liaising with community groups, representing the college on education–business part-nership committees and so on. In this chapter, we discuss the nature of some of the organisations with whom you may be formally required to liaise and work. We also discuss the ways in which these and other organisations can provide you with valuable support in terms of your teaching and professional development.

TRADE UNIONS AND PROFESSIONAL ORGANISATIONS

Two trade unions represent FE lecturers: NATFHE (the National Association of Teachers in Further and Higher Education); and ATL (the Association of Teachers and Lecturers). NATFHE currently has the largest membership. The Association for College Management (ACM) represents college staff in management positions, though some FE principals also belong to the Association of Principals of Colleges (APC) and the Secondary Heads Association (SHA).

Since the incorporation of colleges in 1992, NATFHE, ATL and ACM have spent a great deal of their time and resources fighting the imposition by college governing bodies and the national body representing college employers of controversial new teaching contracts. The long-standing, nationally accepted *Silver Book* agreement which laid down the terms and conditions for lecturers in FE has been replaced by locally devised contracts of employment endorsed by the Colleges' Employers' Forum (CEF).

As we discussed in Chapter 1, many college lecturers have a background in a profession or craft-based occupation and may find it useful to maintain a direct link through an appropriate organisation such as, for example, the Institute of Chartered Accountants. Most occupational sectors are covered by an Industrial Training Organisation (ITO). For example, engineering's ITO is ENTRA, the Engineering Training Association, and details of all ITOs can be gained from NCITO (the National Council for Industry Training Organisations) whose address is listed below. ITOs develop training policies and strategies for their industries and are responsible for devising frameworks for Modern Apprenticeship.

HIGHER EDUCATION

Another way to maintain links with your professional specialism and/or academic interests is through your local HE institutions whose departments may run seminars which are open to external visitors and may also have arrangements for FE lecturers to become research associates. Departments of Education in some HEIs are now encouraging FE staff to have a much closer link with them and will welcome lecturers wishing to pursue research ideas.

As we noted in Chapter 1, some colleges have franchising arrangements with HEIs to run parts of degree courses (see Abramson *et al.*, 1996, for a discussion of this aspect of FE's work). As well as running courses in conjunction with HEIs, some colleges and HEIs have Compact schemes which seek to encourage young people who may not have considered HE to be an appropriate or even realistic option for them to apply to university. Some Compacts, which may be operated through EBPs described below, link university departments to college A level and GNVQ courses or to college-based access courses. Although the idea of Compact appears to very laudable, there are complex issues to be managed when different sectors of education try to work together. Writing about a Compact initiative which has been running in Birmingham since 1987, Bigger notes:

> Post-16 Compact is a simple idea with a challenging agenda: to raise achievement and aspiration by enhancing motivation. This produces a drive for quality which requires effort and enthusiasm in all staff. Its effectiveness is strategic and requires support at the highest level through the institution's mission, vision and strategic plan. Some schools and colleges have found this difficult, so the philosophy of the programme is not regularly matched by the reality of implementation: post-16 agendas can reflect

survival rather than quality. Looking forward, therefore, the priority is to support institutions in developing quality processes.

(Bigger, 1996, p.164)

BUSINESS-RELATED ORGANISATIONS

There are many different forms of business-related organisation in the UK stretching from national bodies such as the Confederation of British Industry (CBI) and the Institute of Directors to local bodies such as Chambers of Commerce and the Round Table. The locally based organisations often have historical roots in their communities, including those which represent the interests of employees rather than those of employers, such as Trades Councils. The CBI has a regional network of branches which meet regularly for seminars and events at which education and training often feature.

At local level, the one organisation which will have the most direct contact and working relationship with an FE college is the Training and Enterprise Council (TEC) or its Scottish equivalent, the LEC (Local Enterprise Company). As we discussed in Chapter 1, TECs and LECs control the funding for government-sponsored training schemes such as, for example, Modern Apprenticeship and Training for Work. They also provide advice and various kinds of financial support to local businesses, usually through their partnership in *Business Link* which they run in conjunction with Chambers of Commerce and local authorities. There are 82 TECs in England and Wales, and 22 LECs in Scotland. Given this funding link with the college, you may have contact with TEC representatives if you are involved in youth and adult training programmes or any other form of TEC-sponsored vocational education initiative.

TECs have a wide brief in relation to their education and training responsibilities. They have a statutory role to work with schools by co-ordinating the annual Work Experience programme for Year 10 pupils and some TECs provide funding for schools' careers libraries and resource centres. TECs may also fund initiatives with a careers education and guidance remit in colleges and sponsor young people to participate in European exchanges. Given their role as a quasi-agent for the DfEE at local level (or in the case of the LECs, the Scottish Office), TECs are constantly charged with introducing new initiatives, many of which have a direct implication for the work of colleges. From the college lecturer's point of view, it may appear that the TEC has too much say in the work of the college but the TEC can be helpful to an individual lecturer by providing funding or expertise to support a creative idea which enhances vocational education and training at the local level. TECs also fund research projects and will work with partners to bid for research and development money from national and European agencies.

The responsibility which TECs have regarding the funding of youth and adult training has been a matter of debate and concern for some time. In late 1994, South Thames TEC went into receivership leaving £5 million in liabilities, much of which was owed to local colleges who had provided off-the-job training for TEC-sponsored trainees. The fall-out from what many people saw as an unthinkable event has resulted in the merger of two London TECs to form the country's largest TEC from April 1997.

Underpinning many of the problems which hinder TECs and colleges in their relationships is the issue of how post-16 education and training is funded at national, regional and local levels and the fact that post-16 organisations are compelled to compete for students and/or trainees. In July 1996, the DfEE launched a consultative document on the funding of 16–19 education and training with the statement:

> Currently the ways in which we fund school sixth forms, colleges and Training and Enterprise Councils are very different. The Government believes that this issue must be addressed and is committed to bringing about greater convergence in these funding arrangements – to create a more level playing field.
>
> (DfEE, 1996, foreword)

Whether this initiative will result in a convergence of funding mechanisms is uncertain, but for the foreseeable future, college lecturers and managers are likely to have to continue negotiating and competing with their TEC colleagues.

A further way in which college staff can meet and work with TEC staff is through membership of a local education–business partnership (EBP) which will include representatives from industry and commerce, the LEA, Careers Service, local HEIs, private training providers, voluntary organisations, trade unions, and schools. EBPs began in 1990 at the same time as the majority of TECs were being established and, at that time, most EBPs were set up and largely managed by TECs. In the mind of the then Employment Department, EBPs were the means to formalise the largely *ad hoc* and voluntaristic links between education and business which, as we noted earlier, have been in existence for many years. The very notion of trying to impose a superstructure on relationships which tended to be organic rather than institutionalised has seemed to some on both sides to be too dictatorial and at odds with the concept of partnership. EBPs have, therefore, developed differently throughout the country ranging from the very successful to those which struggle to get enough people to make meetings quorate.

Where an EBP is successful, the local colleges are likely to be heavily involved. An EBP can provide college staff with an excellent forum for liaising with schools over such matters as managing an effective transition for young people transferring to college at 16 or joint initiatives to raise standards in basic skills. Useful relationships with employers can also be established through an EBP.

The following vignettes illustrate the different ways in which college staff can work together with EBPs.

Chris took over responsibility for running the GNVQ Leisure and Tourism programme in her college. Although she had previously been employed in the travel business, it was some considerable time ago and she felt the need to update her knowledge of the industry. In addition, she was aware that she needed to inform herself about developments in the use of IT in the industry. Her local EBP arranged a week's placement for her with a branch of a national retail travel agent. The placement not only allowed her to gain some 'hands on' experience of the current operation of a travel business but also enabled her to identify work placements for students on the GNVQ programme.

Bob, a lecturer in engineering, was approached by the EBP about the possibility of some of his students undertaking a piece of work for a local engineering company. One of the directors of the company was Chairperson of the EBP and she was anxious to improve the profile of her company, and, at the same time, improve the image of engineering in general by involving students in the company's work. Although initially reticent about the idea, Bob eventually recognised the potential benefits of the link which would allow his students to undertake real tasks to industry standards. Students were given access to the company and completed some of the tasks on site rather than in the college workshops. Bob also had the opportunity of seeing the way in which a small manufacturing company was transforming its production to match new industry standards.

Ranjeep has responsibility for teaching marketing across a range of business courses in his college. For some time, he has been interested in developing a European dimension to the work but has lacked contact with colleges or companies in Europe. The EBP was able to supply the names of several local companies which had links with Europe and the names of local schools involved in European exchanges. Ranjeep followed up these leads and made contact with a vocational school in Belgium which was happy to collaborate in a joint project involving British and Belgian business students. Assignments were developed for a unit on international marketing in which the students exchanged information about their own local economies. Students communicated by fax and e-mail. In future, Ranjeep hopes to extend the project by involving other European partners and, with the help of the TEC, hopes to access some EU funding to finance student exchanges.

Because of the need for local organisations to work together to ensure they make the most of limited resources to finance education and training initiatives, EBPs and similar partnerships rely on individuals who are prepared to put their creative energies to work for the collective good. In some areas, these partnerships may operate under the umbrella heading Strategic Forum.

A 1996 survey by the Education Business Partnerships National Network revealed that three out of four FE and sixth form colleges have developed education link programmes with industry and that many colleges co-ordinate such programmes on behalf of their local schools (see EBPNN, 1996).

As we have described earlier in the book, individual college departments, as well as colleges acting as corporate bodies, have direct links with employers for whom they provide an education and training service. Research by the Institute of Employment Studies in 1995 classified college/employer interaction into two types of activities. The first was based around learners (referred to as learner centred) whilst the second (referred to as planning based) was based around planning and advice, and both could be sub-divided as follows (IES, 1995):

Learner centred

Type A: employer-led training and education – company employees or trainees being trained by the college;

Type B: voluntary, work-related activities with full-time or non-employed students – work experience, work shadowing.

Planning based

Type C: advice and information between individual employers and colleges to aid college planning – for example, governing bodies, curriculum advisory groups;

Type D: activities which aid the planning of education and training in the wider community – local working groups, projects, strategic planning.

NATIONAL AND REGIONAL FE BODIES

Prior to the 1992 FHE Act, colleges were affiliated to their local Regional Advisory Council (RAC), a network of which existed throughout the country. These bodies came within the remit of LEAs but were independent of each other and, although they had some activities in common such as running staff development courses, they were very different in terms of their effectiveness. Where RACs did come together was in their contribution to the work of the Further Education Unit (FEU) which was set up in 1977, under the auspices of the then Department of Education and Science, to help promote curriculum development initiatives and co-ordinate and disseminate good practice in teaching and learning. The FEU was particularly active in the late 1970s and early 1980s when it produced reports such as *A Basis for Choice* (1979) and *Vocational Preparation* (1981) which provided guidance and analysis for colleges in dealing with the sudden dramatic influx of recruits to the newly established government-sponsored youth training schemes. Often working alongside the national Further Education Staff College (FESC), which had been set up in 1963 at Coombe Lodge near Bristol, the FEU produced a wealth of literature, much of it based on action research projects involving colleges, which still carries important and useful messages and ideas for today's college lecturers, managers and support staff.

In April 1995, a new organisation, the Further Education Development Agency (FEDA), replaced both the FEU and FESC and, at the time of writing, is still in the process of establishing its own new identity. FEDA has two offices in London as well as FESC's original premises near Bristol, and has nine regional development officers for England and one in Wales. In one of its early newsletters, FEDA stressed its determination to respond to the needs of staff in the FE sector at local level and at national level offers such services as a GNVQ Support Programme Information and Advice Unit and Information Technology Services (see FEDA, 1996).

Given the incorporation of colleges in 1993 and the establishment of FEDA, the role of the RACs has become confused and some of them have either dissolved or are on the verge of collapse. Along with colleges, RACs left LEA control in 1992 and one of them, the Yorkshire and Humberside Association for Further and Higher Education (YHAFHE), has managed to maintain its regional role through the continued support of local colleges. YHAFHE's 1996 Strategic Plan stresses the importance of a regional voice for FE 'which can effectively reflect regional comment on major educational issues to a national audience' (YHAFHE, 1996, p.4). In similar vein, an editorial in the Spring 1995 edition of *Furthering Education*, a quarterly magazine in which YHAFHE and three other RACs were original stakeholders, castigated what it saw as a 'disappointing and wasteful' attempt by certain national organisations to 'reinvent a regional dimension from a national standpoint' (*Furthering Education*, 1995, p.4). The fight to become the national body for the FE sector subsumes not only FEDA but also two organisations, the Association for Colleges and the CEF. In August 1996, the CEF merged with the Association *for* Colleges, a body whose origins lay in the LEAs which originally controlled the FE sector. At the time of writing, the new body, to be called the Association *of* Colleges, is still defining its role so it is too early to know the extent to which it will be useful or even decide to represent the needs of teaching staff.

USEFUL CONTACTS AND SOURCES OF SUPPORT

The following organisations may prove useful at some time or other during your career in FE. More and more organisations are now placing their details on the Internet and have their own World Wide Web pages.

ACM (Association for College Management)
15 The Beacons
Appley Bridge
Shevington
Wigan WN6 8DU
Tel: 01257 255844

Basic Skills Agency (formerly ALBSU)
Commonwealth House
New Oxford Street
London WC1A 1NU
Tel: 0171 405 4017

BTEC (Business and Technology Education Council) (now EDXCELL)
Central House
Upper Woburn Place
London WC1H 0HU
Tel: 0171 413 8400

Business in the Community (BITC)
44 Baker Street
London W1M 1DH
Tel: 0171 224 1600

CBI (Confederation of British Industry)
Centre Point
103 New Oxford Street
London WC1A 1DU
Tel: 0171 379 7400

Centre for Education and Industry (CEI)
University of Warwick
Coventry CV4 7AL
Tel: 01203 523909

City and Guilds of London Institute
1 Giltspur Street
London EC1A 9DD
Tel: 0171 294 2468

Community Education Development Centre (CEDC)
Lyng Hall
Blackberry Lane
Coventry CV2 3JS
Tel: 01203 638660

Community Service Volunteers (Education)
237 Pentonville Road
Islington
London N1 9NJ
Tel: 0171 278 6601

Council for Industry and Higher Education
100 Park Village East
London NW1 3SR

CRAC (Careers Research and Advisory Centre)
Sheraton House
Castle Park
Cambridge
CB3 0AX
Tel: 01223 460277

For further organisations dealing with education/industry links, consult *The 1996 Directory of Education/Industry Links*, Newbury, Resources Plus.

Department for Education and Employment (DfEE)
Sanctuary Buildings
Great Smith Street
Westminster
London SW1P 3BT
Tel: 0171 925 5000

Education 2000
Corporation Offices
Broadway
Letchworth Garden City SG6 3AB
Tel: 01462 481107

FEDA (Further Education Development Agency)
Head Office
Dunbarton House
68 Oxford Street
London W1N ODA
Tel: 0171 436 0020

Further Education Funding Council (FEFC)
Quinton House
Quinton Road
Coventry CV1 3PJ
Tel: 01203 863000

Industrial Society
Quadrant Court
49 Calthorpe Road
Birmingham B15 1TH
Tel: 0121 454 6769

NACETT (National Advisory Council for Education and Training Targets)
7th Floor
222 Gray's Inn Road
London WC1X 8HL
Tel: 0171 211 5012

NATFHE (National Association of Teachers in Further and Higher
Education)
27 Britannia Street
London WC1X 9JP
Tel: 0171 837 3636

National Foundation for Education Research (NFER)
The Mere
Upton Park
Slough
Berkshire SL1 2DQ
Tel: 01753 574123

NatWest Financial Literacy Centre
Centre for Education and Industry
University of Warwick
Coventry CV4 7AL
Tel: 01203 524234

NCET (National Council for Educational Technology)
Milburn Hill Road
University of Warwick Science Park
Coventry CV4 7JJ
Tel: 01203 416994

NCITO (National Council for Industry Training Organisations)
Unit 10
Amos Road
Sheffield S9 1XX
Tel: 0114 261 9926

NCVQ (National Council for Vocational Qualifications)
222 Euston Road
London NW1 2BZ
Tel: 0171 728 1807

NIACE (National Institute for Adult and Continuing Education)
21 de Montfort Street
Leicester LE1 7GE
Tel: 0116 223 0000

RSA (Royal Society of Arts Examination Board)
Westwood Way
Coventry CV4 8HS
Tel: 01203 470033

Teacher Placement Service (TPS)
Understanding British Industry (UBI)
10 Lakemere Close
Kidlington Business Centre
Kidlington
Oxfordshire OX5 1LG
Tel: 01865 374389

Trades Union Congress (TUC)
Congress House
Great Russell Street
London WC18 3LS
Tel: 0171 636 4030

Workers' Educational Association (WEA)
17 Victoria Park Square
London E2 9PB
Tel: 0181 983 1515

Appendix

National targets for education and training

TARGETS FOR 2000

Foundation learning

1 By age 19, 85 per cent of young people to achieve 5 GCSEs at grade C or above, an Intermediate GNVQ or an NVQ level 2.
2 75 per cent of young people to achieve level 2 competence in communication, numeracy and IT by age 19; and 35 per cent to achieve level 3 competence in these core skills by age 21.
3 By age 21, 60 per cent of young people to achieve 2 GCE A levels, an Advanced GNVQ or an NVQ level 3.

Lifetime learning

1 60 per cent of the workforce to be qualified to NVQ level 3, Advanced GNVQ or 2 GCE A level standard.
2 30 per cent of the workforce to have a vocational, professional, management or academic qualification at NVQ level 4 or above.
3 70 per cent of all organisations employing 200 or more employees, and 35 per cent of those employing 50 or more, to be recognised as Investors in People.

NACETT (1995)

References

Abbott, I. and Huddleston, P. (1995) 'The Development of Business Education: Change or Decay', Paper presented to *International Conference on Developments in Business Education*, Liverpool, 18–20 April.

Abramson, M. *et al.* (1996) (eds) *Further and Higher Education Partnerships*, Buckingham, SRHE/Open University Press.

Ainley, P. (1994) *Degrees of Difference*, London, Lawrence and Wishart.

ALBSU (1991) *Open Learning and ESOL*, London, ALBSU (now Basic Skills Agency).

Ashworth, P. and Saxton, J. (1990) 'On Competence', *Journal of Further and Higher Education*, 14:2, Summer, pp.3–25.

Audit Commission (1985) *Obtaining Better Value from Further Education*, London, HMSO.

Audit Commission/Ofsted (1993) *Unfinished Business – full-time educational courses for 16–19 year olds*, London, HMSO.

Bates, I. *et al.* (1995) 'Special Issue on Competence and the National Vocational Qualifications Framework', *British Journal of Education and Work*, 8:2.

Bateson, M.C. (1984) *With a Daughter's Eye*, New York, William Morrow.

Beaumont, G. (1995) *Review of 100 NVQs and SVQs: A Report submitted to Department for Education and Employment*, London, DfEE.

Belenky, M.F. *et al.* (1986) *Women's Ways of Knowing*, New York, Basic Books.

Berne, E. (1970) *Games People Play*, Harmondsworth, Penguin.

Betts, D. (1996) 'Staff appraisal and staff development in the corporate college', in J. Robson (ed.) *The Professional FE Teacher*, Aldershot, Avebury.

Bigger, S. (1996) 'Post-16 Compact in Birmingham: School and College Links with Higher Education', in M. Abramson *et al.* (eds) *Further and Higher Education Partnerships*, Buckingham, SRHE/Open University Press, pp.154–63.

Bloom, B.S. (1965) *Taxonomy of Educational Objectives*, London, Longman.

Bloor, M. and Butterworth, C. (1996) 'The portfolio approach to professional development', in J. Robson (ed.) *The Professional FE Teacher*, Aldershot, Avebury.

Bocock, J. (1996) 'Take Your Partners', *Times Higher Educational Supplement*, March 3rd.

Boud, D., Keogh, R. and Walker, D. (1985) *Reflection: turning experience into learning*, London, Kogan Page.

Brandes, D. and Phillips, H. (1985) *Gamesters' Handbook*, London, Hutchinson.

Brookfield, S. (1986) *Understanding and Facilitating Adult Learning*, Milton Keynes, Open University Press.

Brown, S. (1994) 'Assessment: a changing practice', in B. Moon and A. Shelton Mayes (eds) *Teaching and Learning in the Secondary School*, London, Open University/Routledge.

Brundage, D.H. and Mackeracher, D. (1980) *Adult Learning Principles and Their Application to Program Planning*, Toronto, Ministry of Education, Ontario.

BTEC (1993) *Implementing BTEC GNVQs: a guide for BTEC centres*, Issue 1, London, BTEC.

Capey, J. (1995) *GNVQ Assessment Review, Final Report of the review group*, London, NCVQ.

Castling, A. (1996) 'The role of the staff development practitioner in the FE college', in J. Robson (ed.) *The Professional FE Teacher*, Aldershot, Avebury.

CBI (1994) *Quality Assessed, The CBI Review of NVQs and SVQs*, London, CBI.

CEDEFOP (1994) *Determining the need for vocational counselling among different target groups of young people under 28 years of age in the European Community*, Berlin, CEDEFOP.

Coats, M. (1994) *Women's Education*, Buckingham, SRHE/Open University Press.

Cohen, L. and Manion, L. (1989) *A Guide to Teaching Practice*, 3rd Edition, London, Routledge.

Corbett, J. and Barton, L. (1992) *A Struggle for Choice, Students with Special Needs in Transition to Adulthood*, London, Routledge.

Cox, A. (1996) 'Teacher as mentor: opportunities for professional development', in J. Robson (ed.) *The Professional FE Teacher*, Aldershot, Avebury.

DE/DES (1981) *A New Training Initiative: A Programme for Action*, London, HMSO.

Dearing, R. (1996) *Review of 16–19 Qualifications; Summary Report*, London, School Curriculum and Assessment Authority.

DES/ED/WO (1991) *Education and Training for the 21st Century*, London, HMSO.

DES/WO (1988) *Advancing A levels* (The Higginson Report), London, HMSO.

DfE (1994) *Participation in Education by 16–18 year olds in England*, Statistical Bulletin 10/94, London, HMSO.

DfEE (1995) *Statistical Bulletin. Award of Vocational Qualifications*, Issue No. 5/95, London, DfEE.

DfEE (1996) *Funding 16–19 Education and Training: Towards Convergence*, London, Department for Education and Employment.

DfEE/FEDA (1995) *Mapping the FE Sector*, London, Further Education Development Agency.

DfEE/The Scottish Office/The Welsh Office (1995) *Lifetime Learning: a consultation document*, London, DfEE.

EBPNN (1996) Colleges and EBPs, report available from Education Business Partnerships National Network, c/o DBEE, Broom Cottages Primary School, Ferryhill, Co. Durham.

ED (1988) *Employment for the 1990s*, Cm. 540, London, HMSO.

Edwards, R. (1993a) 'Multi-skilling the Flexible Workforce in Post-Compulsory Education', *Journal of Further and Higher Education*, 17:1, pp.44–51.

Edwards, R. (1993b) 'The Inevitable Future?: post Fordism in work and learning', in R. Edwards *et al.* (eds) *Adult Learners, Education and Training*, London, Routledge.

Egan, G. (1975) *The Skilled Helper*, California, Wadsworth.

Eisner, E.W. (1985) *The Art of Educational Evaluation*, London, Falmer Press.

EnTra (1993) Unit number UD403: *Selecting Design Options*, Watford, Training Publications Limited.

Eraut, M. (1994) *Developing Professional Knowledge and Competence*, London, Falmer Press.

FEDA (1996) *Inform*, The Newsletter of the Further Education Development Agency, Blagdon, FEDA.

FEFC (1994a) *Quality and Standards in Further Education. Chief Inspector's Annual Report 1993–94*, Coventry, FEFC.

FEFC (1994b) *National Vocational Qualifications in the Further Education Sector in England. National Survey Report*, Coventry, FEFC.

FEFC (1995a) *General National Vocational Qualifications in the Further Education Sector in England. National Survey Report*, Coventry, FEFC.

FEFC (1996a) *Analysis of Institutions' Strategic Planning Information for the Period 1995–96 to 1997–98*, Circular 96/02, Coventry, FEFC.

FEFC (1996b) 'Student numbers at colleges in the further education sector and external institutions in England in 1995–96', Press release, 17 December, Coventry, FEFC.

FEFC (1996c) *Quality and Standards in Further Education in England. Chief Inspector's Annual Report 1995–96*, Coventry, FEFC.

FEFC (1996d) *Inclusive Learning*, Coventry, FEFC.

FEFC (1996e) *Introduction to the Council*, Coventry, FEFC.

FEFC (1996f) *College Responsiveness. A National Survey Report*, Coventry, FEFC.

FEFC (1996g) *The Report of the Learning and Technology Committee, chaired by Sir Gordon Higgonson*, Coventry, FEFC.

Ferguson, M. (1982) *The Aquarian Conspiracy: personal and social transformation in the 1980s*, London, Paladin.

FEU (1979) *A Basis for Choice*, London, FEU.

FEU (1981) *Vocational Preparation*, London, FEU.

FEU (1991) *Flexible Colleges, Part I Priorities for Action*, London, FEU.

FEU (1993) *Introducing General National Vocational Qualifications*, London, FEU.

FEU (1994) *Managing the Delivery of Guidance in Colleges*, London, FEU.

FEU, IOE and Nuffield Foundation (1994) *GNVQs 1993–94: A National Survey Report*, London, FEU.

Fieldhouse, R. and Associates (1996) *A History of Modern British Adult Education*, Leicester, National Institute for Adult Continuing Education.

Finegold, D. *et al.* (1990) *A British Baccalaureate: ending the division between education and training*, London, Institute for Public Policy Research.

Freire, P. (1974) *Education: The Practice of Freedom*, London, Writers and Readers Cooperative.

Furthering Education (1996) 'Regional superhighways in East Anglia', *Furthering Education*, Issue No. 10, Spring.

Gagne, R.M. (1988) *Principles of Instructional Design*, New York, Holt, Rinehart and Winston.

Gibb, J.R. (1960) 'Learning Theory in Adult Education', in M. Knowles (ed.) *Handbook of Adult Education in the United States*, Washington, DC, Adult Education Association of the USA.

Gleeson, D. (1996) 'Post-compulsory Education in a Post-industrial and Post-modern Age', in J. Avis *et al.* (eds) *Knowledge and Nationhood*, London, Cassell Education.

Green, A. and Steadman, H. (1995) *Education Provision, Education Attainment and the Needs of Industry: a review of the research for Germany, France, Japan, the USA and Britain*, London, National Institute for Economic and Social Research.

Harris, S. and Hyland, T. (1995) 'Basic Skills and Learning Support in Further Education', *Journal of Further and Higher Education*, 19:2, Summer, pp.42–6.

Harrow, A.J. (1972) *A Taxonomy of the Psychomotor Domain*, New York, McKay.

Heathcote, G., Kempa, R. and Roberts, I. (1982) *Curriculum Styles and Strategies*, London, Further Education Unit.

HMSO (1981) *A New Training Initiative: A Programme for Action*, Cmnd. 8455, London, HMSO.

HMSO (1994) *Competitiveness, Helping Business to Win*, London, HMSO.

Hodkinson, P. (1996) 'Careership: The Individual, Choices and Markets in the Transition into Work', in J. Avis *et al.* (eds) *Knowledge and Nationhood*, London, Cassell Education.

Hodkinson, P. and Issitt, M. (1995) *The Challenge of Competence*, London, Cassell Education.

Hodson, A. and Spours, K. (1997) Beyond Dearing, 14–19: Qualifications, Frameworks and Systems, London, Kogan Page.

Holloway, W. (1989) *Subjectivity and Method in Psychology*, London, Sage.

Honey, P. and Mumford, A. (1982) *The Manual of Learning Styles*, Maidenhead, Peter Honey.

Huddleston, P., Abbott, I. and Stagg, P. (1995) *Introduction to GNVQs: A Practical Guide*, London, UBI/ED.

Huddleston, P. (1996) *An Evaluation of the Contribution made by the FE Colleges to the Delivery of Rover Group's Integrated Engineering Development Scheme*, Centre for Education and Industry, University of Warwick.

Hyland, T. (1994) *Competence, Education and NVQs: Dissenting Perspectives*, London, Cassell Education.

IES (1994) *Implementing NVQs: The Experience of Employers, Employees and Trainees*, Sussex, Institute of Employment Studies.

IES (1995) *Employers' Use of the NVQ System*, Sussex, IES.

Jackson, C. *et al.* (1996) *Managing Careers in 2000 and Beyond*, Sussex Institute of Employment Studies.

Jaques, D. (1992) *Learning in Groups*, 2nd Edition, London, Croom Helm.

Jarvis, P. (1987) *Adult Learning in the Social Context*, London, Croom Helm.

Jessup, G. (1991) *Outcomes: NVQs and the Emerging Model of Vocational Education and Training*, London, Falmer Press.

Jessup, G. (1994) *GNVQ: An Alternative Curriculum Model*, London, NCVQ.

Johnstone, J.W.C. and Rivera, R.J. (1965) *Volunteers for Learning: A Study of the Educational Pursuits of Adults*, Hawthorne, New York, Aldine.

Kehily, M.J. (1995) 'Self-narration, Autobiography and Identity Construction', *Gender and Education*, 7:1, pp.23–31.

Kidd, R. (1973) *How Adults Learn*, Chicago, Follett.

Knowles, M. (1978) *The Adult Learner: A Neglected Species*, Houston, Gulf.

Knox, A.B. (1977) *Adult Development and Learning: A Handbook on Individual Growth and Competence in the Adult Years*, San Francisco, Jossey-Bass.

Kolb, D.A. (1984) *Experiential Learning*, Englewood Cliffs, New Jersey, Prentice Hall.

KPMG Peat Marwick (1994) *COSH and obstacles to employers implementing NVQs and SVQs*, Sheffield, Employment Department.

Last, J. and Chown, A. (1996) 'Competence-based approaches and initial teacher training for FE', in J. Robson (ed.) *The Professional FE Teacher*, Aldershot, Avebury.

Laurillard, D. (1993) *Rethinking University Teaching*, London, Routledge.

Lauzon, A.C. (1989) 'Educational Transition: A Qualitative Study of Full-time Married Male Students', *International Journal of University Adult Education*, XXVIII:2, pp.34–46.

Lucas, N. (1996) 'Teacher Training Agency: is there anyone there from further education?', *Journal of Further and Higher Education*, 20:1, Spring.

McGiveney, V. (1996) *Staying or leaving the course: non-completion and retention of mature students in further and higher education*, Leicester, National Institute for Adult Continuing Education.

Macleod, D. and Beckett, F. (1995) 'Body and Soul', *Education Guardian*, 6 June.

Mager, R. (1962) *Preparing Instructional Objectives*, California, Fearon.

Marshall, L. and Rowland, F. (1993) *A Guide to Learning Independently*, 2nd Edition, Buckingham, Open University Press.

Miller, H.L. (1964) *Teaching and Learning in Adult Education*, New York, Macmillan.

Minton, D. (1991) *Teaching Skills in Further and Adult Education*, London, City and Guilds/Macmillan.

Mitchell, L. (1989) 'The Definition of Standards and their Assessment', in J.W. Burke (ed.) *Competency Based Education and Training*, Lewes, Falmer Press.

NACETT (1995) *Report on Progress Towards the National Targets*, London, NACETT.

Nash, I. (1992) 'Alliance calls for A level reform', *Times Educational Supplement*, 14 February.

NCET (1992) *Special Update*, Coventry, National Council for Educational Technology.

NCVQ (1995) *GNVQ Assessment Review*, Final report of the review group chaired by Dr John Capey, London, NCVQ.

NCVQ (1996) *Data News*, Issue 2, winter 1996–7, London, NCVQ.

Payne, J. (1995) *Routes Beyond Compulsory Schooling*, England and Wales Youth Cohort Study, Sheffield, Employment Department.

Payne, J. and Storran, J. (1995) *Further and Higher Education Progression Project Final Report*, London, Division of Continuing Education, South Bank University.

Quicke, J. (1996) 'The Reflective Practitioner and Teacher Education: an answer to critics', *Teachers and Teaching: Theory and Practice*, 2:1, pp.11–22.

Rees, S.A. (1995) 'Students with Emotional and Behavioural Difficulties: Coping with a Growing Tide', *Journal of Further and Higher Education*, 19:2, Summer, pp.93–7.

Richardson, W., Spours, K., Woolhouse, J. and Young, M. (1995) *Learning for the Future, Initial Report*, London, Institute of Education and Centre for Education and Industry, University of Warwick.

Richardson, W., Woolhouse, J. and Finegold, D. (1993) *The Reform of Post-16 Education and Training in England and Wales*, Harlow, Longman.

Robinson, J.E., Such, S., Walters, C., Muller, D. and Stott, D. (1996) 'Researching in Further Education: An Illustrative Study from Suffolk College', in M. Young *et al. College as Learning Organisations: The Role of Research*, Unified 16+ Curriculum Series, Number 12, London, Institute of Education.

Robson, J. (1996) (ed.) *The Professional FE Teacher*, Aldershot, Avebury.

Rogers, A. (1986) *Teaching Adults*, Buckingham, Open University Press.

Rogers, A. (1994) *Teaching Adults*, Buckingham, Open University Press.

Rogers, J. (1992) *Adults Learning*, 3rd Edition, Milton Keynes, Open University Press.

Rowland, S. (1993) *The Enquiring Tutor*, London, Falmer Press.

Rowntree, D. (1990) *Teaching Through Self-Instruction: How to Develop Open Learning Materials*, London, Kogan Page.

Sacks, O. (1986) *The Man Who Mistook His Wife For a Hat*, London, Pan Books.

Satir, V. (1983) *Conjoint Family Therapy*, 3rd edn, Palo Alto, California, Science and Behavioural Books.

Schon, D. (1983) *The Reflective Practitioner: How Professionals Think in Action*, New York, Basic Books.

Schon, D. (1987) *Educating the Reflective Practitioner*, San Francisco, Jossey-Bass.

Skinner, B.F. (1968) *The Technology of Teaching*, New York, Appleton-Century-Crofts.

Smith, J.J. (1989) 'Judgements in Educational Assessment', *Journal of Further and Higher Education*, 13:3, pp.115–19.

Smith, R.M. (1982) *Learning How to Learn: Applied Theory for Adults*, New York, Cambridge University Press.

Smithers, A. (1993) *All Our Futures: Britain's education revolution*, London, Channel Four Television.

Spours, K. (1995) *The Strengths and Weaknesses of GNVQs: Principles of Design*, Learning for the Future Working Paper 3, London, Institute of Education and Centre for Education and Industry, University of Warwick.

Squires, G. (1987) *The Curriculum Beyond School*, London, Hodder and Stoughton.

Stenhouse, L. (1975) *An Introduction to Curriculum Research and Development*, London, Heinemann.

Tedder, M. (1994) 'Appraisal and Professionalism in Colleges', *Journal of Further and Higher Education*, 18:3, Autumn, pp.74–82.

TES (1994) 'Rivalry set to increase as colleges woo young', 1 April, London, *Times Educational Supplement*.

TES 2 (1995) 'Drama out of a crisis', 20 September, London, *Times Educational Supplement*.

TES (1996) 'Perils of penguin-like star gazing', 9 February, London, *Times Educational Supplement*.

Tough, A. (1971) *The Adult's Learning Projects*, Toronto, Ontario Institute for Studies in Education.

Training Agency (1989) *Development of Assessable Standards for National Certification*, Guidance Note No. 1, Sheffield, Employment Department/Training Agency.

UDACE (1991) *What Can Graduates Do? A Consultative Document*, Leicester, UDACE.

Unwin, L. (1992) 'Enabling Learning: Raising the Profile of Staff Development', in I. McNay (ed.) *Visions of Post-Compulsory Education*, Milton Keynes, SRHE/Open University Press, pp.94–103.

Unwin, L. (1993) 'Training Credits: the pilot doomed to succeed', in W. Richardson *et al.* (eds) *The Reform of Post-16 Education and Training in England and Wales*, Harlow, Longman.

Unwin, L. (1994) 'I'm a real student now: access to and the use of library services by distance learning students', *Journal of Further and Higher Education*, 18:1, Spring, pp.85–91.

Unwin, L. (1995) *Staying the Course: Students' Reasons for Non-completion of Full-time Education Courses in South and East Cheshire*, Middlewich, South and East Cheshire Education–Business Partnership, 42 pages.

Unwin, L. and Edwards, R. (1990) 'The Tutor-Learner Relationship: Making Sense of Changing Contexts', *Adults Learning*, March, pp.197–9.

Wildemeersch, D. (1989) 'The Principal Meaning of Dialogue for the Construction and Transformation of Reality', in S.W. Weil and I. McGill (eds) *Making Sense of Experiential Learning*, Stony Stratford, SRHE/Open University Press.

Wilmot, M. and McLean, M. (1994) 'Evaluating Flexible Learning: A Case Study', *Journal of Further and Higher Education*, 18:3, Autumn.

YHAFHE (1996) *Helping Education to Succeed*, Dewsbury, Yorkshire and Humberside Association for Further and Higher Education.

Young, M. *et al.* (1995) *Teacher Education for the Further Education Sector: Training the Lecturer of the Future*, London, Post-16 Education Centre, Institute of Education.

Young, M. *et al.* (1996) *Colleges as Learning Organisations: The Role of Research*, Unified 16+ Curriculum Series Number 12, London, Institute of Education.

Further reading

PART I FURTHER EDUCATION IN CONTEXT

Chapter 1 Where will I teach?

Abramson, M., Bird, J. and Stennett, A. (1996) *Further and Higher Education Partnerships*, Buckingham, SRHE/Open University Press.

Funnell, P. and Muller, D. (1991) (eds) *Vocational Education and the Challenge of Europe*, London, Kogan Page.

McGinty, J. and Fish, J. (1993) *Further Education in the Market Place*, London, Routledge.

Raggatt, P. and Unwin, L. (1991) *Change and Intervention, Vocational Education and Training*, London, Falmer Press.

Richardson, W., Woolhouse, J. and Finegold, D. (1993) (eds) *The Reform of Post-16 Education and Training in England and Wales*, Harlow, Longman.

Chapter 2 The student body: who will I teach?

Bates, I. and Riseborough, G. (1993) *Youth and Inequality*, Buckingham, Open University Press.

Calder, J. (1993) (ed.) *Disaffection and Diversity: Overcoming the Barriers for Adult Learners*, London, Falmer Press.

Chitty, C. (1991) (ed.) *Post-16 Education, Studies in Access and Achievement*, London, Kogan Page.

Coles, B. (1995) *Youth and Social Policy*, London, UCL Press.

Corbett, J. (1990) (ed.) *Uneasy Transitions, Disaffection in Post-Compulsory Education and Training*, London, Falmer Press.

McGiveney, V. (1996) *Staying or Leaving the Course, Non-completion and Retention of Mature Students in Further and Higher Education*, Leicester, NIACE.

Chapter 3 Diverse curricula: what will I teach?

Halsall, R. and Cockett, M. (1996) *Education and Training 14–19, Chaos or Coherence?*, London, David Fulton.

Hodgson, A. and Spours, K. (1997) *Beyond Dearing, 14–19 Qualifications, Frameworks and Systems*, London, Kogan Page.

Hyland, T. (1994) *Competence Education and NVQs*, London, Cassell Education.

Pring, R. (1995) *Closing The Gap, Liberal Education and Vocational Preparation*, London, Hodder and Stoughton.

PART II TEACHING AND LEARNING

Chapter 4 Approaches to learning

Anderson, G., Boud, D. and Sampson, J. (1996) *Learning Contracts*, London, Kogan Page.

Boud, D., Cohen, R. and Walker, D. (1993) (eds) *Using Experience for Learning*, Buckingham, SRHE/Open University Press.

Curzon, L.B. (1995) *Teaching in Further Education*, 4th Edition, London, Cassell.

Soden, R. (1994) *Teaching Problem-Solving in Vocational Education*, London, Routledge.

Chapter 5 Teaching strategies

Ashcroft, K. and Foreman-Peck, L. (1994) *Managing Teaching and Learning in Further and Higher Education*, London, Falmer Press.

Baldwin, J. and Williams, H. (1988) *Active Learning: A Trainer's Guide*, Oxford, Blackwell Education.

Coats, M. (1996) *Recognising Good Practice in Women's Education and Training*, Leicester, NIACE.

Ollin, R. and Smith, E. (1996) *Planning, Delivering and Assessing GNVQs*, London, Kogan Page.

Rogers, A. (1996) *Teaching Adults*, 2nd Edition, Buckingham, Open University Press.

Rowntree, D. (1991) *Teaching Through Self-Instruction: How to Develop Open Learning Materials*, London, Kogan Page.

Chapter 6 Assessment and recording achievement

Ecclestone, K. (1994) *Understanding Assessment: A Guide for Teachers and Managers in Post-compulsory Education*, Leicester, NIACE.

Hargreaves, A. (1989) *Curriculum and Assessment Reform*, Milton Keynes, Open University Press.

McKelvey, C. and Peters, H. (1993) *APL: Equal Opportunities for All*, London, Routledge.

Wolf, A. (1995) *Competence-based Assessment*, Buckingham, Open University Press.

PART III PROFESSIONAL DEVELOPMENT

Chapter 7 Evaluation, reflection and research

Carr, W. and Kemis, S. (1986) *Becoming Critical*, London, Falmer Press.

Schon, D. (1991) *The Reflective Practitioner: how professionals think in action*, Aldershot, Avebury.

Young, M. *et al.* (1996) *Colleges as Learning Organisations: The Role of Research*, Unified 16+ Curriculum Series, No. 12, London, Post-16 Centre, Institute of Education.

Chapter 8 Professional development

Eraut, M. (1994) *Developing Professional Knowledge and Competence*, London, Falmer Press.

Hodkinson, P. and Issitt, M. (1995) (eds) *The Challenge of Competence*, London, Cassell Education.

Robson, J. (1996) (ed.) *The Professional FE Teacher: Staff Development and Training in the Corporate College*, Aldershot, Avebury.

Young, M., Lucas, N., Sharp, G. and Cunningham, B. (1995) *Teacher Education for the Further Education Sector: Training the Lecturers of the Future*, London, Institute of Education.

Chapter 9 Networks and support agencies

CIHE (1996) *Colleges and Companies: Sharing Great Expectation*, London, Council for Industry and Higher Education.

Gibbs, B. *et al.* (1991) *The Reality of Partnership*, Harlow, Longman.

Index

A levels (GCE) 5–6, 9; awarding bodies 33, 34, 35; curriculum 35–7; debate over standards 133; results by type of institution (1994) 36

ability, range of 21–2

access: flexibility of 12; programmes to HE via FE 21; to learning 109–10

accommodation pressures 16

accountability 14, 16–19

accreditation 9–10

accreditation of prior learning (APL) 21, 49, 133, 157

achievement: not age-related 31; recognition of 113; recording 111–33; statements of 42

action research 158

adaptability 88–90

administration 14

adult education: basic education in 52–3; curricula 52–4; definition 52; funding for 22, 52–3; informal 52, 53; scope 52; teacher training for 153

adult education centres 7

adult learning, theories of 64–8

Adult Literacy and Basic Skills Unit (ALBSU) 115, 125

adulthood, concept of 62–4

adults: compared with children 65–6; returners to learning 6, 14

Adults Learning (Rogers) 125

advisors 82

affective domain learning 68, 97

ages of students 20, 31, 62–4

agricultural and horticultural colleges 6, 13

aims 92–3, 95–6, 99

andragogy 65–6

anxiety 59, 107

'Applied A levels' 39

appraisal: teacher 155; workplace 53

apprentices 7, 77, 106

art and design colleges 6

assessment 111–33; competence-based 125–9; emotions and formal 140; methods of 112–29; the role of 111–13, see also formative assessment; summative assessment

assessor awards 16, 130–2, 146, 154

assignments 101–6, 123–5; designing 101–2; features of 101; grading and criteria and marking 123

Association for College Management (ACM) 160–1, 166

Association for Colleges 166

Association of Colleges 166

Association of Principals of Colleges (APC) 160

Association of Teachers and Lecturers (ATL) 160–1

attendance: modes of 31; patterns of 21; and responsibility 106

attitudes of students 23–8

attitudes to students, schools compared with further education 63

audio cassettes 110

Audit Commission 11

authoring of distance learning materials 110

awarding bodies 10, 33–5; job-specific 45

awards, academic separate from applied and vocational 35

banking 38

basic education 3; adult education and 52–3

basic literacy and numeracy skills 6, 21, 53, 115

Basic Skills Agency (formerly ALBSU) 166

Basis for Choice (FEU) 165

Bateson, M.C. 156

behavioural problems 106–7

behaviourism 60
Belenky, M.F. 63
Berne, Eric 78
Bigger, S. 161–2
biographical accounts, of professional
    experience 156–7
Birmingham College of Food, Tourism and
    Creative Studies 5
Bloom, B.S. 68, 97–8
Bloor, M. 156–7
Boards of Governors 5
Bobbitt, Franklin 96
Bocock, J. 10–11
Boud, D. 137
brainstorming 99
Brookfield, Stephen 59, 64
Brown, S. 111
Brundage, D.H. 65
BTEC 10, 35, 38; *add.* 167; assessment in
    123; Certificate in Management Studies
    (Education Management) 153; Higher
    National Diploma courses 10;
    performance evidence and supplementary
    evidence 126–7
budget management 14
bullying 107
business administration, NVQ 120–1
Business in the Community (BITC) 167
Business Link 162
business short courses 11
business studies 8
Business and Technology Education *see*
    BTEC
business-related organisations 162–5
Butterworth, C. 156–7

candidate 77
Capey, Sir John 129
career development, for teachers in FE
    155–9
careers guidance 162
Careers Research and Advisory Centre
    (CRAC), *add.* 168
Castling, A. 149, 150
catering, NVQ 121, 124
CEDEFOP 71
Centre for Education and Industry (CEI)
    167
Centre for the Study of Comprehensive
    Schools (CSCS) 171
Certificate in Education (FE) 16, 152, 153
Certificate of Pre-Vocational Education
    (CPVE) 38

Certificate for Teachers in Adult Education
    153
Chadbrook College 114
Chambers of Commerce 162
Cheshire, barriers to learning for 16–19
    year-old FE students 71–4
children, compared with adults 65–6
China 64
Chown, A. 153–4
City and Guilds: 926 Adult Trainers' Award
    153; courses 35, 38; Teacher's Certificate
    (7306) 16, 153; Teacher's Certificate
    (7307) 16, 152
City and Guilds of London Institute (CGLI)
    45, *add.* 167
class size 14
Coats, Maggie 74–5
cognitive domain learning 68, 97
cognitive models of learning 64
Cohen, L. 118
collaborative mentoring 155
college culture, and staff development
    154–5
college staff *see* staff in colleges
colleges, in competition with private
    training and company in-house training
    50
Colleges' Employers' Forum (CEF) 161,
    166
collegiality 80
communication, core skills performance
    criteria 122
community: links with 160; needs of the 13,
    22
Community Education Development
    Centre (CEDC) 167
Community Service Volunteers (Education)
    167
Compact schemes 161–2
companies: in-house training 50;
    partnerships with 104; perceived barriers
    to implementation of NVQs 46; projects
    for 103
company-specific training programmes 11
competence 112, 129; definition of 40;
    levels of 40
competence-based approach 9–10, 39–44,
    60, 62, 93, 117, 153; application to
    teacher training for FE 153–4
competence-based assessment 125–9
competitiveness 29
Competitiveness Helping Business to Win
    (White Paper 1994) 6

completion rates for courses 17, 70
computer-based learning 31
computers, interactive 110
Confederation of British Industry (CBI) 162, *add.* 167
confidence, lack of 59
confrontation, dealing with 108
continuing education 52, 53
continuing professional development (CPD) 53, 151
continuing professional education (CPE) 151
continuous assessment 104–5, 113
contracts: local for lecturers in FE 161; negotiation of new teaching 14, 161
core skills, within vocational areas 123–4
correspondence courses 60, 109
Council for the Curriculum, Examinations and Assessment (CCEA) in Northern Ireland 34
Council for Industry and Higher Education, *add.* 167, 172
counselling 14, 22, 31, 49, 108
counsellors 82; three-stage model of the skilled helper 83
courses: completion rates 17, 70; students and 7–14
coursework assessment 36, 37; in GCSEs 118
Cox, A. 155
creativity 102–5, 118
criterion referencing 132
Crompton College of Further Education, projected income distribution 5
curriculum 29–55; combining of elements 35; continuum from holistic to aggregative 51; control of the 30; FEFC grading of 18; modularisation of 49; stakeholders in the 29–30; traditions 29–35; use of term 95
Curriculum and Assessment Authority for Wales (ACAC) 34
curriculum design, influences on 30–1 Fig. 3.1
curriculum development, objectives of 96–8
curriculum planning 95–6

day-release courses 7, 45
Dearing Review (1996) 33–5, 36–7, 39, 44
deficit model of provision 22
degree courses 10, 50–2

degrees: debate over standards 133; 'two plus two' 21
delivery, devolved 51
Department for Education and Employment (DfEE) 35, 153; *add.* 168; funding of 16–19 education 163
dependence on teacher 59
destination data, questions based on 17
development plan 12
Dewey, John 61, 77
dialogue 113
difficult students, handling 106–10
disabled students 12, 22
disciplinary procedures 106–10
disruptive students 106–10
distance learning 14, 21, 96, 109–10, 157; materials 110
doctoral programmes 157–8
Doctorate in Education (EdD) 157–8
domestic life, and learning 69–70
drop outs, mature students 70
'drop-in' centres 31, 115
drop-out rates 14

East Anglia 110
Education 2000 168
education, banking concept of 61
'education for all' 20
Education and Training for the 21st Century (1991 White Paper) 36, 38
education-business partnership (EBP) 161, 163–5; National Network 164, 174; organisations listed with addresses 171–6
Edwards, R. 14, 110
EDXCELL 10
Egan, G. 83
ego states 78
electronic communications 110
Elton, Ben 75–6
emotional problems, students with 106–7
empathy 107
employer-funded training 11, 45
employer-led part-time training 21
employers: assistance with assignments 104; links of colleges with 164–5; partnerships with 49
Employment for the 1990s (1988 White Paper) 39–40
employment, preparation for 53
employment patterns, in colleges 14
empowerment 112
engineering 7, 8, 32, 49, 161; GNVQ units 115–17; NVQ 126–7

Engineering Council 173
England 4, 33, 162; college staff 15; number of FE colleges in 3; student profile 21
Enquiring Tutor, The (Rowland) 138
enrolment: by gender 21; by mode of attendance and source of funding (1993–4) 7; increased 16; numbers and types of students 30
Enterprise Education World Centre of Excellence 173
Enterprise and Industry Education Unit 173
enthusiasm 76
entry qualifications 10–11
Eraut, Michael 149, 151
essays 118–19
Europe, closer links with 32
European Business and Language Centre 32
European Commission (EC) 110
European exchanges 162
European Social Fund (ESF) 52
European Union 71; funding 4
evaluation 137–47
evening classes 45
event organisation in college 103
evidence 117, 133; in assessing GNVQs 123, 124; validity of 126–7
examination boards, for A levels and GCSE 36, 37
examination pass list 133
examinations 115–18; numerical marking beside questions 119, 120; resitting 36, 37
exclusions policy 106
expectations: of curriculum and timetable 72; of students 21, 92–3; teacher of student 107
experiential learning 61

facilitator 76, 125
family: accommodating the learner 69–70; support or otherwise 73–4
financial pressures, on young adults 73, 74
financial support, advice on 82
flexibility 11, 14, 49, 88–90
flexible college 49
flexible contracts 14, 161
flexible learning 19–10, 62
flexible teaching approach 14, 22
flexistudy 109
formative assessment 113–15, 133

foundation learning, targets 170
franchising agreements of FEs with universities 6, 10, 50, 51, 161
freelance professionals 14
Freire, Paulo 61
'full-cost' courses 4–5, 11
full-time students 21, 30–1
functional analysis 40, 154
fund allocation 11–12 Fig. 1.5
funding 4–5, 11, 16, 30, 53, 163; for adult education 22, 52–3; by employers 45; from TECs 162–3; and needs of the local community 33; for research degrees 158; for staff development 149–50
further education: growth rates in 6, 11, 22; national and regional bodies 165–6; nature and scope of 3–7; policy of 'all inclusiveness' 3; relationship with higher education 7, 50–2, 146–7, 161–2; teaching qualifications 151–4
further education colleges: number by region 3–4 Fig. 1.1; types of 6
Further Education Development Agency (FEDA) 154, 165–6, *add.* 168
Further Education Funding Council (FEFC) 4, 146; *add.* 168; assessment inspection process 16; Chief Inspector's Report (1993–4) 6; funding 6, 11–12, 106; on human resource development 150; inspections 17–19, 150: grading scales 17–18; Inspectorate 123, 124–5; Quality Assessment Committee 17; work placements in care sector 128
Further Education Staff College (FESC) 165
Further Education Unit (FEU) 102, 149, 165
Further and Higher Education Act (1992) 4, 11, 165
Furthering Education 166

Gagne, R.M. 67–8
gender 79; enrolment by 21; impact on learning 74–5, 79
General Certificate of Education (GCE) Advanced levels *see* A levels
General Certificate of Secondary Education (GCSE) 6, 9; assessment 118; awarding bodies 33, 34; curriculum 37; debate over standards 133
general education 5; curricula 35–7; qualifications 9
General National Vocational Qualification *see* GNVQ

general vocational education, curricula
    37–50
Gibb, J.R. 64
GNVQ: Engineering mandatory units
    115–17; Human Resource Management
    98–101; Information Technology Services
    166; Support Programme Information
    and Advice Unit 166
GNVQs 9; assessment in 123, 124, 128–9,
    154; awarding bodies 33, 34, 35, 129;
    core skills questions 119–20, 122;
    curriculum 38–45; defining features 41;
    internal and external verification 131;
    mandatory and optional units 42,
    115–17; performance criteria 43, 98, 113,
    129; student portfolios 44, 113, 129;
    unit-based 42–3; vocational and core
    skills 42, 44; work experience for 104
goals 96, 99
government policy 30
government-sponsored training programmes
    22; funding for 106, 162
grading: final analytic schemes 118; GNVQ
    themes 123; NCVQ themes 129;
    numerical and literal 119; scales for cross-
    college provision 17–18
graduate teachers, in FEs 158
Grant for Educational Support and Training
    (GEST) 149–50
group assessment 124–5
group learning 80–2
group management, training for staff in 108
group presentations 122
group teaching, types of aims and purposes
    in 81 Fig. 4.3
guidance 22, 31, 49, 82; map 84 Fig. 4.4
guidance team, influence on learner's
    pathway through college 85 Fig. 4.5

Harris, Steve 115
Harrow, A.J. 98
Haycocks Report (1975) 152
Headteachers into Industry (HTI) 173
Heathcote, G. 95–6
Her Majesty's Inspectorate (HMI) 149
Hertford Regional College 83–6
Higginson Report (1996) 31
high technology initiatives 31
higher education 5; curricula 50–2; growth
    in 6; qualifications 10; support agencies
    161–2
Higher Education Funding Council
    (HEFC) 5

higher education institutions (HEIs):
    collaboration with FE 7, 50–2, 146–7,
    161–2; departments of education 161;
    research ratings 158
Higher National Certificate (HNC) 10, 50
Higher National Diploma (HND) 10, 50
holidays 12
Holloway, W. 157
Honey, P. 138
How to Make a Curriculum (Bobbitt) 96
Huddersfield Technical College 3
human resource development (HRD) 148,
    150
human resource management, GNVQ
    98–101
hybrid roles 14, 102, 151–2

Illich, I. 30
inclusive learning, concept of 22
income distribution 5
incorporation (1992) 4, 16, 160, 166
independent self-study 65, 109
individualised learning programmes 31–2
induction: need for continuing 87;
    programmes for new staff 106; types of
    programmes 86–7
Industrial Society 168
Industrial Training Organisation (ITO)
    161
Industry in Education 174
information technology 32, 129, 166
initial professional education (IPE), for FE
    teachers 151, 152–4
initial teacher education (ITE): for FE 16,
    152–4; for schools 152
Institute of Chartered Accountants 161
Institute of Directors 162
Institute of Employment Studies 165
Institute of Marketing 10
interactive computer programmes 110
International Partnership Network (IPN)
    174
Ireland, Northern 4, 33, 34, 35; number of
    FE colleges in 3

Jackson, C. 155
Jaques, D. 80–2
Jarvis, P. 60–1
job titles 16
job-specific training 9, 45–50
Johnstone, J.W.C. 65
Joint Council of National Vocational
    Awarding Bodies 35

Kennedy Commission Report on widening
    participation viii
Kidd, R. 63, 65, 77, 82
Knowles, Malcolm 65–6
Knox, A.B. 65
Kolb, D.A. 60–1, 67

labels, power to determine behaviour 76
labour market 17, 22, 71, 74; local 8, 12,
    33
Last, J. 153–4
lateral thinking 94–5
Lauzon, A.C. 69
Lead Bodies 40
learner-centred teaching styles 62, 109
learning: approaches to 59–87; barriers to
    60, 68–75; areas of concern 71–4;
    different patterns of 31; Gagne's eight-
    stage model of 67–8; Kolb's definition
    60–1; model for effective 105 Fig. 5.3; as
    a transaction 77; ways of 64–8
learning by doing 101
learning cycle (Kolb) 60–1 Fig. 4.1; 67
learning difficulties, students with 12, 13,
    22, 31, 115
learning organisation 148
learning outcomes 92–101
Learning Resource Centres 31, 49
learning role, terminology 76
learning styles: changes in 72; types of 138
Learning Styles Inventory (Honey and
    Munford) 138
lecturers 76, 77
leisure and recreational classes 11, 22, 53
life experiences 10–11
lifelong learning 31, 52, 148
lifetime learning, targets 52, 170
listening 82
literacy, basic skills 6, 21, 53, 115
local education authorities (LEAs) 149, 165;
    funding from 4
Local Enterprise Company (LEC) 7, 162
low income students 12
Lowestoft College 3
Lucas, Norman 151–2

McGiveney, V. 70, 82
Mackeracher, D. 65
McLean, M. 62
Mager, R.F. 96–7
Man Who Mistook His Wife for a Hat (Sacks)
    156
management, and cost-effectiveness 62

Managing Careers in 2000 and Beyond
    (Jackson) 155
Manion, L. 118
manufacturing, example of GNVQ in
    43–4
marketing 14, 21
marking, standardised 118–19
Marshall, L. 125
Master of Arts (MA) 157
Master of Science (MSc) 157
Masters in Education (MEd) 157
mature students 4, 10–11, 51; drop outs 70;
    problems for 74–5; reflections on learning
    experiences 141–2
Mechanics Institute 3
media 110
mentors 155
micro curriculum, negotiation of a 93
Miller, H.L. 64
mining 8, 32
minority groups 13
Minton, D. 120
mixed-ability teaching 21
moderation 132
Modern Apprenticeship 7, 54–5, 161, 162
modular programmes 12, 32, 36–7, 49, 51,
    62
motivation of students 22–8
MPhil 158
multi-skilled teaching 14, 148
Mumford, A. 138

National Advisory Council for Education
    and Training Targets (NACETT) 6, 146;
    add. 168; targets for 2000 6, 169
National Association of Teachers in Further
    and Higher Education (NATFHE)
    160–1, add. 169
National Council for Educational
    Technology (NCET) 22, 168, 174
National Council for Industry Training
    Organisations (NCITO) 39, 161, 168
National Council for Vocational
    Qualifications (NCVQ) 34, 35, 93, 123;
    add. 168, 174; framework 33–4 Fig. 3.2;
    grading themes 129; on outcome based
    model 41
National Curriculum: compulsory
    assessment 111; testing at key stages 31
National Foundation for Education
    Research (NFER) 169
National Information System for Vocational
    Qualifications (NISVQ) 45, 46

National Institute for Adult and Continuing Education (NIACE), *add.* 170

National Vocational Qualification *see* NVQ

networks 160–9

New Training Initiative (MSC 1981) 39

non-compulsory education 63

Norfolk study of disruptive students 106–7, 108

norm referencing 132–3

Northern Ireland Office 4

numeracy, basic skills 6, 21, 53, 115

NVQ: Business Administration questions 120–1; Catering questions 121, 124; Engineering unit 126–7

NVQs 9–10, 21; assessment within 48–9, 126–7, 128, 154; awarding bodies 33; curriculum 45–50; elements 47; impact on college provision 49–50; influence on GNVQs 39; internal and external verification 131; number of (1991–5) 46; production of evidence 117; units of competence 46–8

objectives 93, 95, 96–8, 99; negotiation of 93, 98

occupationally specific training, qualifications 9

Ofsted 152

open learning 14, 21, 62, 109–10

'open systems information superhighway further education network' 110

Open University 51, 52, 109

oral tests 122

order, maintaining 77–8

Origami, reflection on 66–7

outcome-based model of education 39, 41, 103, 104, 112, 123

outcomes of learning *see* learning outcomes

outreach centres 6, 22, 160

overseas students 21–2

part-time staff 14, 15

part-time students 31

Patten, John 39

payment by results 53

pedagogy 151

peer assessment 125

peer group, problems with 73

peer mentoring 155

performance criteria: in GNVQs 43, 98, 113, 129; in NVQs 47

performance indicators, output-related 16

performing arts colleges 6

personal and professional development 52, 53

personal tutors 108

personality, of teacher 77

PhD 158

Piaget, Jean 61

portfolios: student *see* student portfolios; teachers' of professional experience 156–7

post-16 education, need for reform 29

post-compulsory education, participation rates 146–7

post-Fordism 110

Postgraduate Certificate in Education (PGCE) 16, 152, 153

postgraduate degrees, in teacher education 157–8

pre-course guidance 12

pre-vocational education, in schools 38

Prince of Wales Business Leaders Forum 175

prior experience of learning 21, 28, 59

prior learning, *see also* accreditation of prior learning (APL)

private training providers 50

professional development 52, 53, 135–69, 148–59; barriers to 154–5; pathways to 155–9; via distance learning 110

professional organisations 160–1

professional role, duality as teacher and expert 151–2

professional teaching qualification; in FE 151–4; no statutory requirement for FE 15–16, 151

professionalism, concept of 149

profile, student 114, 133

programmed learning 60

psychomotor domain 97, 98

public accountability 14, 16–19

publication of destinations of qualified students 17

qualifications 33–4; categories of 8–10; competence-based 117; professional teaching *see* professional teaching qualification; range of 5; vocational 38–50

Qualified Teacher Status (QTS) 152

quality control 16–17, 51, 104, 150

questions, multiple-choice 120

Quicke, J. 144–5

race 79

record, of professional experience 156–7

recording of achievement 111–33

recreational classes 11, 22, 53
Rees, Sue 106–7, 108
reflection 137–8; on barriers to learning 69;
    on diversity of curriculum provision 33;
    on impact on learning of gender 75; on
    induction programme 86; on learning
    experience 60, 139–41; on learning needs
    and student feelings 23–8; on learning
    outcomes 94–5; on mixed curricular
    model 54–5; on modularised curriculum
    50; on Origami 66–7; on professional
    development 159; on sense of self 64;
    structured 137–45; for students 138–41;
    on teacher-learner relationship 80
reflection-in-action 61, 137
reflective diary, constructing a 141–5
reflective practitioner 137, 145
Regional Advisory Councils (RACs) 165,
    166
regulation, of award-bearing courses 33
regulators 33–4
research 145–7; collaboration between FEs
    and HEIs 158; funding for 147
research degrees 158
residential weekend study 110, 157
resource-based learning 109
resources pressures 16
respect 108
responsibility 108; and attendance 106; for
    own learning 63
responsiveness of college 13, 22, 49
retention rates 11, 106
returning learners 22
risk factors 8–10 Figs. 1.3 and 4
Rivera, R.J. 65
Robson, J. 150
Rogers, A. 92–3
Rogers, Jenny 125
role play 100
'roll-on, roll-off' programmes 12
Round Table 162
Rowland, F. 125
Rowland, Stephen 138
RSA 35; add. 168, 175; Certificate for
    Vocational Preparation Tutors 153;
    Diploma in Teaching and Learning in
    Adult Basic Education 153
RSA Examinations Board (RSAEB) 38, 170

Sacks, Oliver 156
Schon, D. 61, 137, 145
School Curriculum and Assessment
    Authority (SCAA) 33, 35

School Curriculum Industry Partnership
    (SCIP) 175
school-leavers 14
schools: compared with further education
    63; partnerships with local 160; pre-
    vocational education and vocational
    education in 38
Scotland 4, 7, 33, 162; number of FE
    colleges in 3; staff in FE colleges 15
Scott, P. 10–11
Scottish Office 4; Education and Industry
    Department 175
'second-chance' education 5–6, 21
Secondary Heads Association (SHA) 160
self, sense of 63–4
self-directed learning 65
self-discipline 78
self-evaluation 125
self-study texts 110
seminars 11
service industries 32
Silver Book agreement 161
simulated work environments 49, 103, 128,
    132
sixth form colleges 6, 7, 16; risk factors
    10
skills updating 6
Skinner, B.F. 60
Smith, J.J. 112
Smith, R.M. 65
social backgrounds of students 21
social class 79
social interaction 63
special access courses, in HE 51
special educational needs in FE viii 22
specialist designated colleges 6, 7
specific learning needs, students with 31
Spours, K. 39, 44
Squires, G. 29–30, 51, 53
staff in colleges 14–16; roles of 14–15; types
    of 15
staff development: funding for 149–50;
    programmes for assessor awards 130; use
    of term 149–50
staff-student ratios 14
standards, debate over 133
Standards Methodology Unit, Department
    of Employment 40
Standing Conference on Schools' Science
    and Technology (SCSST/SATRO) 176
statements of achievement 42
Stenhouse, Lawrence 145
Strategic Forum 164

strategic plans 11–12, 33, 150
student portfolios 104–5; GNVQs 44, 113, 129, 131; grading themes 105
student-centred approach 44–5, 101, 103, 138
students 20–8; as consumers of learning 62; and courses 7–14; diversity of 20–2; internal pressures on 107; needs of 22–8
subjectivity 118
subjects, balance of 7–8 Fig. 1.2
Suffolk College, all-graduate teaching staff target 158
summative assessment 115–18, 133
support agencies 160–9
support staff 14, 152
support for students: defined 83–6; services 49, 63, 82–7
support for teachers 106; sources of listed 166–9

targets for 2000 6, 170
Taxonomy (Bloom) 97–8
teacher education 16, 151–4; postgraduate degrees 157–8; *see also* initial teacher education
Teacher Placement Service (TPS) 170
Teacher Training Agency (TTA) 152
teacher-student relationship 75–80; external pressures on 79 Fig. 4.2
teachers: effect on people's lives 75–6; as facilitators of learning 31; guidance roles 22, 82; and involvement of students in learning process 107–8; mentoring 155; personality of 76, 77; as researchers 145–7; roles of 22, 124, 151–2; who create barriers to learning 68–9
teaching functions 77
teaching hours, non-traditional 14
teaching plan 98–101
teaching qualifications in FE 151–4
teaching role, terminology 76
teaching strategies 88–110; choosing 90–2, 105–6; range of 99–101
teaching styles: and approaches to learning 59; learner-centred 62
team teaching 109
Technical Teacher's Certificate *see* City and Guilds Teacher's Certificate (7307)
Technical and Vocational Education Initiative (TVEI) 38
Tedder, Michael 149
teenagers 70–4
terminology 76, 93, 98, 120

tertiary colleges 6, 7
test, teaching to the 36, 112–13, 120
testing 112–13
tests: external 129; multiple-choice 129; objective 120; oral 122; short-answer 120–1, 129; written 119–21
theory: and reflective practice 144–5; role in professional development 148–9
time: for research 147; spent in collecting and collating assessment evidence 129
Times Educational Supplement (TES) 13–14, 75
Tomlinson Committee Report (1996) viii, 22
Tough, Allen 65
trade unions *see* unions
Trades Councils 162
Trades Union Congress (TUC), *add.* 168, 170
trainee 77
Training Credits *see* Youth Credits system
Training and Development Lead Body (TDLB) 16; standards as basis of FE teacher training 153, 154; units and elements of standards 130–1
Training and Enterprise Councils (TECs) 4, 7, 50; education and training responsibilities 162–3
Training for Work 52, 162
transactional analysis (TA) 78
Trident Trust 176
tutor bias 122
tutors 77
'two plus two' degrees 21
Tyler, Ralph 96

UK, concept of adulthood 64
undergraduates 3, 21, 51
Understanding British Industry (UBI) 176
Understanding Industry (UI) 176
unemployment: long-term adult 52; youth 7
unions 159, 160–1
Unit D32, assessment standards 130, 153
Unit D33, as national standard for assessor awards 130–1, 153
Unit D34, as the internal verifier award 131, 153
Unit D35, as the external verifier award 132
universities 50–2, 146–7, 152

value system 68
verification, internal and external 131–2
verifier awards 16, 130–2, 154
video-conferencing 110

videos, instructional 100, 110
vocational awards, number of (1991–4)
    46
vocational education 5; in schools 38
Vocational Preparation (FEU) 165
vocational qualifications 9, 38–50;
    traditional 45

Wales 4, 33, 34, 35, 162; number of FE
    colleges in 3
weekend study 12, 110, 157
welfare 108
Welsh Funding Council 4
Wildemeersch, D. 80
Wilmot, M. 62
women: and family concerns in learning 70,
    74; returners to work 52
women-only courses 74–5
work experience 103, 104, 162
work placements 128; in NVQs 48–9

work shadowing 103
work-based learning activities, examples
    103
Workers Educational Association (WEA) 52,
    add. 170
workloads 146–7
workplace assessment 128
workplace training 21, 60
workshops 11, 32

Yorkshire and Humberside Association for
    Further and Higher Education (YAFHE)
    166
Young, M. 153
young adults 70–4
Young Enterprise 176
Youth Credits system 7
Youth Training (YT) 7; funding for NVQs
    48
youth unemployment 7